OFFSIDE

The Battle For Control Of Maple Leaf Gardens

Theresa Tedesco

VIKING

VIKING
Published by the Penguin Group
Penguin Books Canada Ltd, 10 Alcorn Ave, Toronto, Ontario, Canada
M4V 3B2
Penguin Books Ltd, 27 Wrights Lane, London W8 5TZ, England
Viking Penguin, a division of Penguin Books USA Inc., 375 Hudson
Street, New York, New York 10014, U.S.A.
Penguin Books Australia Ltd, Ringwood, Victoria, Australia
Penguin Books (NZ) Ltd, 182-190 Wairau Road, Auckland 10, New
Zealand

Penguin Books Ltd, Registered Offices: Harmondsworth, Middlesex,
England

First published 1996
10 9 8 7 6 5 4 3 2 1

Printed and bound in Canada on acid-free paper ∞

Canadian Cataloguing in Publication Data

Tedesco, Theresa
    Offside: the battle for control of Maple Leaf Gardens

ISBN 0-670-86734-9

1. Maple Leaf Gardens Ltd. – History.
2. Sports facilities – Ontario – Toronto – History.
I. Title.

GV416.T67T43 1996   790'.06'871354109   C96-930276-2

Visit Penguin Canada's web site at www.penguin.ca.

For my mother and father,
Carolina and Michael

Contents

Acknowledgments   ix

The Players   xii

Chronology   xiv

Preface   xix

1 "C'mon Harry!"   1

2 The "BaGa" File   26

3 Harold Ballard's Legacy   51

4 Drawing the Battle Lines   85

5 The Salvage Plan   112

6 Billy Come Lately   138

7 Stavro's Hat Trick   159

8 Hunting Leafs   183

9 The Carlton Street Cash Box   200

10 Charities at the Gate   228

11 Overtime   241

Epilogue   276

Index   283

Acknowledgments

The idea for this book first came to me while I sat in the gold seats of Maple Leaf Gardens watching the hockey team practise on-ice skating drills during the 1994 pre-season training camp. By this time the future ownership of the team and the arena had been thrown into legal limbo by the court and I was assigned to cover the story for the CBC's business show "Venture."

This was one of those assignments that seem to take on a life of their own. Every time I scratched the surface, new, compelling (even shocking) pieces of information would spring up, sending me rushing off into different directions—often at the same time, it seemed. The cast of characters who enter and exit the stage of this drama are studies in contrasts: complex, fascinating and at times extraordinary. It was not long before I realized the battle for control of Maple Leaf Gardens was a book in the making.

This chronicle is the result of more than a hundred interviews that extended over countless hours during the past sixteen months. That journey is bookended by Steve Stavro: his was the first interview I sought and he was the last to consent to speak to me. I would like to thank all those who generously made themselves available, offering their time for lengthy—often numerous—interviews and who were always unfailingly polite, especially Brian Bellmore for his frankness, J. Perry Borden, Frank Newbould and George Engman for their enormous patience explaining very complicated financial and legal scenarios. As well, my gratitude goes to Donald Crump for his poignant and often humorous recollections of Harold Ballard and to Terence Kelly for insights into the reclusive Mr. Stavro.

Others, such as Norman Seagram and especially Rosanne Rocchi, were expansive and particularly generous with their time and their assistance. They welcomed my requests to relive a part of their lives they had stored away, sharing their experiences and insights even though they had very little to gain personally from the exercise. Christopher Dundas, Claude Lamoureux, Jeffrey

Leon, John McKellar, David Roebuck, Harry Ornest, Jim Devellano and David Peterson also provided important observations and clarification.

There are many others whose names you will not find on any of the book's pages, but their valuable contributions are scattered all over the text. They remain anonymous because they could not speak candidly. For some, the events are still too sensitive, the memories still bitter and for some, distasteful. Yet they all felt strongly enough about this endeavour that they agreed to speak on a strictly background basis. I am grateful for their co-operation. Only a handful of those whose names are mentioned in this book declined repeated requests for interviews. Their actions and words are a matter of public record and have been confirmed by others.

Fortunately, there was a wealth of research and reference material among the vast number of books and newspaper articles written about Maple Leaf Gardens and the Toronto Maple Leafs. Among those especially helpful were those authored by Scott Young, William Houston, Jack Batten, Brian McFarlane, Andrew Podnieks and Tony Van Alphen.

Although this book bears my name, it would not have been possible without the help of the talented and supportive group at Penguin Books, especially Cynthia Good, who embraced this project with lively interest from the very beginning, Lori Ledingham, Scott Sellers, David Kilgour and Wendy Thomas. The unflappable Peter Jacobsen kept me on the right side of the law and offered constructive advice.

In researching this book, I owe deep gratitude to Gaelyne Leslie and an honourable mention to Caroline Eberts and Kim Brown. Special thanks to Carlos Esteves for his keen eye and his uncompromising perfectionism.

There are many friends to thank for helping me along the way: Ann Shortell, who was the first to encourage me to take on the project, and Mark Piesanen for helping me harness the story's potential back in the early days. Large bouquets to my executive producer, Joy Chrysdale, senior producer Linda Sims and the rest of my colleagues at CBC's "Venture" for their unflagging support. As well, my special appreciation to Kevin Doyle, John MacFarlane and the wonderful David Steinberg.

I am especially indebted to Caroline van Hasselt and Mitchell Merowitz, whose faith and friendship buoyed my spirits.

Caroline's independent knowledge of business was immeasurable in its importance to the book; her loyalty and selfless efforts on my behalf were much appreciated.

Mitchell's confidence never wavered nor diminished despite my constant demands on his time. His seemingly infinite tolerance set new boundaries of friendship.

Enduring thanks to my family—my parents, my siblings and their spouses, Tullio, Natalie, Peter, Joseph, Angela, Michael, Doris, Linda, David, and my nieces and nephews—for their cheerful enthusiasm. I am especially grateful to my sister Rosemary and my brother-in-law Albert for offering me their refuge of solitude and kindness.

Lastly, to my dear friend Angela Ferrante for her enduring friendship. Her sensitive criticisms helped shape the contents of this intricate—and often unwieldy—tale. Without them, this book would not have been possible.

Theresa Tedesco
August 1996
Toronto, Ontario

The Players

Constantine Falkland Smythe – founder of Maple Leaf Gardens Ltd. in November, 1931.

Harold Edwin Ballard – late controlling shareholder of the Gardens from 1972 until he died in 1990.

William Ballard – eldest son of Harold, rock concert promoter long thought to be the heir apparent.

Rosanne Rocchi – Harold Ballard's personal and business lawyer who wrote his disputed last will and testament.

Steve Stavro – grocery-store magnate and executor of Harold Ballard's estate who made a controversial takeover bid for Maple Leaf Gardens.

Donald Giffin – millionaire businessman who aided Harold Ballard in obtaining the crucial financing that helped Ballard secure control of Maple Leaf Gardens. Giffin battled Stavro for the company after Ballard's death.

Donald Crump – dour-looking chartered accountant who kept Ballard in control and out of trouble. As an executor after his boss's death, Crump played an instrumental role in determining the company's fate.

Terence Kelly – Oshawa criminal lawyer and long-time Ballard friend who replaced Donald Giffin as executor.

Hugh Paisley – the Public Trustee of Ontario from 1987 to 1993.

Susan Himel – Public Trustee who replaced Paisley in 1993 and challenged Stavro's takeover bid in court.

Eric Moore – director of the Charitable Properties Division in the Public Trustee's office who was charged with overseeing the administration of the Ballard estate.

Frank Newbould – senior lawyer at Borden & Elliot who was hired by the Public Trustee to build a case against Stavro.

Brian Bellmore – journeyman lawyer and trusted friend of Stavro whose emotional defence of his client would raise eyebrows in the courtroom.

Norman Seagram – former executive vice-president of the Molson Companies Ltd., who spearheaded the company's long-standing involvement with Maple Leaf Gardens.

Harry Ornest – feisty Beverly Hills millionaire who was the single largest shareholder in Maple Leaf Gardens at the time of Stavro's takeover bid. His deft manipulation of the media helped spark the storm of controversy surrounding the offer.

James Devellano – senior vice-president of the Detroit Red Wings and second largest shareholder in the Gardens; refused to sell his shares to Ballard six years before Stavro's offer.

Yolanda MacMillan – Fort William, Ontario, native who barged her way into Ballard's office in the early 1980s and terrorized the Gardens denizens while she played nurse and companion to Ballard.

Chronology

1903   Harold Edwin Ballard is born in Toronto.

1927   Conn Smythe founds Toronto Maple Leaf hockey club.

1931
Feb.   Maple Leaf Gardens Ltd. is incorporated.
Nov.   Opening night for Carlton Street arena.

1944   Ballard incorporates a private company called Harold E. Ballard Ltd. (HEBL).

1952   Canadian Broadcasting Corp. starts "Hockey Night in Canada" telecasts.

1961   Ballard, Stafford Smythe and John Bassett get control of Maple Leaf Gardens Ltd.

1966   Ballard reorganizes corporate structure of HEBL creating a succession vehicle for his three children.

1971
June   Ballard and Stafford Smythe are charged with tax evasion, theft and fraud.
Sept.   Ballard and Smythe buy out their partner Bassett. Stafford Smythe dies of health complications.

1972   Ballard buys Smythe's shares and seizes control of Maple Leaf Gardens before being hauled off to prison.

1980   Ballard signs a fifteen-year broadcast deal with Molson. Ballard borrows money from Molson and gives the company a 20-percent option on his controlling block of Gardens stock and a right of first refusal on the rest.

1981 Yolanda MacMillan pleads guilty to conspiracy to commit fraud and perjury.

1984 Ballard signs his first will.
Yolanda is ensconced in Ballard's life.

1988 Ballard declares that his children are cut from his will.
Molson begins making plays to take over Maple Leaf Gardens.

1989
Jan.   Harold begins buying out his children, financed by huge amounts of debt.
Bill Ballard launches a $70-million lawsuit against his father, Crump, Giffin and his younger brother.

1990
Jan.   Harold Ballard is in a coma in a Florida hospital; MLGL's board of directors takes temporary control.
Crump resigns to become Commissioner of the Canadian Football League.
Feb.   Ballard is declared mentally incompetent by a Surrogate Court, which names his three executors as guardians of the Gardens.
Apr.   Harold Ballard dies.
Crump, Giffin and Stavro run the arena and hockey operations, purge the board of Ballard's cronies.
Nov.   Molson exercises its 1980 option and seizes Gardens shares from Ballard's estate.
Dec.   Molson creates a trust to house its MLGL shares at behest of National Hockey League governors.
The controversial Mellanby Report is tabled.

1991
Jan.   Fierce battle within estate between Giffin and Stavro.
Feb.   Executors take their battle before five different judges.
Mr. Justice James Farley rules in favour of Bill Ballard in his court case from 1989.

Mar.	Stavro snares an option to buy for himself all of the estate's controlling block of Maple Leaf Gardens shares.
June	Cliff Fletcher is hired as president of Gardens.
Sept.	Bill Ballard sells his one-third interest in HEBL to his late father's estate for $21 million.
	Stavro and Molson sign a put/call agreement.
Oct.	Giffin is purged from the board as new directors are appointed; Stavro becomes chairman.
	Giffin's son Philip and a group of friends begin their own campaign to unseat Stavro and take a run at the company for themselves.

1992 Donald Giffin dies of cancer and Terence Kelly is appointed as his replacement as executor of Ballard's estate.

1993

Jan.	Stavro declares he's interested in exercising his option.
Feb.	Morgan Guaranty Trust in New York is hired as financial adviser to Philip Giffin's group.
Mar.	Brokerage firms RBC Dominion Securities and Burns Fry Ltd. are retained to produce evaluations of the Gardens.
Sept.	Stavro starts assembling his takeover team.
Oct.	Two investment firms produce their evaluations which average $29 to $34 a share, which are filed with the Public Trustee's office.
	Cliff Fletcher hires Barry Frank at the International Management Group to begin negotiating a new local broadcast deal with Molson.
Dec.	Yolanda Ballard receives millions in an out-of-court settlement with her late companion's estate.
	Stavro secures a $33-million loan from the TD Bank for his proposed takeover bid and entices the bank's investment arm, TD Capital, to become an equity partner.

1994

| Mar. | Estate of Harold Ballard agrees to sell its 60.3-percent controlling block to Stavro for a total of $75 million. |
| | Molson agrees to sell all of its 20-percent block to Stavro for $25 million. |

Apr.	Stavro, TD Bank and Teachers make a $125-million takeover offer for all of the outstanding shares in Maple Leaf Gardens for $34 a share.
	Gardens board of directors urges shareholders to accept Stavro's offer.
	Harry Ornest and Jim Devellano, the Gardens' two largest public shareholders, refuse and begin attacking Stavro's offer in the press.
	Rival bidders plan a strategy to counter Stavro's bid.
Summer:	Public Trustee of Ontario and the Ontario Securities Commission investigate Stavro's bid.
Aug.	Public Trustee asks an Ontario Division Court to grant an injunction prohibiting the amalgamation of Gardens' shares with Stavro's private company. Request is granted.

1995

Jan.	MLGL shareholder files a class-action suit on behalf of minority shareholders against Stavro.

1996

Jan.	Mandatory mediation begins at the Hilton Hotel for an out-of-court settlement.
Feb.	Bill Ballard launches a $100-million lawsuit against his late father's executors and TD Bank.
Apr.	Out-of-court settlement sees Stavro and his business partners pay $23.5 million to Public Trustee for charities, and $49.50 a share each to Ornest and Devellano.
May	Class-action suit settled based on similar offer as the one to Ornest and Devellano.
Aug.	Going private meeting is held to squeeze out remaining shareholders who have not yet tendered their shares.
Sept.	Conn Smythe's 65-year-old public company passes into the hands of Stavro and his business partners.

Preface

"So this is Shangri-La."

That hackneyed line tumbled from the mouth of a $400-an-hour lawyer to a predictable round of self-satisfied guffaws. The audience, twenty-four in all, was a group of mostly well-paid commercial trial lawyers, the peacocks in the zoo that makes up the legal community.

It was the middle of January 1996, and the group had gathered in the Shangri-La Room, high above downtown Toronto on the thirty-second floor of the Toronto Hilton Hotel. Lawyers from a dozen firms, a handful of bureaucrats, a financial adviser from a small Bay Street firm, the general manager of a professional hockey team, bankers, a pension fund honcho, a grocer, an accountant, a small-town criminal lawyer and two court-appointed mediators mingled nervously among the bamboo and rattan furniture. This cross-section of Canada's legal and financial elites had gathered behind closed doors to try to fast-track an out-of-court settlement that would end their long and bloody legal battle.

Most of the combatants looked decidedly out of place. After all, this group of blue-ribbon lawyers was accustomed to the quiet halls and understated boardrooms scattered throughout the country's largest financial community. The hotel suite, with its fireplace and pool table, was not exactly the forum in which this group of congenitally immodest litigators prefers to do battle—and especially not in this case, which is a courtroom voyeur's dream: a smooth mixture of white-collar misdeeds, big bucks and the opiate of the masses, professional sports. It's not often that those elements conspire to bring a case before Her Majesty's bench.

Suite number 3202 was the pivotal stop on an eighteen-month journey to sort out the legacy of Harold Edwin Ballard. The crusty, foul-mouthed former majority shareholder of Maple Leaf Gardens Ltd. and the Toronto Maple Leafs hockey club had died on April 11, 1990, amid mystery, intrigue and cheap drama. More importantly, he left behind an estate in financial disarray and a complicated three-part will that would be poked and prodded by dozens of lawyers and judges, costing millions of dollars to unravel.

Ownership of Maple Leaf Gardens was Ballard's curse and his legacy. Time and time again, the patriarch of the dysfunctional Ballard clan had threatened to cut his rebellious children out of his will. He finally made good on his promise when he left final instructions that his assets were to be sold and the proceeds divided among a group of charities. Ballard's parting shot allowed his three hand-picked executors—grocery magnate Steve Stavro, sheet-metal millionaire Donald Giffin and career accountant Donald Crump—not only to referee the eventual selloff but also to step in and buy the assets for themselves. Before his death, the always mischievous Ballard had cackled to one of his executors that "You're going to be in court for years on this one." Indeed. The master of the game of divide and conquer would have chuckled at the spectacle that ensued from his handiwork.

Ballard had left the field wide open for the predators who had been circling for years even before his death. His three executors jockeyed for position in anticipation of the long-awaited auction of the fabled franchise and the arena; Ballard's prodigal son William plotted his revenge and a handful of corporations hedged their bets and curried favour with the likely contenders to succeed Ballard. There were other Maple Leaf Gardens shareholders, such as Harry Ornest and Jim Devellano, who had their own notions about the value of their investments in what had been a very public institution. Even the eight charities named in Ballard's will coyly waited on the sidelines. All the while standing guard was the sleepy watch dog, Ontario's Public Guardian and Trustee, whose responsibility it was to protect the interests of the charities and make sure they would receive something—anything—from Ballard's estate. All in all, you needed a Maple Leaf Gardens souvenir program to keep track of all the players.

The prize that Ballard had tossed up for grabs was the jewel of Canadian sports and one of the most treasured companies in this country. If there is a national sports team, most would say it's the Toronto Maple Leafs. There are other Canadian teams—most notably the Montreal Canadiens—but no team delivers the Saturday night crowd like the Leafs. In fact, Toronto accounts for 40 percent of the National Hockey League's total annual broadcast revenues, and it ranks third among all twenty-six teams in merchandising sales even though the team has only recently tapped into the riches of modern marketing. As a result, Maple Leaf Gardens has assumed mythical status, a heart throb for young boys and titans of industry alike.

Yet under Ballard, the Gardens had been a big-league company run by minor-leaguers who played out at the fringes. The financial wizards of Bay Street had dismissed Maple Leaf Gardens as a consistent underperformer, never rising to balance-sheet greatness under the aegis of the nickel-squeezing Ballard. Worse, the old curmudgeon didn't look or sound like one of them; nothing about Ballard was smooth or polished. But he played hard—sometimes illegally, as a stint in jail proved—and he knew how to get the most out of his position as the patriarch of a public company.

Ultimately, it was the quiet executor who carried the big financial stick who had launched the major assault on Ballard's estate. It had been Steve Stavro's offer to buy Maple Leaf Gardens in April 1994 and then take the company private that had led to the gathering at the Shangri-La in January 1996. His takeover offer had been challenged in court by the Attorney General of Ontario and the Public Guardian and Trustee. Since then, the reclusive grocer—whose pugnacious style more closely resembles that of Conn Smythe than Ballard—has been the subject of intense public scrutiny.

A fierce legal war had led to the peace talks in the Hilton Hotel. In forty-one days of examinations for discovery, more than seven thousand pieces of evidence had been marked in the Commercial List Court. Many of them had resulted in dozens of appearances before Mr. Justice John (Jack) Ground, the methodical judge assigned to manage this very complicated piece of commercial litigation to trial. Claims and counterclaims, dozens of snippy, sarcastic, abrupt letters, bearing the logos of some of the clubbiest establishment legal firms in the country, have been exchanged and filed in the eight boxes that made up the public record. And the verbal brawling, the unkind cuts and the haggling over costs are constant reminders that there is more than just a hockey team on the line.

During the morning gathering at the Hilton Hotel, the lawyers prowled nervously, each staking out their clients' turf for the final showdown. The inaugural meeting was the first of many closed-door sessions over four months that finally settled the fate of Maple Leaf Gardens. Two years to the day after he launched his takeover bid, Steve Stavro was crowned the new king of Carlton Street by virtue of the play he orchestrated with the help of his business partners.

That Stavro prevailed was anti-climactic. During a lengthy interview at his home, Stavro later said he believed Ballard wanted *him* to take the company. "I figured he believed in me and I could do something with the club." He justified his victory by saying his trusted lawyer, Brian Bellmore, had told him that Ballard's will was unique. "Look it, it's yours—if you want to give to the charities, give it. If you don't want to give them anything, don't give them anything. He [Ballard] left us a carte blanche with the whole thing ... you want to buy it with cash or without cash, you know what I mean? You know, with a dollar down or whatever you want. Make your own terms." Stavro did just that—taking a page out of Ballard's own book.

More important than his triumph is the bitter-sweet saga of how Stavro stickhandled his way to victory. This is a play-by-play account of one of the messiest, nastiest takeover battles in Canadian corporate history. It stars some of the biggest names in the country's financial, legal and sports establishments, players who were motivated by personal ambition, rampant ego and corporate greed. It is a chronicle of how high-priced legal and financial vigilantes spun clever and complicated business transactions and then dared the courts to shoot them down. The protracted battle for the Gardens delves into the broader issues of duty, conflicts of interest, and the conduct of a regulatory body which acted too slowly and too timidly for the public good. Mostly though, this is a straight-up yarn about the business of hockey and the extraordinary characters it seduces with its mixture of boyhood fantasy and grown-up profits.

CHAPTER ONE

"C'mon Harry!"

"Fuck the Teachers and fuck the Toronto Dominion Bank!" – HARRY ORNEST

IT WAS 6:30 A.M. and the telephone was ringing inside the grey stucco house across the street from Nancy Sinatra's. That the phone was sounding at such an unseemly hour of the morning was not unusual for Harry Ornest, one of the titans of industry and celebrities who live in the world's most exclusive five-and-a-half-square-mile enclave just west of the Hollywood Hills. The seventy-one-year-old transplanted Edmontonian, a pioneer in the vending machine business, is perhaps best known in Canada as the former owner of the Toronto Argonauts football team and the National Hockey League's St. Louis Blues. These days, Ornest is vice-chairman of Hollywood Park Inc., a Los Angeles race track that boasts such luminaries as TV mogul Aaron Spelling on its board of directors.

On the morning of Monday, April 4, 1994, as he was making his way to the main-floor study, Ornest registered the time. About now, he thought, the bells are sounding the start of trading on the New York and Toronto stock exchanges. Ornest couldn't help but wonder if the timing of this call might be a bit ominous.

"Harry!" exclaimed the familiar voice on the line. "You're gonna get $34 a share." It was Steve Stavro, the sixty-six-year-old chairman and chief executive officer of Maple Leaf Gardens Ltd., the entertainment company that owned and operated one of the most revered hockey shrines in Canada, bearing its name, and the fabled Toronto Maple Leafs Hockey Club. Stavro had been running the Gardens for the better part of four years, since Harold E. Ballard

1

died in April 1990. For many, that was a day that ended almost twenty years of tyranny at Maple Leaf Gardens, a legacy left by Conn Smythe that had become a private playground under Ballard. Stavro has been a director of the public company for thirteen years—nine of them under Ballard. And as one of three executors of Harold's estate, Stavro had waged his own power struggle to ensure he would be part of the lineage of Maple Leaf Gardens owners.

A shrewd, solid administrator, Stavro owns Knob Hill Farms Ltd., the largest independent retail food chain in Canada. He built this multi-million-dollar private empire without personal publicity. Once regarded as the worst-run business in the National Hockey League under Ballard's proprietorship, the Toronto Maple Leafs had regained a semblance of their winning tradition under the quiet, hands-on tutelage of Stavro. The team that once had the dubious distinction of collecting the most at the box office but paying the least to its players now boasted one of the highest payrolls in the NHL.

The last time Ornest had seen Stavro had been during the 1993 Stanley Cup semi-finals between the Leafs and the Los Angeles Kings. Ornest had invited Stavro and his entire board of directors, along with their wives, for a day at the Hollywood Park race track while they were in town visiting with the hockey club. Ornest had even named a race the Maple Leaf Cup and had brought Stavro and his wife, Sally, down to the winner's circle to present the prize.

With the Leafs looking respectable and the company's balance sheet as solid as ever, nobody seemed in a hurry to sell the Gardens. Back then, Ornest had figured management would continue to build a better team and fetch a higher price years down the road. At least that's what they'd told Ornest the few times he'd asked.

He was understandably caught off guard by Stavro's early-morning call. Ornest, his wife, Ruth, and four children were the largest individual shareholders in the company with 3.55 percent of the outstanding shares—130,640 in all. Ornest had owned the shares since mid-1990, just after Ballard's death, and benefited handsomely from dividends that flowed annually. So he was a little jarred when the CEO of the company casually talked share price from three thousand miles away. Of course, what Ornest didn't know yet was that Stavro, with the help of two partners, was about to launch a surprise bid to take over the company that Conn Smythe had built sixty-five years ago and then to take it private.

The lifeline of any good businessman is an ability to anticipate events. That Ornest didn't see it coming was deliberate. In business parlance, it means he was frozen out of the action, and that was the unspoken dialogue between the two men. The wily Ornest mustered his best "What are you talking about?" The response from his old friend confirmed his worst fears: "Harry, I wanted to phone you and tell you we're syndicated." That may have sounded cryptic but Ornest knew exactly what it meant: Stavro had assembled his own group of investors to take over Maple Leaf Gardens. And now, they wanted Ornest's shares.

Ornest was out of sorts. "Steve, I'm not in to do the selling." Now it was Stavro's turn to conceal his surprise. This should have been easy. Everyone in the hockey world knew Harry Ornest had never met a dollar he didn't like. At $34 a share, Ornest would net a tidy profit of about $1.1 million, considering he bought most of his shares in the mid- to high twenty-dollar range. Besides, not since Ornest sold the St. Louis Blues and The Arena in 1986 for an $11.6-million (U.S.) pre-tax profit, had he ever shown a real interest in purchasing another major league professional hockey team, let alone trading in that world-famous southern California zip code for Toronto winters.

"C'mon Harry! You'll always have a friend in Toronto," Stavro guffawed. Some friend, deadpanned Ornest silently. He'd been miffed for years that Stavro hadn't invited him to join the company's board of directors. Not that Harry would have accepted such an offer; at his age making the cross-continent trips for meetings would be physically taxing. But to Harry, a gesture was still a gesture.

Through bouts of silence, Ornest began to figure out that it was the hard-nosed Stavro who wanted to take a run at Maple Leaf Gardens Ltd. for himself. A sports buff, Stavro already owned several race horses, and he had dabbled in a professional soccer league thirty years ago, which was how he met Ballard. Adding the cachet of the Toronto Maple Leafs, described by Robert Goodenow, executive director of the National Hockey League Players' Association, as "the Mona Lisa of Canadian sports," would yield the kind of ego boost Stavro needed to slake the thirst for credibility he had long craved within the sports and business establishments. Fine. But if

Ornest, whose family controlled 40.36 percent of the remaining 20 percent that Stavro didn't already own, couldn't be on the team, then his friend the grocer would have to pay a hell of a lot more than $34 a share to get Ornest to play the game.

"I ain't selling, Steve. I'm gonna stay in." With that, Ornest drew the first battle line in the fight against Stavro's advance on Maple Leaf Gardens, a resistance that gathered momentum in the months ahead and garnered Ornest the sardonic title "Beverly Hills Tycoon," courtesy of Stavro's lawyer, Brian Bellmore.

After a momentary pause, Stavro tried to reason: "Harry, you can't stay in, because I got the Teachers and I got the Toronto Dominion Bank." But Ornest, who had whipped himself into an oratorical frenzy, barked back: "Fuck the Teachers and fuck the Toronto Dominion Bank."

For the cool-headed Stavro, this was a courtesy call gone awry. More importantly, it was the first sign of defiance he would encounter and, remarkably, underestimate. Who could blame him? Stavro figured he was on the verge of a done deal, so Ornest's intransigence wasn't about to unsettle him. Besides, if all went according to plan, Stavro wouldn't need Ornest or, for that matter, much of the loose stock in the hands of public shareholders, most of whom owned fewer than a hundred shares each.

The self-made multi-millionaire had the coveted shares in the estate of the late Harold E. Ballard—a controlling 60.3 percent—irrevocably locked up. Just days before his call to Ornest, Stavro had successfully stickhandled his way through a series of manoeuvres that would consolidate his control and guarantee the success of his blockbuster takeover bid.

The final details came together during a series of hushed weekend meetings at Stavro's rambling forty-nine-room mansion on Teddington Park Avenue in North Toronto (formerly belonging to Colonel Eric Phillips, who co-founded Argus Corp. with horse-breeding legend E.P. Taylor), forty-eight hours before the public offer was announced. On April 2, Stavro finally snared the 19.99-percent block (735,575 shares) owned by The Molson Companies Ltd. (the company that owns Molson Breweries) which it had received as part of a loan agreement with Harold Ballard in 1980. That

Molson owned a slice of the Leafs was one of the few secrets Ballard ever kept. It was not surprising, then, that when John Ziegler, then president of the National Hockey League, was informed in December 1988, he went ballistic. After much angst and conference calling among NHL governors, the company (which already owns the Montreal Canadiens) was ordered to unload its stake in the Leafs *tout de suite* because NHL regulations prohibit the same owner having a stake in two teams.

For the next two years, the thirty-sixth floor Toronto offices of Marshall "Mickey" Cohen, Molson's chief executive, resembled a sultan's tent where suitors vying for the single largest block of shares outside Ballard's estate paraded their wares. In the end, from the dozen or so who were entertained and ultimately spurned, Stavro emerged the victor. His heft as an executor made him really the only choice for Cohen, whose own motives were to maintain friendly relations with the Gardens and protect his brewery's exclusive broadcast agreements with the Leafs.

The two inked a deal in September 1991 that had to be consummated by April 15, 1994. Almost two weeks before that deadline, Stavro's private company, Knob Hill Farms Ltd., would pay Canada's largest brewery about $21.3 million (or $29 a share) for almost 20 percent of Pal Hal's hockey palace. Not a bad return for Molson, whose original investment for the shares was $10,000 in 1980.

Having secured the Molson shares, Stavro then grabbed the controlling rein. Ballard's estate, which was represented by three named executors (J. Donald Crump, Terence V. Kelly and Stavro), agreed to sell the entire controlling block of shares in the late owner's estate to Stavro for just over $75 million (or $34 a share).

That Stavro appeared to be in a conflict of interest as both buyer of the estate's shares and, at the same time, seller as one of the custodians (not to mention that he was also chief executive officer of Maple Leaf Gardens) seemed a moot point at the time. Reported mostly by sports writers lulled by the sanity that prevailed at Maple Leaf Gardens in the post-Ballard era (for which Stavro had been given full credit), the prospect of a non-arm's-length deal seemed to go unchallenged. Even the regulators who are supposed to ensure these deals pass the so-called smell test didn't get a whiff of controversy until well after the offer was floated.

Concerns about fiduciary or even fiscal responsibility were rarely raised publicly, and when they did surface, the loquacious Brian Bellmore would nullify them by proclaiming that Stavro abstained from voting on the sale of the estate shares and had no influence on the timing of the decision. In what would become his mantra, Bellmore's defence would always include a reference to the last will and testament of Harold E. Ballard—specifically, how it clearly states that an executor of the estate can purchase the shares at "fair market value," as long as they are "supported by two independent appraisals."

However, what Bellmore didn't explain—nor in fairness was he asked then or at any time before—was how he and his long-time friend and client had spent the previous four years laying the groundwork to secure the votes eventually cast by Crump and Kelly.

By the time the Toronto Stock Exchange halted trading on Monday, April 4, Stavro already controlled a hefty 80.3 percent of Maple Leaf Gardens. The last time the thinly traded stock changed hands before the takeover announcement was on March 31—and the shares closed at $28.50. The $34-a-share offer Stavro would tender to the company's public shareholders, although required by Ontario securities law, at the time looked like a mop-up job, though in fact it was a necessary step for Stavro's final move to take the company private. In fact, technically Stavro only needed 10 percent of the outstanding shares to reach the 90-percent mark he needed to take the company private as set out by Ontario's Business Corporations Act.

In a terse press release, the public was told that Stavro had teamed up with the Ontario Teachers' Pension Plan Board (the most actively invested pension plan in Canada, with almost $40 billion in assets), and TD Capital Group, the investment-dealer arm of the Toronto Dominion Bank, and together they intended to take control of Maple Leaf Gardens. Strictly for the purpose of the deal, an acquisition company called MLG Ventures Ltd. was incorporated a week before the takeover offer.

This is how Stavro's team looked on paper: Ontario Teachers' Pension invested $44.3 million and owned 49 percent of MLG Ventures; the remaining 51 percent was controlled by a company called MLG Holdings Ltd., which was 80 percent owned by Stavro's Knob Hill Farms (it brought $39 million to the table) and 20 percent by TD Capital, which threw $9.75 million into the pot. TD Bank provided the remaining $35 million in financing via a five-year loan. In effect, Stavro maintained a controlling interest in the new company and was listed as the only one holding official titles as president and secretary. If all the shares were tendered by May 2—the deadline for the offer—the total tab to acquire one of Canada's most treasured sports institutions would be just over $128 million. (The lawyers and financial advisers would fetch a hefty $3 million for their services.)

Soon after that announcement, Maple Leaf Gardens' 2,500 shareholders, who combined owned 3.2 million shares (or almost 20 percent of the institution), received a twenty-six-page prospectus circulated by Bay Street investment firm Midland Walwyn Inc. in Toronto. Most of the company's disparate shareholders clutched small, symbolic batches of Maple Leaf Gardens stock, a rite of passage handed down from one hockey-loving generation to the next. For those lucky enough, owning a piece of 60 Carlton Street carried an emotional attachment, making the Gardens no ordinary public company.

The company's board of directors knew this when they dispatched their recommendation urging the neophyte shareholders to accept the offer. According to their circular dated April 15, the seven-man board reached that decision after studying an internal report by an independent committee made up of three directors (George Whyte, Ron Pringle and Ted Nikolaou) who were not officers or employees of Maple Leaf Gardens. However, these same directors were all hand-picked by Stavro (who abstained from the vote) after he became chairman of the board and chief executive officer in November 1991. Together, the seven-member board (not including the shares represented by the estate) owned a paltry 1,850 shares in the company—hardly putting their money where their mouths were. Until Stavro acquired the estate's shares and the Molson block, his financial interest in the company was the same as when he joined in 1981— five hundred shares.

That's what really galled Ornest. Moments after giving his parting shot to Stavro, Ornest was back on the blower communicating through fibre optics again. This time, he was talking to Jim Devellano, his long-time friend, who was general manager and senior vice-president of the Detroit Red Wings. The fifty-one-year-old bachelor had been hanging around hockey rinks all his life and had begun buying shares in the Gardens twenty years earlier. A close acquaintance of Ballard, Devellano was the second largest individual shareholder in Maple Leaf Gardens, with 1 percent or 32,375 shares, right behind Harry Ornest.

Ornest regaled Devellano with the highlights of his chat with Stavro. Devellano informed his friend that he too had had an early morning call. Brian Bellmore, who was also a director of Maple Leaf Gardens, had phoned to deliver the "good news that Steve [was] going to buy the company." Jimmy D., as he is known in hockey circles, didn't think it was such a great idea. "Geez, I don't find that real good news at all," he recalls telling Bellmore. "Harold Ballard offered me $42 a share." That was back in 1988 during a dinner at an NHL governors' meeting, the last one Pal Hal attended before he died. An intense, cherubic man, Devellano told Stavro's lawyer that he was happy to remain on the sidelines collecting his dividends. He asked Bellmore to "go back to Mr. Stavro and see if anything can be worked out so that I can hold my stock in the company. Don't force me to sell at $34 a share. I'm not looking to cause you any trouble but at the same time, I don't want to get short-changed, Brian, okay?"

No, it was not okay, came the response. "Jim, I don't think we can do that because we have to treat all shareholders alike." Bellmore explained that Stavro was going to take out all the shareholders because he intended to take the company private.

Devellano didn't like what he was hearing. "I don't care who owns it. I just don't agree with the price. Harry, you're not going to settle for $34 a share. This is bullshit. The Raptors paid $155 million [Canadian] for a team without as much as a jock strap. Holy cow, this is Maple Leaf Gardens—a national heritage, a debt-free profitable company." Later, he would say, "They should have left me in. They were so arrogant. 'We don't care that you invested your life savings in the company.'

They didn't show a lot of respect for me as an executive in the league."

Ornest and Devellano made a blood pact to hold out for more money by refusing to sell their shares. With any luck, they could get a bidding war going; an auction, they figured, would fetch $70 a share. To do that, they needed to prod the regulators into launching an investigation into Stavro's offer. So they conspired to attack Stavro's offer through the Toronto news media from their respective homes in Los Angeles and Detroit. For the next three weeks, the holdouts received a lot of ink for their protests, most of it nasty one-liners that amounted to a thinly veiled character assassination of Stavro and his supporters.

Ornest and Devellano saw the deal as undervalued and accused Stavro of using his position as executor to create a sweet deal, the result of being both buyer and seller. Soon, the two men became the embodiment of the resistance against Stavro's offer. When fielding telephone calls from dozens of MLGL shareholders in Canada and a few in the United States, they advised them to hang tough and not be intimidated to sell to Stavro.

Their adversary used whatever levers he could to muzzle his opponents. Stavro complained to Mike Ilitch, owner of the Detroit Red Wings, about Devellano's public comments. At the same time, NHL Commissioner Gary Bettman stepped into the fray, delicately admonishing Devellano for bad-mouthing another owner. "He said something like, 'Jimmy, I know you have a lot of money invested in this but it's before the courts,'" Devellano recalled. "But it was my dough that was at stake and I had to do whatever it took to get it." Behind the scenes, Ornest and Devellano were getting some unexpected help from a group of would-be players, who for years had been waging a clandestine campaign to break Stavro's hammerlock on Ballard's controlling shares.

In the days following Stavro's offer, Ontario's Office of the Public Guardian and Trustee, a quiet corner of the Attorney General's office created in 1919 to protect charitable properties under estates in the province, was bolted out of its complacency. The backlash from some of the high-profile shareholders paraded in press reports was making the bureaucrats uneasy. More specifically, senior civil servants in the department were starting to ask questions, including Susan Himel, the acting Public Guardian and Trustee. But their interrogations were not about Ornest's quest for a higher share price. They wanted to know whether the executors of Ballard's estate were acting in the best interests of the charities designated to receive benefits. One of the main reasons for Himel's $120,599 annual salary, courtesy of Ontario taxpayers, was to ensure that the rights of charities weren't being jeopardized. Stavro's offer would have left little (if anything) to charities, which were the ultimate beneficiaries of Ballard's estate. The insiders who had crafted the deal knew that, but Himel and her staff didn't, at least not at the time Stavro made his overture.

Eric Moore, the director of the Public Trustee's charitable properties division who'd been handling the Ballard estate file since 1990, was at the centre of the gathering storm. He was away on vacation when the offer hit the street, and other than a telephone voice-mail message left in his absence by the Ballard estate lawyer, John McKellar, Moore had been caught completely off guard by the public offering. Following his return on April 11, he'd been scrambling to review his voluminous file. While he pored over a copy of the offer and the directors' circular urging shareholders to accept the offer from Stavro, he deployed a newly arrived articling law student to make telephone calls to Ornest, Devellano and Tony Van Alphen, a business reporter at the *Toronto Star* who had been covering the backlash from Stavro's offer. After a couple of days of listening to the irate shareholders, the fact-finding mission of Mary Elizabeth Julian-Wilson would provide the government agency with its first taste of the bitter controversy surrounding the administration of the Ballard estate. Julian-Wilson briefed Moore in a memo dated April 25, and that led to a showdown between the high-ranking civil servant and his bosses.

That's when the paper-pushing kicked into high gear. In a six-page letter sent to John McKellar at Weir & Foulds on April 28, Moore listed a series of questions that he wanted answered within ten days—enquiries that amount to a blanket request for information about events and deals that had taken place within the estate since Ballard's death four years earlier. Much of it was information that Stavro and his co-executors should have handed over earlier— but nonetheless, it was knowledge the Public Trustee would have acquired if it had been meticulously carrying out its own duties. "He said, 'Here are some questions. We want to know your answers to these questions and you have ten days to answer,'" McKellar says of Moore's missive. "It was not a stop-work order and it was a little late obviously, but here it was and I was happy to answer the questions." In fact, Moore didn't assert that the estate had to seek prior court approval for the sale to Stavro before closing the deal. Instead, in his letter he merely asked whether the executors were intending to seek court approval for their sale of the MLG shares to Stavro and, "if so, when. If not, please explain why not." The Public Trustee's office knew Stavro's offer was set to close on May 2—just four days after Moore's letter was sent. It was a little disingenuous considering Moore hadn't been served with the necessary court papers he knew Stavro would have had to file before making an appearance before any judge.

Meanwhile, Stavro was oblivious to the bureaucratic flourish. On the morning of April 29, he was off to a meeting at the NHL head office in New York City with Gary Bettman. A special conference call with the league's twenty-six governors was scheduled later in the day at 2:30 P.M. when Stavro expected to win their blessing as the new owner of the most important and storied franchise in the league. Stavro; Brian Bellmore; Claude Lamoureux, chief executive officer of the Ontario Teachers' Pension Plan Board; Michael Lay, the portfolio manager who negotiated the deal for Teachers; Chris Dundas, Stavro's chief financial adviser; and William Brock, a vice-chairman at Toronto Dominion Bank, met at Pearson Airport's Terminal 2 for their Air Canada flight to the NHL head office.

Surprisingly, it was the first time Lamoureux, whose pension plan had committed to funding almost half of the deal, had ever met Stavro. During the ninety-minute flight, Stavro and Lamoureux, who were seated next to each other, exchanged pleasantries while the others huddled, trying to anticipate what questions they'd be asked by the other owners. The NHL Board of Governors is a tough crowd, made up of an eclectic group of wealthy, white American men who jealously guard entry into their cosy club. Given that most of them already knew Stavro through his long affiliation with the Leafs (and that they shared a collective loathing for Harold Ballard), the meeting should have been a formality. Still, the plan heading into LaGuardia Airport was to get Bettman on side and he'd take care of the rest. And that's exactly what happened.

But it didn't get off to a good start. Stavro and company were late arriving at Bettman's office located on the Avenue of the Americas in midtown Manhattan. As the five men piled into their taxi from the airport, Lamoureux gave directions to the cabbie which seemed natural given that he'd worked in New York for years with the Metropolitan Life Insurance Company. He instructed the cab driver to head to 50th Street, fully expecting to impress Stavro with a quick tour. Forty-five minutes into the drive he began to recognize the buildings of his old neighbourhood on 15th Street. It seemed the cab driver had tripped over Lamoureux's accent, and it took another half-hour to get uptown.

Luckily for them, Bettman had a light morning schedule. The group met in the commissioner's top-floor office and were joined by Jeffrey Pash, senior vice-president and general counsel for the league. A lawyer by training, the crafty Bettman zeroed in on Lamoureux. "Claude, you work for a union," said the commissioner, who was obviously preoccupied with the upcoming collective bargaining with the NHL Players' Association. "What are you going to do if there's a strike?" A number of governors had already privately whispered their concerns about the spectre of a union having a part ownership in one of the teams, especially at a time when they could vote to let the players strike.

Lamoureux was surprised at the misunderstanding and used his self-effacing charm to disguise his amazement while explaining how he ran a pension fund whose contributing members belonged to a union. Bettman seemed consoled, even relieved, when the actuary told him that he really worked for the Ontario government.

A few hours later, there were two items on the agenda for the NHL governors. Bettman began the meeting with the customary roll call and then announced the first: the approval of a new owner for the Toronto Maple Leafs. As Lamoureux and Stavro sat on a sofa directly across from Bettman, Bellmore described the deal over the speaker phone. Bettman weighed in with his own favourable opinions and to ward off any potential opposition, he sprinkled in highlights of their morning discussion. Most notably, he told the group that the NHL's own lawyers were satisfied that all of their concerns had been adequately addressed. All in all, it was the best Stavro could have hoped for and after a few cursory questions, the decision was unanimous.

Stavro and company lingered for the remainder of the conference call. Next up on the agenda was what to do about Bruce McNall, former chairman of these same governors and owner of the Los Angeles Kings, who was facing numerous charges, including breaching securities laws, by the Securities Exchange Commission in Washington.

At that point, Bellmore left the room to deal with an urgent matter. During the conference call, several letters were faxed within minutes of each other from Toronto and delivered to David Zimmerman, one of the NHL's lawyers. The first was a copy of the eleven-page original sent to Susan Himel by Local 847 of the International Brotherhood of Teamsters, the union representing 450 full- and part-time employees at Maple Leaf Gardens. The letter, signed by Bill Gillett, vice-president of Teamsters Local 847, urged the Public Trustee to investigate Stavro's offer on behalf of the 450 employees who were potential beneficiaries of Ballard's will through the Maple Leaf Gardens Scholarship Fund. (Ballard's will designated eight charities, including a scholarship fund and bursaries for current and former employees of the Gardens, to share in proceeds from the estate's assets.) The Teamsters wanted to make sure there was enough in Stavro's offer to pay the estate's debts and still leave enough in the kitty for the charities.

The second fax was a two-page letter written by John Perry Borden, a Toronto lawyer specializing in trust and labour law, addressed to Edward Waitzer. The letter urged Waitzer, chairman of the Ontario Securities Commission, the provincial agency that regulates Canada's largest capital market, to halt the takeover by Stavro. Borden, whose father was a former Gardens director, wrote of his concern that the beneficiaries of Ballard's estate were not receiving proper value for the assets. Borden wanted the OSC to open up a public auction of the shares because a bidding war was the only way to determine fair market value.

The third letter was a copy of the letter Eric Moore had sent to the executors via their lawyer, John McKellar, the day before.

As the faxes were delivered to Zimmerman during the conference call, he and Bellmore exchanged glances. The potential irony of the discussion about McNall was not lost on Zimmerman, who by now appeared disturbed. Soon after the governors rubber-stamped Stavro's takeover, Bellmore and Zimmerman quickly bolted to another room where the feisty Toronto lawyer dismissed the letters as nuisance claims by disgruntled charities.

Meanwhile in Toronto, Susan Himel was starting to scramble. She'd just received the Teamsters' letter although she didn't read it until much later. Making matters worse, the answers to Eric Moore's requests for more information from the Stavro camp weren't coming in fast enough for his liking. Moore's enquiries were related to documents Brian Bellmore and John McKellar had filed with the Public Trustee's office in November 1993—six months before Stavro's offer. These papers included valuations of Maple Leaf Gardens done by two Bay Street brokerage firms. Documents that combined with those already in the file—including Stavro's 1991 option agreement with Ballard's estate that gave him the right to buy its 60.3-percent block—would have given even the Gardens' Zamboni driver a pretty clear idea of where Stavro was headed.

Yet until now, the Public Trustee's office had never once raised a red flag about Stavro's potential conflicts. In fact, that was the problem; it had been saying absolutely nothing. That silence had been interpreted by many—not only Stavro—as a sign of acquiescence. Himel wasn't in a strong position to be throwing her weight around, especially in the middle of the offer. Besides, she was fully aware that her predecessor had supported Stavro in court on this matter three years earlier. Today, the best Himel could hope for was that the publicity-shy businessman would try to get court approval for his takeover. That would conveniently let everyone involved off the hook. But so far, Stavro was giving no indication of co-operating, which was why lawyers in the trustee's office were poring over the province's Charitable Gifts Act trying to find a way to force him to appear before a judge.

On May 2, two hours after Stavro's offer closed at 11 A.M., Moore dispatched copies of a two-page letter to Michael Melanson, the lawyer for MLG Ventures at Fasken, Campbell, Godfrey, Bellmore and McKellar, advising them that according to Section 5 of the 1980 provincial act that outlines the statutory guidelines of the Public Trustee's office, Stavro needed court approval to close the sale. Moore seemed to be under the impression that the offer was on the table until 5 P.M. that day. McKellar found the faxed message waiting on his desk when he returned to his office after the estate signed off on its deal with Stavro and immediately called Moore. "Eric, I have your letter but the deal is closed."

When an assistant snatched Moore's missive off the fax machine, Bellmore couldn't believe his eyes. Talk about "bureaucratic ass-covering," he thought as he punched Moore's telephone number. Too late, came Bellmore's reply to Moore, we've already closed the deal.

Bellmore knew he was being a little hasty. Stavro had amassed 89.5 percent of the shares, just shy of the 90 percent he needed to take the company private under Ontario's Business Corporations Act. His offer to minority shareholders was extended another two weeks.

In the meantime, the OSC was the first to publicly step into the fray. On May 6, the commission announced it was taking a closer look at the controversial offer. More than a few eyebrows were raised when this one hit the street. The OSC is legendary for its ability to avoid tackling prickly, high-profile issues.

That may explain why a few days later the Public Trustee decided to look beyond her own legal staff for a hired gun to figure out what her department had been doing with the Ballard file until then. First, she called Maurice Cullity, arguably the most reputable trust lawyer in Canada, who had been one of Himel's law professors at Osgoode Hall at the University of Toronto during the 1970s. Cullity begged off because of a conflict. His firm, Davies, Ward & Beck, was representing one of the two investment houses that produced the appraisals used in Stavro's bid. In fact, by the time Himel made her rounds, most of the blue-chip law firms in the city had already been drafted by the other teams involved in the deal.

After a few more enquiries, Himel called Frank Newbould, a senior partner at Borden & Elliot. The fifty-four-year-old commercial litigator had just successfully represented the Trustee's office in a complicated estate closing involving potential land fraud and had made a good impression. Strong in arguing important theoretical points of law, Newbould's courtroom skills, not to mention his firm's vast resources, would prove invaluable in what would become a high-profile, if not embarrassing case for the Public Trustee's office. Borden & Elliot was one of the largest law firms in Canada with more than two hundred lawyers, whose extensive clientele already included governments and many financial institutions (which would prove helpful during the course of the lawsuit).

Newbould was hired on May 10 at the government rate of $240 an hour to review the takeover bid even though the blue-ribbon firm where he worked had a potential conflict of its own. The previous year, three of his firm's former partners, including the same J. Perry Borden who had written to the OSC, had been representing another group of investors who were interested in the Gardens. At the time, the rival bid that was being assembled gave rise to serious disputes within the firm and particularly among the three lawyers, mostly because it was time-consuming. Eventually the disagreement caused the three partners to leave Borden & Elliot. In a bizarre twist, the Public Trustee was hiring a law firm with a past, to probe—and possibly attack—Stavro for conflicts of interest.

Thus began the exchange of courtesy letters, telephone calls and lawyers' meetings. When McKellar, who was well respected within the legal community, learned that Newbould was on the Public Trustee's payroll, he immediately called to ask for a meeting. The next day, on May 11, the two camps met at McKellar's office in the Exchange Tower in downtown Toronto. Bellmore; Donald Crump (one of Ballard's executors); David Matheson, the lawyer for Maple Leaf Gardens; and Wolfe Goodman, a founding partner of Goodman & Carr and a trust law expert, were present representing Stavro and Ballard's estate. Newbould brought along his colleague at Borden & Elliot, Robert Russell, and the Public Trustee's Eric Moore, Jay Chalke and Dana DeSante, a lawyer who worked in the charitable properties division.

At the meeting, Newbould described his client's starting position as a fact-finding mission. Bellmore balked at his use of the word "investigating" and played hard ball from the beginning by raising the spectre of Borden & Elliot's conflict. Newbould stared it down, openly declaring the conflict a red herring. The animosity between the two seasoned litigators and their personal clashes would influence the course of this legal scuffle. Repeated requests for specific information, such as the Master and Subscription agreements signed by Stavro, Ontario Teachers and TD Bank, were flatly denied. The meeting quickly deteriorated from politely cordial to barely civil. Newbould was aware of the reference in the offering circular to a proposed amalgamation of Maple Leaf Gardens and Stavro's MLG Ventures. He lobbed a few cursory questions but Bellmore said the details of that transaction were not finalized. At a meeting in the second week of June, the Maple Leaf Gardens board of directors announced the proposed merger in a press release and set aside Monday, August 9, for a special shareholders' meeting to finally seal the deal and take the company private. That prompted Newbould to ask Stavro and his business partners to delay the deal until the Public Trustee had had a chance to review all the information. The answer was a resounding no.

And so it went. While all of this was unfolding in the glass towers of the financial community, on the ice, the Leafs had bowed out of the Stanley Cup semi-finals against the Vancouver Canucks by mid-May in rather disappointing fashion.

Away from the rink, Stavro's chances of winning looked better. The OSC confirmed everyone's worst opinions by bailing out of the controversy four days after it announced its investigation. At this point, Stavro had 91.2 percent of the company (enough to squeeze out the remaining dissident shareholders) and appeared headed for a shutout. At least that's what they had planned.

The summer of 1994 would rekindle amusing memories of the circus atmosphere that engulfed Maple Leaf Gardens during the last decade of Harold Ballard's reign. Only this time it would all play out away from the Gardens. Devellano and Ornest were still at it, turning the heat up by spreading their criticisms around to include the Public Trustee. "I challenge Stavro to publicly face the media and explain his takeover grab at $34 a share," Devellano charged in the *Globe and Mail*. "This is a guy who owned all of five hundred shares until April 1994, leveraged his executive and estate control with the blessing of a subservient board of directors to pull off a deal at this low price." Although the agency's jurisdiction didn't include shareholder interests, these two unhappy stakeholders knew its actions could indirectly affect their own pocket-books.

Newbould was still being stymied. He couldn't get the estate or anyone else in Stavro's camp to hand over documents, not even to the independent business valuator, Richard Wise, he hired from Montreal. Stavro's people knew Wise's job was to help the Public Trustee evaluate the $34-a-share offer. So they'd have to think about acceding to his requests for interviews with Gardens management and its auditors at Peat Marwick. Nonetheless, the court-appointed independent valuator produced a preliminary report on July 6, severely criticizing the two appraisals assembled for Stavro's takeover offer by Bay Street brokerages RBC Dominion Securities Inc. and Burns Fry Ltd. However, Wise was unable to determine a fair market value because he didn't have pertinent information. Newbould shoved Wise's report in the faces of his legal counter-parts and received a tentative reaction: Stavro and Maple Leaf Gardens would provide access to management and the information Wise needed.

The latter never happened. In mid-July, Wise met with senior representatives of the two brokerage houses, who weren't accustomed to having their work criticized. "Mr. Wise, I resent all this. No one questions our evaluation opinions," was how Wise recalled George Dembroski, vice-chairman of RBC Dominion Securities Inc., greeted his firm's visitor. He was the same honcho who had suggested that Gardens director George Whyte "take the money and run," when Whyte met with him as chairman of the independent committee assessing Stavro's offer for the Gardens shareholders. It was a view shared by Marianne Anderson, who prepared the RBC Dominion appraisal, and Grant Haynen, a lawyer with Davies, Ward & Beck sitting in on the meeting for the broker, as well as by David Matheson, the Gardens lawyer who was an old acquaintance of Wise. Matheson was a tax lawyer at Aird & Berlis and had met Wise when the Montreal evaluator was working as a special assistant to Herb Gray, minister of national revenue during the early 1970s Liberal government of Pierre Trudeau. In fact, Matheson did the rounds with Wise, following the former senior partner at Deloitte Touche to the afternoon session with Robert Bellamy, vice chairman and executive vice-president of Burns Fry Ltd., and Jeff Watchorn, an associate who co-authored the Burns Fry report. And Matheson was also present when Wise met with the independent Gardens directors. The meetings didn't change the findings of Wise's initial critique and he was still not able to assemble his own appraisal.

Inside the Public Trustee's office, they were searching for plausible legal arguments to haul Stavro into court. The problem was that Ballard's will didn't say that court approval was necessary for the sale of the estate's shares. Stavro wasn't about to volunteer getting it, and still seemed to be under the impression that it wasn't necessary. At least that's what his lawyer said the courts had decided back in 1991. It seemed the Public Trustee's only hope was again the Charitable Gifts Act, a thirty-seven-year-old law designed to protect charitable organizations. It was one of the rule books that outlined the fiduciary role of executors. And it was in this piece of legislation that Newbould believed he'd found a case against Stavro.

In late July, Frank Newbould had requested a standstill agreement, which meant that if Stavro went ahead with the privatization meeting, the public shares in MLGL would not be cancelled. The Public Trustee's silver-haired attorney had received an unequivocal thumbs down. Then, Newbould asked if Stavro and his business partners would delay their deal until the Public Trustee had a chance to review all the material. Again, he was denied. It became apparent that something drastic would have to be done. It may have been too late to stop Stavro from buying outright ownership of Maple Leaf Gardens but there was still time to preserve the shares. If the Gardens and Stavro's MLG Ventures were amalgamated, it would be virtually impossible to undo the deal and restore the companies after they'd been dissolved. Thus Newbould decided to enlist the court's help. "We were not prepared to see the shares, about which we were conducting an investigation, amalgamated with another company and cancelled," explains deputy Public Trustee Jay Chalke.

On August 4, five days before the special Maple Leaf Gardens shareholders' meeting, in an attempt to prevent Stavro from taking the company private, the government agency's lawyer filed a claim with the Ontario Court (General Division) suing Ballard's executors for breach of their fiduciary responsibilities. By now, the Attorney General of Ontario had joined the lawsuit on Himel's side. A hearing before Justice Sidney Lederman was scheduled for 10 A.M. Monday, August 8. Once again, the Ballard circus was coming to town and would be played out before a judge.

In the meantime, some charities started calling their own lawyers. The seven charities and one bursary listed as beneficiaries in the will, dated March 30, 1988, were: Wellesley Hospital, Princess Margaret Hospital, the Charlie Conacher Throat Cancer Fund, the Salvation Army, Ontario Crippled Children's Centre (today known as the Hugh MacMillan Rehabilitation Centre), Hockey Canada, the Canadian Association for the Mentally Retarded, and the Maple Leaf Gardens Scholarship Fund.

Who would have figured that the bombastic Ballard would be true to his promise and bequeath part of Maple Leaf Gardens to charity, just as he had often threatened to do during his much-publicized battles with his three children? In fact, if Ballard hadn't been such a posthumous philanthropist, Stavro would probably have walked off with his prize with no opposition, much as Ballard had done back in 1972.

Still, the charities were sideline players to the public spectacle unfolding before them. To be sure, just by being named in the will papers, the charities found themselves in an awkward position. Ever mindful of their public image, they couldn't appear to be greedy, but at the same time, they were expected to act in the best interests of the people who benefited from their organizations. Needless to say, it was a delicate balance.

At 4:22 P.M. on the Friday before Newbould was set to stand before Justice Lederman, Marie DunSeith received a call from Newbould's office. DunSeith, president and chief executive of the Toronto Hospital Foundation and an undisputed heavyweight in philanthropic circles, had received a call from the Public Trustee's office around the time Stavro's offer was first tabled in April. Back then, the caller asked if she knew anything about a charity called the Charlie Conacher Throat Cancer Fund. The caller hit paydirt; it was one of the organizations DunSeith oversaw at Toronto Hospital. DunSeith was told her non-profit organization had been named as one of the beneficiaries in part of Ballard's will. Months later, in early August, the Public Trustee's office called her again to inform her that the government agency was going to court in less than seventy-two hours to defend the rights of the charities. She was then asked if the organization's lawyers would appear in court to support the Public Trustee on Monday morning. This would be no small feat to accomplish at the best of times, and DunSeith was annoyed at the arrogance of the request. Virtually ignored by the Public Trustee since the débâcle had begun months earlier, now the government agency wanted her to suddenly appear in court with the hospital's blue-chip lawyers—at the charity's own expense.

A copy of the Statement of Claim filed by Newbould was sent over to DunSeith's University Avenue office and in the meantime, she received instructions from John Warren, the vice-chair of the Toronto Hospital Foundation Board and another partner at Borden & Elliot. By 6 P.M. DunSeith was rushing off to another firm, Stikeman, Elliott, where William Innes waited for her arrival. Innes (who would later join the firm representing Stavro and his co-executors) and a junior lawyer named Katherine Kay would spend the entire weekend poring over the legal papers to sort out a strategy. By Sunday, the decision was made to send someone to court because "from the charity's perspective, this whole thing smelled bad. What we're saying is we'd like to get to the bottom of this," explains one of the lawyers. But when Katherine Kay called Robert Russell (Newbould's cohort) a potential problem surfaced. Kay and Innes expected that because the case was on the Commercial Court List, Justice James Farley would oversee the proceedings. Russell told them not so, that Justice Sidney Lederman would be presiding over the hearing. The problem was, Lederman, who had been just six months on the bench, had previously worked as a litigation partner at Stikeman Elliott. Kay, a relative newcomer, phoned all the lawyers on both sides to declare the potential conflict, which everyone waived without a problem.

Uptown, Darrell Gregersen, executive director of the Hugh MacMillan Children's Foundation (and therefore in charge of the crippled children's rehabilitation centre), had already made the decision to send a lawyer to protect the interests of her organization. Formerly with the Wellesley Hospital, Gregersen knew which charities were listed in Ballard's trust because she already had a copy of the will. On the Friday before the injunction hearing,

Gregersen phoned Jay Chalke to inform the Public Trustee's office that she would send Stephen Grant from the Toronto law firm Gowling, Strathy & Henderson to make a cameo appearance before the judge. "Great," came Chalke's response, "we'd really appreciate that."

Meanwhile, Newbould was scrambling too. If he was to secure an injunction and stop the proposed amalgamation, he'd have to prove to the judge that the estate could fetch more than $34 a share. For that, he went to his law school friend David Peterson, the former premier of Ontario and now a senior partner with Toronto law firm Cassels, Brock & Blackwell. Peterson was also chairman of the Toronto Raptors Basketball Club Inc., which owns the National Basketball Association's Toronto Raptors basketball franchise, and was a director of a fistful of Canadian companies. The Raptors had made a number of overtures to Stavro in recent months about a possible joint-venture arena. Newbould tried all weekend to track down Peterson with the help of John Bitove Jr. (who is Stavro's second cousin), majority owner of the Raptors. At 10 P.M. Sunday—twelve hours before his debut before Justice Lederman—Newbould located Peterson at his farm outside London, Ontario. They agreed to meet at seven-thirty the following morning in Newbould's office, where Peterson would later give the Public Trustee's lawyer a crucial affidavit with which to strut into Her Majesty's court.

By the time the phalanx of lawyers convened in Courtroom Six at 145 Queen Street West in downtown Toronto on August 8, the dynamics of the case had already changed. Suddenly, Stavro (who did not make an appearance) was no longer taking on a spineless branch of government acting on behalf of a bunch of timid charities. He was now up against the custodian of the legal system in the province, the Attorney General, and the rarefied crowd of bank presidents, billionaire retailers and industrialists that made up the charities' boards of directors.

"When you sat in that courtroom and you looked at that side of the room, the defendant side of the room, who did you have? Well, you had independent counsel for the three executors," muses one of the eleven lawyers present. "Next you have MLG Ventures and Knob Hill Farms. Well, that's Stavro. Then you have Maple Leaf Gardens supporting that side. Well, who is basically calling the shots at Maple

Leaf Gardens? We say Stavro. So you know, that's a lot of hats."

It took little time before the lead litigators began the sniping that would intensify during the next year and a half. Newbould argued that Stavro's obligation to the estate was to pay fair market value for the shares. And without testing the market or initiating a serious bidding war, there was no way of determining whether the highest price was being paid for the estate's shares. The threshold for convincing the judge was much lower when seeking an injunction. All Newbould had to do was demonstrate that there were serious questions about the deal.

A shrewd litigator, Bellmore knew this only too well. That was why he harboured such resentment towards Peterson for his last-minute affidavit in which he claimed that had there been a solicitation for bids, the Raptors would have been prepared to make "an initial bid which was significantly higher than the $34 a share" that Stavro had offered. Bellmore knew that Peterson's sworn testimony breathed life into the Public Trustee's case against his client, which until that time had been little more than a bunch of high-priced lawyers squawking at one another. For now, all the crafty lawyer could do was counter Newbould's argument: Ballard's will clearly stated that no public auction was necessary. More important, Stavro had made a deal with the estate in 1991 allowing him to get first crack at buying the shares through a private sale.

The two men were on their feet constantly, interrupting their respective arguments with sophomoric bickering, prompting Newbould to snidely remark to Justice Lederman, "Well, I don't get as uptight about this because I'm not a board member of Maple Leaf Gardens."

The estate's litigator, Bryan Finlay, fared no better in the eyes of his own clients. His argument was clear: if Stavro's co-executors, Donald Crump and Terence Kelly, had gone out to beat the bushes to snare other suitors, that would mean the estate was breaching the option agreement it had signed with Stavro. As well, canvassing the marketplace would have been fruitless anyway because it was well known publicly that the estate's shares were up for sale. And still, no offers ever surfaced. Lederman wouldn't buy any of it, prompting a very annoyed Donald Crump to request that Gardens lawyer Bernie McGarva find a suitable replacement for Finlay.

After two days of listening to accusations and denials, Justice Lederman reserved judgment until the following week. Just after noon on August 15, he handed down a fifteen-page ruling in favour of the Public Trustee, and unlike those of his peers on the judiciary who had previously handled cases involving the Ballard estate, Lederman's words were blunt. "It is recognized that Stavro is caught in a conflict between his fiduciary obligation to maximize the value of the estate's interest in MLGL and his personal interest in minimizing that value," he wrote. "His paramount obligation, however, is to the estate and he must be scrupulous in satisfying that duty. The evidence before me raised some questions about that." The judge even hinted at the sense of scandal that would engulf the high-profile case in the months ahead. Quoting that famous onerous line from the 1970s—"In short, on this issue, in the parlance of Watergate, there remain the questions: What did Stavro know; and when did he know it?"—Justice Lederman ruled that "there would be irreparable harm to the plaintiff if the amalgamation proceeded and the shares were eliminated." With that, he placed an interlocutory injunction on Stavro's plan to take the Gardens private until there was a trial because "in the circumstances before me there is enough of an issue to warrant one."

Within a month, the Public Trustee amended its statement of claim and began the process of scrutinizing the deal-making that had allowed Stavro to put together his takeover offer. Stavro; his company, Knob Hill Farms Ltd.; and his co-executors, Crump and Kelly, were sued by the Attorney General's office. (Conspicuous was the fact that Ontario Teachers and TD Bank were not named, although the bank would face that prospect almost eighteen months later.) In November, Ornest and Devellano convinced the court to allow them to add their names as plaintiffs to the Public Trustee's ticket.

That was followed by a class-action suit, launched by a homemaker in the west Toronto suburb of Etobicoke named Gwen Maxwell, who had sold Stavro her four thousand shares at $34 each after talking to brokers at three different firms.

By November, Stavro was counter-suing the Public Trustee for breaching *its* responsibilities. For Stavro, it was a stunning turn of events. All he was really doing was repeating history, helping himself to the estate's shares just as Ballard had done back in 1972 when he bought out the shares of his late partner Stafford Smythe. No one had complained twenty-two years ago.

This time, though, the game to win control of Maple Leaf Gardens was headed into overtime.

CHAPTER TWO

The "BaGa" File

"It's all going to eventually end up in the courts anyway." — HAROLD GARNER BALLARD

HAROLD EDWIN BALLARD WOULD be genuinely peeved. And not for the reasons you would think. Mischievous to the end, Harold loved controversy, especially the kind he could orchestrate and manipulate to fashion his own notoriety. By the time the eighty-six-year-old despot died in his sleep at Wellesley Hospital in Toronto on April 11, 1990, he had become a millionaire celebrity with a cantankerous public persona and a scandalous private life that scored him more newspaper headlines than his product on the ice ever did.

Thus, it would stand to reason that the late owner of Maple Leaf Gardens would be deriving some perverse satisfaction from the ownership chaos engulfing the company he left behind. In death as in life, Harold managed to court public attention. His parting salvo, his sixteen-page last will and testament, would, upon its unveiling in April 1990, close out a life that left behind a warped legacy of betrayed hopes, thwarted ambitions and a set of last instructions that would pave the way for a protracted legal battle that invited dozens of Bay Street lawyers into the fray.

That's the part Ballard would loathe. All those high-priced legal parasites in their fancy suits, racking up hundreds of bill-able hours—and millions of dollars—at his expense. Ballard knew a thing or two about that when he was alive. He carried a lot of wannabes on his dime then and he continued doing it from the grave.

Only Ballard's lawyers—Robert Sedgewick and Rosanne Roc-chi—at the Toronto firm Miller Thomson Sedgewick, Lewis and Healy knew as far back as 1979 that the bulk of Ballard's estate was earmarked for charity. That's when he first instructed Sedgewick to begin drafting a new will to replace the previous document loosely assembled in the 1960s by Campbell Burgess, a former Gardens director. Back then, Ballard was part of a triumvirate that ran the Gardens, headed by Stafford Smythe (son of Conn Smythe, who founded MLG Ltd.) and John W. Bassett, then owner of the Toronto *Telegram* newspaper.

Ballard's MLGL shares were housed in a private company, Harold E. Ballard Limited (known as HEBL), which he incorporated in 1944. At that time, Ballard was only dabbling in hockey (mostly on the organizational side) while managing the highly successful machinery company he had inherited from his father, Sid, in 1936. Born in 1903, Ballard, the only child of Sid and Mary, loved sports, especially speedskating, motor boats and hockey. He dropped out of Upper Canada College. In 1928, he became one of the assistant coaches with the Canadian Olympic hockey team in Switzerland. Four years later, the irascible Ballard managed the National Sea Fleas hockey team to the world hockey championships in Prague, where they became the first Canadian hockey team to lose a world title.

By the 1940s, Ballard had made his way into the Toronto Maple Leaf organization, helping Stafford Smythe, son of Con-stantine Falkland Cary (Conn) Smythe, the tough-minded, self-made president of Maple Leaf Gardens Ltd. He was a man Ballard revered but who showed him little more than contempt in return. "I would not give [Ballard] a job at ten cents a week," Smythe wrote in his autobiography about the man he dismissed as "an old fashioned buccaneer."

A small, stout man raised by an alcoholic mother and deeply religious father, Conn Smythe was a decorated World War I fighter who had received a Military Cross for his valiant efforts with the 25th Battery Canadian Field Artillery. He'd even been taken prisoner after his fighter plane was shot down in 1917 and spent time in a POW camp until the end of the war. When not in military garb, Smythe operated his own profitable sand and gravel business in Toronto. A perennial underdog, Smythe loved sports.

At thirty-two years of age, Conn Smythe formed the Toronto Maple Leafs hockey team on February 14, 1927, after convincing a group of investors, including wealthy mining magnate Jack Bickell, to purchase the last-place St. Patricks franchise of the National Hockey League. The price: $160,000. It was during the infant days of the NHL, which was set up in 1917, when there were just four teams: the Montreal Canadiens, the Montreal Wanderers, the Toronto Arenas (which Smythe would later purchase under their new name Toronto St. Patricks) and the Ottawa Senators.

Smythe made two notable changes that still distinguish the team today. First, he changed the squad's jersey colours from green and white to the blue and white he had worn as a player with the varsity team at the University of Toronto. Four years later, he moved the Leafs out of a dank, eight-thousand-seat rink on Mutual Street and into a spanking new thirteen-thousand-seat arena at the corner of Church and Carlton streets. The new facility was hailed in typical Toronto fashion as "world class," perhaps because the building was put together in less than six months and stayed within its budget of $1.5 million. The property was bought from the T. Eaton Co. for $350,000 and financing came from the Bank of Commerce, Sun Life and a handful of public shareholders who'd bought stock when Maple Leaf Gardens Ltd. was incorporated in February 1931. In fact, one reason the arena went up so quickly— and stayed within budget—was that Smythe was also a shrewd businessman. He gave the electricians, carpenters and bricklayers added incentive by partially paying them with Gardens stock.

On opening night, November 12, 1931, more than 13,500 fans paid as much as $2 for the best seats in the house. For those who couldn't watch the pageantry of the 48th Highlanders and the Royal Grenadiers march onto the ice on that inaugural evening— and subsequently watch the home team lose 2–1 to the Chicago Blackhawks—there was the legendary Foster Hewitt giving the play-by-play on local radio from the gondola fifty-six feet above ice level. Hewitt's game calls would make him Canada's first sportscasting celebrity and the Toronto Maple Leafs the favourite team in all of English Canada. (Sadly, Ballard would later tear down that piece of hockey tradition with the same reckless disregard he showed for the once-proud Leaf hockey team and arena. After all, Ballard said he wasn't in the historical business; out went Smythe's sign in the dressing room "Defeat Does Not Rest Lightly On Their Shoulders"—followed years later by the team's best players, including the only three fifty-goal scorers it has ever had, all because of disputes with the boss.)

Until the early 1950s, the Leafs were either winning Stanley Cups or seriously contending for the prize. But by the time the Canadian Broadcasting Corporation began telecasting "Hockey Night in Canada" on Saturday evenings in 1952, the team's fortunes had begun to sag. For the first time, Conn Smythe was openly criticized. With his health failing, requiring the warm Florida sun to soothe his aches and pains during the hockey season, Conn became more interested in racehorses and charitable works. He stepped down as general manager of the hockey team in 1955 and created the Silver Seven, a group of MLGL directors that were supposed to act as a committee on matters regarding the hockey team.

Stafford Smythe was chairman of the group, whose members included Bassett; George Mara, president of William Mara and Co., a wine importing business; George Gardiner, president of Gardiner Watson Ltd., a stock brokerage firm; Robert Amell, vice-president of Robert Amell and Co. Ltd., a large jewellery manufacturing firm; William Hatch, vice-president of McLaren's Food Products; and Harold Ballard, who had entrenched himself in the front office of the Leafs' junior team, the Toronto Marlboros, the direct result of his friendship with Smythe, whom Ballard befriended while the youngster worked as a stick boy for the Leafs in the early 1930s.

The significance of the Silver Seven in the development of the modern-day Toronto Maple Leafs is debatable. However, undoubtedly the group's influence has historical implications in the evolution of the company. Ultimately, it became the vehicle for an official opposition to Conn Smythe's iron-fisted rule at the Gardens. Led by his son Stafford (who had made a secret pact with Ballard and Bassett to buy his father's controlling shares if they were ever put on the sale block), Conn Smythe was facing relentless pressure to relinquish control of the whole company, not just the hockey team.

His eldest son had been pestering him for years. A shy asthmatic, Stafford was educated at Upper Canada College, had served in the navy and put in time running the family gravel business, and was the convenient target of his domineering father's criticisms. Conn even found fault with Stafford's choice of bride, Dorothea. Although he developed a severe inferiority complex, Stafford found in his new buddies the courage to ask for a shot at running his father's hockey business.

Finally, in November 1961, Conn Smythe succumbed, grudgingly ceding control of Maple Leaf Gardens to his son Stafford, Ballard and Bassett. The trio, which had been quietly accumulating MLGL shares for years in what amounted to a creeping takeover, bought control of the Gardens in a $2-million leveraged buyout.

The ever-resourceful Ballard arranged for the loan from the Bank of Nova Scotia, using his own assets and the shares he was about to purchase from Conn as collateral. In the end, the three bought 45,000 shares at $40 apiece to add to the 42,000 they already owned. Together, they amassed a whopping 87,000 shares, which represented a tidy block worth 60 percent of MLGL's outstanding common shares.

The new ownership regime gave each partner 20 percent of the arena and hockey team. Stafford became president but his sole responsibility was operating the hockey side of the business. Ballard (who was considered the junior member of the trio) received the title of executive vice-president, in charge of front office, and Bassett took on the role of chairman of the board. As part of their arrangement, the triumvirate signed another pact whose implications would resonate a decade later. Ballard, Smythe and Bassett agreed on a survivorship clause: if one partner died or wished to bail out, the other two would have the right of first refusal on purchasing his shares.

By 1966, Ballard was noticeably wealthier. He had transferred his MLGL stock to HEBL, the company used to house his various business interests. A reorganization of the holding company's corporate structure was necessary because it had effectively become a succession vehicle for his three children, Mary Elizabeth, William Owen Sidney and Harold Garner, known as Harold Jr. In an attempt to minimize inheritance taxes, he froze the value of the estate by eliminating ninety-seven of the original two hundred HEBL shares issued back in September 1944. The remaining shares were divided equally among the three children; 102 shares were split evenly, each child receiving 34 common shares held in trust for which they each paid $340. Ballard's wife, Dorothy, received the extra one common share (which Harold inherited upon her death in 1969), while Ballard himself owned 308,029 preferred shares, which were worth about $3.2 million.

Estate taxes were avoided because a freeze essentially allowed Ballard to let the appreciation of the company's assets accrue to the benefit of the children so that when he died, the taxes they would have had to pay on his death would have been deferred. The ownership of HEBL's equity was vested in the common shares. Each common and preferred share held one vote. So it's not hard to figure out which Ballard wielded absolute control over the company. However, back then the trust provided that upon his death, ownership of the Gardens would remain with the children.

But the decade after HEBL's corporate restructuring was tumultuous. Management at the Gardens refocused the business from merely selling hockey tickets, to flogging circuses, rock concerts, even conventions. The Leafs won their last Stanley Cup in 1967 and after that, its winning tradition became a fast-fading memory.

Yet the company's overall balance sheet was awash in black ink. Revenues tripled, the share price shot up to $114.75 in the mid-1960s before the stock split five for one. The company's shares had been trading at $26.50 just before they bought out Conn. And those all-important dividends skyrocketed from $176,539 in 1960 to $2.28 million in 1967.

The financial windfall was mostly due to Ballard's tireless marketing and blatant disregard for tradition. As boss of the arena, he crammed in another three thousand smaller seats wherever he could find the space, including tearing down a picture of Queen Elizabeth hanging in the rafters, saying, "What the hell position can a Queen play?" He also created a licensed restaurant called the Hot Stove Lounge on the southeast corner of the building in 1964. It became an overnight success and a private members' club which today boasts about a thousand members. Conn Smythe cringed at the sight of alcohol at his beloved Gardens. Had he lived long enough to witness Stavro's takeover, he'd be no less pleased to hear of rumours to convert the Hot Stove Lounge into a family hamburger eatery called JJ Muggs, which is owned by a Gardens' director. The company already caters the meals served in the private boxes, the press box and the directors' lounge.

Predictably, the Gardens stock became a darling among investors, making it a prime target for a takeover. That power play came from inside the arena. Bassett was agitating for control of the company, especially after learning that Smythe and Ballard were being investigated by the Royal Canadian Mounted Police and the Department of National Revenue in 1968. The search centred on hundreds of thousands of dollars that were allegedly skimmed from the Gardens coffers and deposited into a joint account set up by Ballard and Stafford in 1964. The police determined the two men had deposited Gardens money into unauthorized accounts, using MLGL money to pay for renovations to their homes and cottages. (A similar ruse would be unveiled after Harold's death.) Not surprisingly, Ballard and Smythe stuck together in their own defence.

When the Attorney General of Ontario weighed in with its own examination, Ballard and Smythe were formally charged with tax evasion, theft and fraud totalling a little more than half a million dollars in June 1971. Out on bail at $50,000 each, their trial was set for October that year. (Until the day he died, Ballard hated the RCMP and wouldn't let them into the Gardens to watch games for free in the standing room only sections, even though members of other police forces were always welcome.)

A month before the trial was set to begin, Bassett made one last effort to take control of the company. But his two partners—both already ousted from the board of directors—proved formidable. In the end, they still had too many allies. After five months of heated boardroom battles, Bassett bailed out, selling his 20-percent stake to Smythe and Ballard for about $5.9 million or $30 a share.

Twelve days before his day in court, Stafford Smythe, ravaged by alcoholism, died of a massive haemorrhage at fifty years of age. For the first time in almost thirty years, Ballard found himself truly alone: a new widower, on his own to stand trial, without his closest friend and cohort, and more importantly, alone to finally snatch for himself control of the company he had coveted for forty years.

Indeed, Ballard was finally going to step out from the long shadow cast by the Smythe family.

Because of the clause in their ownership agreement, Ballard was entitled to the right of first refusal on Stafford's MLGL shares. As executor of his late friend's will, Ballard facilitated the sale of those shares to his own company, HEBL, at fair market value, just as stipulated in Stafford's will. The Toronto Dominion Bank came through with a loan of $7.4 million and by February 1972, Ballard owned a commanding 71 percent of Maple Leaf Gardens stock. Thus, Conn Smythe's wish that his grand house would be passed along to another family member was shattered. Worse, the Gardens fell into the hands of a sixty-eight-year-old man whom Smythe despised, and it was soon to become known as Pal Hal's Palace. More importantly, MLGL became another in a long line of well-known Canadian companies controlled by patriarchs and wealthy families through elaborate corporate structures that flowed upstream to privately held holding companies, except that MLGL's structure was less cumbersome than most.

Ballard's first days as undisputed boss of the Gardens were interrupted when he was sentenced to three years in jail on forty-seven charges of fraud and theft. He began serving his sentence at Millhaven Penitentiary in October 1972 and on a three-day pass made national headlines when he told reporters that Millhaven was like a country club, complete with steak dinners and colour televisions. He was back at his Carlton Street stomping ground twelve months later, released on parole for good behaviour.

By the end of the 1970s, Ballard was inducted into the Hockey Hall of Fame as a builder of hockey. More importantly, his financial status appeared—at least in public—to have improved dramatically. Only a handful knew that his fortune was tenuous at best, that he'd leveraged almost everything he owned to finance his rise to the offices of chief executive officer and president. Ballard's altered financial state required a new will.

From 1979 until the summer of 1984, Ballard's "last wishes" changed constantly while his lawyers made almost daily visits to Ballard's second-floor apartment at the Gardens. Like most people, Ballard had a psychological hang-up about dealing with his own mortality. For him, signing a will was like taking one step into the grave. Yet by the time he died, Ballard had inked his signature on four different versions.

Ballard was fickle, abetted by a habit of backing off whenever he felt he was being pushed to do something. In the case of his will, Ballard kept vacillating. He became mired in the details of choosing which charities were worthy of his largesse; the children's trust, which held their equally divided shares in HEBL; and even, at times, what to leave his four grandchildren.

Back then, although the children grew up in the shadow of the colossus that was their father's checkered life, they remained deeply loyal to Harold. Bill was a lawyer and operating his own concert productions company with his partner, Michael Cohl. Mary Elizabeth, the eldest child he once referred to as a "reptile," had been employed as a physiotherapist and had married wealthy. Harold Sr. always seemed distraught about "Junior," the sensitive one who just couldn't seem to make anything of his life. Although he graduated from university, he never pursued a particular career. He dabbled in art, attending the Ontario College of Art in Toronto, a world his acutely critical father could not understand nor respect ("only flakes go to art school"). From time to time Harold Jr. worked at Davis Printing, a subsidiary of MLGL, only to be fired by his father for allegedly telling a reporter that "my dad once stuck my finger in a light socket when I was young and then told my mother he was 'just giving the kid some juice.'"

Unlike his brother, Bill, Junior wasn't a chip off the old man's block. Worse for his father, he was always hard up for cash, courtesy of sustained unemployment, a drinking problem and a nasty divorce settlement. The elder Ballard was worried that because his youngest progeny owned valuable shares in the family holding company, he would be easy prey. He wanted Sedgewick and Rocchi to devise a plan to dole out his wayward son's inheritance piecemeal to prevent him from blowing it all at once.

On other days, the topic was Yolanda Babic-MacMillan, a sixty-three-year-old bottle-blonde divorcée with a criminal record, who browbeat her way into the heart of a severe diabetic by camping outside his office with a cake and declaring to all that she craved the old man's body. Within weeks, the Fort William native was comfortably ensconced as the so-called First Lady of the Gardens, much to the chagrin of Harold's vassals.

Yet Ballard was such a miser, he couldn't decide how much to leave Yolanda, if anything at all. After much reasoning, he first agreed to $25,000 a year, but Rocchi managed to cajole him to cough up $50,000. (For years after that, Rocchi would carry a codicil in her briefcase that would have bolstered Yolanda's annual stipend to $75,000, but she never did get Harold to agree to sign it before he died.)

Not that Rocchi or Sedgewick particularly liked Yolanda. In fact, they were deeply suspicious of the woman whose parents had emigrated from Czechoslovakia in the 1920s. And with good cause. Yolanda had a track record: she had pleaded guilty to charges of conspiracy to commit fraud and perjury in the Supreme Court of Ontario in 1981. The charge stemmed from a forged will dated in 1977—and supposedly executed in Las Vegas—which was intended to defraud the beneficiaries of the estate of William Donald Lloyd, a small businessman in Chatham, Ontario, for whom Yolanda worked as a property manager in the 1970s. Yolanda met Robert Irwin, Lloyd's lawyer, ten years after her divorce from prominent Windsor lawyer William MacMillan. Irwin soon became her lover, and together they purchased the St. Clair Golf & Country Club in Wallaceburg, Ontario, with designs on refurbishing it into a resort. However, their dream soon became a sink hole creating serious cash-flow problems for the pair. So when Lloyd became ill, Irwin hatched a scheme to rewrite his client's will, leaving the bulk of his $3-million estate not to his only child (as he had stipulated), but rather to his second wife, Marion, who had agreed to go along with the plan in exchange for a million dollars and a new car every two years. When Lloyd died in 1978, the new will surfaced with Yolanda's signature as one of two witnesses (the second was a Windsor realtor).

But it was a suspicious-looking document: for example, Lloyd's name was spelled incorrectly. Soon the group was pleading guilty to a number of charges. Yolanda and Irwin were both convicted; he received four years while she first was handed three, later reduced to two on appeal. In a stinging pre-sentence report, Yolanda's former husband, William MacMillan, described her as "a compulsive liar, adept at deception with manipulative skills." Yolanda served four months at the Prison for Women at Kingston Penitentiary. That Mrs. MacMillan, née Babic, was capable of rattling the cage would be a staggering understatement.

While Ballard dithered, his lawyers fretted. They knew how precarious their client's financial situation had become as a result of crippling interest payments he was making to the Toronto Dominion Bank for loans he'd taken on to buy out Bassett and Stafford. And more importantly, they knew about a secret deal Ballard had made with the company that owned the country's largest brewery.

Ballard and the brewery fell into bed clandestinely. Ballard originally borrowed from the TD Bank at a floating rate of interest hovering around 6.5 percent. But inflation skyrocketed during the 1970s and, of course, so did interest rates. By 1980, loan rates were as high as 22 percent. Ballard was using his dividends from MLGL stock to pay back the loan. Still, they weren't generating enough revenues to keep pace with the ever-rising payments, even though MLGL had one of the best average returns of any publicly listed Canadian company. Worse for Ballard was that his controlling block of Gardens stock was used to secure the loan in the first place. By the end of the decade, Pal Hal was in serious danger of defaulting on his loan—and losing his hockey shrine.

Enter Donald Giffin, a self-made millionaire contractor who began apprenticing in the sheet-metal trade after his arrival in Toronto from Brockville, Ontario, before World War II. He had been a director of MLGL since 1970 and it was Giffin who introduced Ballard to senior officials at the TD Bank to help him buy control of the Gardens after Stafford's death. Giffin had met Ballard in 1950 through Stafford, and they became close friends after years spending summers as neighbours in Thunder Beach (on Georgian Bay in northern Ontario) where the two men owned cottages.

Giffin was going to play matchmaker again. He brought his good friend Norman Seagram to visit Ballard in early 1980. Seagram, who was executive vice-president of The Molson Companies Ltd., which had a considerable vested interest in advertising and broadcasting at the Gardens, had a proposition. Molson would provide much-needed financial relief by taking care of Ballard's burdensome interest payments on the $8.8 million he still owed on the TD loan. The caveat: Harold would have to reduce the principal on the loan by at least $600,000 a year.

Here was the rub. In exchange, Molson asked for and received an option to purchase 147,115 common shares (or 19.99 percent) in the Gardens owned by HEBL for $10,000. Molson could exercise that option within thirty days of October 31, 1990. Not only that, Molson also received a right of first refusal on the rest of Ballard's MLGL shares, entitling the company to pay 103 percent of any other offer Ballard might entertain for the shares in his holding company. Molson's right to match any bona fide third-party offer for Ballard's shares would only disappear if the company divested itself of the option.

Subsequent to that agreement, in 1986, MLGL underwent a five-for-one split, increasing Molson's stake to 735,575 shares.

At the time of the agreement in 1980, Seagram, Ballard and Sedgewick were not breaching NHL by-laws with their private arrangement. However, in 1982, the league changed the cross-ownership rules, forbidding any person or company to own an interest in more than one NHL team. As owner of the Montreal Canadiens, Molson was in a conflict of interest. But Ballard was never one to play by the rules, and he needed the money, so no one fessed up to the league or, for that matter, to the Ontario Securities Commission, whose disclosure rules were much more lax at the time.

Molson would later say publicly that it had no interest in controlling Maple Leaf Gardens. The Molson family had a long tradition with the Montreal Canadiens and wasn't interested in selling the team. Molson's goal was to protect its hammerlock on the broadcasting rights in Canada's most populous—and richest—market. Its plan was known as the "BaGa" file (an abbreviation of Ballard and Gardens) by a very small group within Molson's executive suites. Molson's agenda was to "ensure that the franchise pass to competent, interested professionals that were friendly to Molson." Company officials were desperate to keep their major competitor, John Labatt Ltd., out of Maple Leaf Gardens. At the time, Labatt had a cosy relationship with Bill Ballard, who many thought was the heir apparent. Later, that suspicion would heighten when Labatt purchased 45 percent of Bill's company, Concert Productions International, for $20 million in 1987. Bill was involved directly with the enemy and now he was making noises about taking over the Gardens. Molson didn't like that for two reasons. "We didn't think they were the appropriate people to manage that franchise," a senior Molson executive said later. And secondly, "The affiliation with Labatt. So that was motive enough."

For his part, Donald Giffin harboured his own motives. He convinced himself that both Molson and Ballard were indebted to him for bringing them together and that there were greater rewards for him down the road. A framed picture showing Giffin, Ballard and Edward Lawrence (a long-time MLGL director) at the signing with the TD Bank hung in his office as a constant reminder of his contribution to Ballard. Another picture of Ballard hung on the wall in Giffin's rec room in his north Toronto home. (Years later when Giffin attempted to call in the favours for his yeoman services, he would be crushed with disappointment.)

So the arrangement remained a dirty little secret the boys at Molson and Ballard kept from everyone until late 1988. When Ballard's health took a serious turn for the worse, Seagram and Donald Crump, the Gardens secretary-treasurer, flew to New York on December 1 to break the news to NHL president John Ziegler. Through it all, Ballard kept a poker face but his lawyers knew he had a tenuous hold on his hockey shrine.

On May 4, 1984, Ballard was finally jolted out of his complacency. Bob Sedgewick, his trusted lawyer and confidante, died suddenly of a heart attack at fifty-nine years of age. The Harvard-educated Sedgewick was a respected litigator, who was a stabilizing influence on Ballard and his children without smothering him with advice, as many others in his entourage attempted to do constantly. Sedgewick was also highly regarded in business and sports circles as secretary and vice-president of the NHL. As the alternate governor for the Toronto Maple Leafs, Sedgewick also served as a human buffer between the combative and tempestuous Ballard and the other NHL owners.

Ballard, who shrank from public displays of intimacy, was devastated by the loss, not least because he had selected Sedgewick to be one of his executors. So distraught was Ballard, he beckoned Rosanne Rocchi and Arthur Gans (one of Sedgewick's partners), to bring the draft of the will to his apartment for immediate signing. But there was a problem. One of the sticking points in the past was that Ballard couldn't decide on who to name as third executor alongside Donald Crump, the fifty-one-year-old accountant who had joined the Gardens two days before Ballard and Smythe had been hauled away in handcuffs, and the recently deceased Sedgewick. Now, because Ballard had not signed the document before his lawyer died, he had to find two trustees to make the quorum of three he needed.

Ballard, Rocchi, Crump and Gans deliberated over a shortlist of candidates that included Paul McNamara, chairman of MLGL's board of directors. A lawyer by training who never practised law, McNamara was one of the few who remained loyal to Ballard while he was in prison. But many in Ballard's court said that he ruined his own chances when he audaciously asked a grieving Ballard if he could be named as the Leafs' new alternate NHL governor. Worse for the chairman of the board, he made his request before mourners gathered for Sedgewick's wake. Harold was incensed. McNamara was quickly banished from the list of candidates for having the temerity to act like a jock sniffer.

Ballard finally signed the elusive document a month after his lawyer's untimely death. Gans replaced his late colleague and the third name added to the will was the newest member of MLGL's board of directors: Steve Stavro, a Macedonian immigrant who met Ballard in sporting circles during the 1960s. Stavro was appointed to the Gardens board in 1981, but he had not yet figured prominently in the affairs of the company.

One of Harold's few joys in life was detonating bombs of the verbal kind. On New Year's Eve heading into 1988, as he was leaving town with Yolanda for his annual winter vacation in Florida, Ballard flicked his most explosive grenade. He made good on his threats to cut his bickering children out of the will entirely. He told his friend Milt Dunnell, a sports columnist with the *Toronto Star*, that he was leaving the whole business—his entire block of shares that controlled Maple Leaf Gardens in HEBL—to a handful of charities.

At the time, the children owned all the common stock in HEBL, worth $120 million, and 80 percent (or about three million shares) of the Gardens. Because their father owned all the preferred shares—remember, each had a vote—he controlled HEBL. As well, Ballard owned an additional 10 percent of Gardens shares on his own. In what appeared to be an uncharacteristically selfless act, Ballard said he was going to bequeath all his wealth to charity by setting up a trust with representatives from each named organization to operate the Gardens and the hockey club.

Needless to say, everyone from the Gardens' ushers to the crippled children were stunned. After all, the prevailing wisdom was that Ballard was worth in the range of $100 million. What would charity do with all that money? Besides, the Charitable Gifts Act of Ontario prohibits any one charity from owning more than 10 percent of a business. At the time, the Canadian Cancer Society was the only charity ever publicly named. Overnight, non-profit organizations across the country began jockeying for position. Experts were sought and the demand curve for tax lawyers started heading north.

Then, as if on cue, Ballard suffered a heart attack three days later at the West Palm Beach home of Steve Stavro. While he recuperated at the Miami Heart Institute, the vultures began circling.

The announcement to the *Star* was vintage Ballard, always angling for the greatest shock value. In truth, his kids had been written out of the will for years during the document's third incarnation dating from March 1986. He never gave them credit for having the ability to actually manage the company, and he was concerned that their ill will and sibling battles would eventually cannibalize his beloved legacy. In the end, he'd grown weary of his stormy relationship with the children, much of it induced by their hostility towards his tumultuous relationship with Yolanda. The children were highly suspicious of her unbridled ambition. In fact, they viewed Yolanda simply as a gold digger, conveniently blaming her for reducing the family to the public farce that it had become by the late 1980s. "It was noisy, chaotic, it was pathetic and it was very uncomfortable for an outsider to see inside this dysfunctional family," was how one observer saw the feuding clan.

But Ballard wouldn't listen to any of it. Besides, he figured his children didn't need an inheritance because they were already millionaires by virtue of their common stock in the holding company. Each still owned thirty-four common shares in HEBL and, like their father, had benefited handsomely from the stock's rise over the years. "He didn't want the children fighting over Maple Leaf Gardens," explains Rocchi, the legal author of Ballard's will. "He knew that each of his children had different interests and different needs. He was concerned that the different needs couldn't be accommodated if they were left to sort out matters on their own."

Mary Elizabeth and Bill refused to comment. But Harold Jr. had a few prescient words to say. "This is against the arrangement with us guys that it remain my brother, my sister, my father and myself," he told reporters. "It's all going to eventually end up in the courts anyway." No truer words were ever spoken.

Ballard signed the fourth—and final—version of his last will and testament on March 30, 1988, four months before he was scheduled to undergo major heart surgery. His health was deteriorating faster than his hockey team, so on the eve of his eighty-fifth birthday Ballard wanted to put his house in order.

Although the family patriarch may have had overwhelming control over the holding company, he couldn't strip his children of the shares he'd given them over twenty years ago. If he wanted their shares, he'd have to buy them. And Ballard needed them. Badly. He still wanted to solidify his own position, which had been eroded as a result of his earlier deals. By the end of the 1980s, Ballard was convinced (and with good reason) that there were forces conspiring to overthrow him, including Molson, Labatt and even singer Anne Murray, who had made an offer in 1982.

Ballard's paranoia was fuelled partly by an incident with a businessman from Manitoba named Michael Gobuty. A former owner of the Winnipeg Jets (when the team belonged to the World Hockey Association), Gobuty was introduced to Ballard by Yolanda in 1984. For the next few years, they did the couple thing: Ballard and Gobuty (who took the late King Clancy's place next to Harold during the games) bonded while their respective mates, Yolanda and Adrienne, went shopping. The men talked business; most of the time Gobuty was looking for handouts. His leather company, Gobuty & Sons, was taken over by the liquidators; his Assiniboia Race Track in Winnipeg had failed; and his latest venture, a garbage container pickup service called Canus Containers Corp., desperately needed refinancing. (It too would fall into receivership in 1988.)

In August 1987, Ballard put up a $5-million guarantee to back a revolving operating loan, worth $2.5 million, Gobuty had taken out from the National Bank of Canada to pay off his debts at Lloyds Bank of Canada. Curiously, Harold appeared to receive nothing in return for this gesture and he never mentioned the guarantee to Crump (his trusted bean counter) or his lawyers, who learned about it when Harold checked into the hospital for his quintuple-bypass surgery.

At the same time Gobuty had secured the guarantee from Harold, he had also cut cheques of his own to Yolanda. The most notable one was worth $75,000 drawn on a Lloyds Bank of Canada account. Yolanda would later explain under oath that she received the money in return for "[her] mother's precious jewellery." It was the same line she had given Maple Leaf Gardens four years earlier when they investigated a mysterious $25,000 cheque deposited from Ballard's account to her own at the Canadian Imperial Bank of Commerce. The cheque from Gobuty would haunt Yolanda again in 1990 when she sued Ballard's estate for more money.

Whether Ballard knew he was being played for a fool is not clear. Gobuty's intention had been to use the same money the old curmudgeon helped him secure to stage a friendly takeover of Maple Leaf Gardens. Ballard would later claim it was all a joke. But National Bank wasn't laughing. When it called in the loan, Gobuty didn't have the money. Naturally, the bank sued Gobuty and Ballard as the guarantor.

The trial degenerated into a spectacle with Yolanda at the centre delivering typical grist for the gossip mill. In the end, the Ontario Court of Justice ordered Gobuty to pay National Bank $3.4 million (including interest). But because Ballard had guaranteed the loan, he was on the hook for the money. His estate eventually paid over $3 million to settle with the creditors. The incident heightened everyone's paranoia about Yolanda while many couldn't help but notice how obvious Gobuty's motives appeared to be. The Gardens' denizens increasingly viewed this as a sure sign that the crafty Harold was declining. "I didn't worry too much until the discovery of the guarantees that he had signed in favour of Gobuty," recalls Rocchi. "That was when the trouble started and that was when many of us became very protective of him."

Around the same time, Donald Giffin was looking for a hat-trick. Having successfully helped Ballard stickhandle out of tight financial corners twice before, Giffin was trying for a third shot at playing matchmaker. For as long as anyone could remember, the seventy-three-year-old soft-spoken man cradled a not-so-secret desire to one day control the Carlton Street arena. Giffin never wanted to actually own it. Always proud of his association with the company, he wanted to be part of it—a player. But the father of six sons, Giffin didn't have the money, or the valour, to fulfil his dream alone. His only real hope rested with his friends at Molson, who included Mickey Cohen, the former federal bureaucrat who took over as chief executive officer and president in 1988. By acting as Molson's emissary while still playing loyal foot soldier to Ballard, Giffin covered both ends of the rink.

For Molson, Giffin was perfect. "He was the one single person that could work with each of the three children individually or collectively, with Harold and with ourselves. He was the only one who could bring Yolanda to some sort of common meeting with the kids, and he was driven by an honest wish to make the place a better place," is how Norman Seagram describes Giffin. "He shared Molson's objective. He saw the franchise and the business disintegrating because of Harold Ballard's management style. And he too wanted MLG to pass into competent hands."

Molson was less sure of the others. "There was always concerns with Donald Crump," explains another Molson executive. "What you see is not always what you get. He was always obliging until he had to do something. And since he was someone who'd pass things back and forth, you couldn't rely on him for accurate information." In the end, they underestimated the man who introduced Giffin to Seagram in the first place. Stavro was still an unknown factor, one that Molson would try to figure out only later. "He was completely invisible," the Molson executive continued. "He was just not a factor or wasn't a name that ever appeared on anybody's radar." "It wasn't until Harold Ballard took sick and became incompetent [that] Steve Stavro started to get involved."

Molson was constantly prodding Ballard, testing his resolve to hold onto the company. Norman Seagram, a slim, taut fifty-four-year-old engineer with a quarter-century of experience in the beer business, developed close personal relations with most of the Gardens' denizens. Although he didn't have standing orders from Molson's board of directors to officially pursue anything specific with Ballard, Seagram floated a lot of ideas over the years, and not necessarily always with the company's blessing. His ultimate goal was to protect his brewery's exclusive sponsorship rights at Maple Leaf Gardens. "Norman may have seen his role as an attempt to try to identify the impossible in Mission Impossible," deadpans a former Molson colleague.

But Seagram, who was well liked by everyone, saw his mission clearly. "It goes back to the basic objective that really drove Molson in the first place," he explains. "Here we had what had been an extremely valuable advertising and promotional property in Maple Leaf rights, but audiences were dropping off, people didn't give a damn, radio audiences were off.

"Everybody was down on Harold. Everybody was waiting for the future, and the future involved Harold getting out of it. Sure, Harold was a rascal, he was an unusual character, and everybody admired him because he didn't give a damn what people thought about him or said about him. The more controversial it was, the better he liked it and if it wasn't controversial enough, he would make it controversial. He liked to stick it to people and people sort of admired that but in fact, they hated the way the club was going. And despite his belief in his own invincibility, we even recognized that Ballard was going to eventually die and he better bloody well get his affairs in order. We did not like the idea, for one moment, of it passing into the hands of Bill Ballard and Michael Cohl."

Giffin was very useful in Molson's endeavour. He could deliver the vital details of Ballard's will. As part of their overall plan to influence the new ownership of the Gardens, Molson officials needed to know how the estate would be carved up. Apart from Rocchi and Ballard, the only people who actually knew the details were Donald Crump and Steve Stavro—and they weren't talking.

When a bereaved Ballard had signed the will back in 1984, he directed that a trust be established to house his controlling shares in HEBL and his majority stake in Maple Leaf Gardens. The three executors would act as trustees and were also named directors of

HEBL. Among their required duties, the executors were instructed to operate the business affairs of the company, dissolve HEBL, and sell its MLGL shares at a time they deemed appropriate, but no later than twenty-one years after Ballard's death. In the meantime, Ballard listed the names of eight non-profit and humanitarian organizations to receive donations from the dividends being accrued in the trust from the MLGL shares. All the while, Ballard's name would remain publicly associated with Maple Leaf Gardens while further perpetuating his other image as a grand philanthropist. Once the trust was liquidated and the Gardens shares sold, the proceeds of that sale were to be used to pay off the estate's debts—which would total about $60 million by the time Ballard died. Whatever remained would be transferred to the Harold E. Ballard Foundation, a registered charity and from there the funds were to be disbursed for philanthropic purposes to be decided by the Foundation's directors—Stavro, Crump and Giffin.

Stavro and Crump knew about Ballard's last instructions in 1984 when, as named executors, their signatures were needed on the paperwork to set up the trust. Giffin's name was added three years later, the result of a falling-out between Ballard and lawyer Arthur Gans.

Once his name was on the will, Giffin was constantly badgering Rocchi for a copy, which she refused to give him. However, Ballard's lawyer did oblige by giving him highlights of the will's contents. Whatever bits of information Giffin learned were invariably passed on to his buddies at Molson.

Giffin and Seagram shared a common perspective. To them, hockey wasn't just dollars and cents, it was like religion. Giffin could only watch with envy at the way Molson operated the Montreal Canadiens, all that tradition, integrity, and honour, the very attributes missing from the Toronto Maple Leafs under Ballard's reign. Giffin figured Molson could restore the team to its glory days, maybe even before Harold died.

To that end, he would give the Molson boys access to the increasingly reclusive Ballard, parading Seagram and Doug Love, Molson's in-house lawyer, around the Gardens every few weeks. Usually they'd watch the team practise from the red seats with Ballard, whose health was taking a decided turn for the worse. The talk would inevitably turn to Ballard's shares. Molson wanted the old man's stock but they never said so overtly. At least not at first. They'd be non-committal when talk turned to what Molson intended to do with its option.

Mindful of the tight grip the brewery had on him, Ballard humoured them, stringing them along. In April 1988, Molson's lawyers had already assembled and delivered to Ballard a fourteen-page checklist fleshing out a proposal in the event Harold actually decided to sell during his lifetime. Although no specific numbers and values were cited, the document prepared by Osler, Hoskin & Harcourt outlined a strict timetabled step-by-step process to first purchase Ballard's HEBL shares and then offer to buy out MLGL's other shareholders. The proposal also called for the company to be split into two separate entities, known as the "butterfly" reorgani-zation. (That idea would be floated again after Ballard's death.)

Harold also knew that Molson, through Giffin, was quietly courting his children's shares. They were already talking with Harold Jr. in November 1988 about buying out his thirty-four HEBL shares for $15.3 million (based on a market value of $40 a share). Although the youngest Ballard bailed out, Mary Elizabeth decided to cash out. Her lawyer John McKellar enquired whether Giffin might discuss a similar offer to the one he was negotiating with her brother. Sure thing, came the reply. But first, the loyal foot soldier would have to clear it with her father.

A tacit blessing was given and Giffin offered up a $50,000 deposit as a sign of good faith. But on the eve of consummating the deal, Mary Elizabeth's tax lawyers did some number crunching. They claimed that she'd be on the hook for millions of dollars in capital gains taxes if she sold to Giffin. However, a sale to her father would result in a tidy tax deferral because she would be redeeming shares and receiving a deemed dividend from a non-arm's-length company. On January 20, 1989, Mary Elizabeth severed all ties to the family by selling her thirty-four HEBL shares to her father for $15.5 million. Giffin got his $50,000 back with interest.

Guess who bankrolled this deal. When an infuriated Ballard learned that Giffin wasn't using his own money to buy out his daughter (but was being financed with an interest-free loan from Molson), he went straight to Molson himself. Ballard got the loan with the help of Giffin and Mary Elizabeth's shares. But it didn't come cheap either for Ballard. In return for opening its vault, Molson secured its loan to Ballard with Mary Elizabeth's shares, which Ballard warehoused in 810756 Ontario Ltd., a numbered company he indirectly owned and created for this transaction. Finally, Molson had its hands on a third of the company that controlled Maple Leaf Gardens and a string on the other shares.

Once again, the mercenary wound up playing the bridesmaid. Only this time, Giffin's disappointment was eased with a consolation prize. He was named to the board of HEBL, replacing Bill Ballard, who was unilaterally ousted by his father after yet another blowout over Yolanda.

Two months later, in March 1989, Molson switched gears. Moving from their informal chats with Ballard, Seagram and Love scratched something down on paper. "What we were trying to do was determine well, is there a ball park? Have we got anything really to talk about? So we tried to put something concrete into his mind," Seagram recalls. That came in the form of a two-page memorandum they asked Rocchi to deliver to her client.

According to the transaction points outlined, Molson would purchase Harold's one common and 308,029 preferred shares in HEBL and his 350,320 common shares in MLGL (which he held directly) for $34.5 million based on Molson's assessment that Maple Leaf Gardens was worth $160 million at the time. As well, Molson intended to make a follow-up offer of $43.60 a share to all the outstanding shares in MLGL held by the public after vetting the proposal with John Ziegler. If the offer was accepted, there were also plans to shake up the Gardens board of directors and HEBL, adding Seagram and Marshall Cohen to the holding company's board. Having done that, Molson planned to split the company into the so-called "butterfly" and then flip the team to a friendly third party (Seagram kept an active list of potential suitors). Molson, which says it prides itself on treating its employees with compassion, would allow Harold to continue living in his second-floor apartment; however, the corporation wanted to buy Ballard's house in Etobicoke, the condo on 130 Carlton Street that he had purchased in 1985, and his cottage in Georgian Bay.

The proposal, however, had not been discussed by Molson's

board of directors, although Cohen was always informed about the BaGa file. According to the Molson proposal, Giffin's contributions were also singled out for future consideration: "G's role in this and other transactions will be recognized in a separate compensation arrangement, still to be determined." Later, Giffin would be greatly disappointed.

Looking back, Giffin seems pathetic in how much he underestimated Ballard. Given the forty-year history between the two men and their families, he should have known that Ballard would never sell the team, the arena or any other part of the company while he was still alive. Ballard craved public attention and used outlandish behaviour to draw attention to his team—and himself. Always the crafty marketer, Ballard wasn't going to give up the very forum that allowed him to emerge as a public figure with a national profile. Instead, Giffin inadvertently set in motion the process that would ultimately banish him from the arena he fought so hard to get.

Ballard was insulted by Molson's proposal. "It was rejected, completely, absolutely and totally as being ridiculous," recalls one of those involved. Ballard bellowed that he wanted $300 million for his shares alone. Then again, "Harold never distinguished between what we had an option on, what the public owned and what he owned either directly, or in fact, controlled but not owned. He always believed he owned the whole thing, lock, stock and barrel."

Perception became the reality. Ballard confirmed his long-held suspicions that the brewery wanted to steal the company away from him and complained to his fellow governors about the company's bold overture. In fact, he even tried to buy back the option on his shares that he had signed over to Molson back in 1980. And although his later moves were meant to entrench his own position, they'd provide opportunities for others who sought to wrest control of his company. His deal with Mary Elizabeth further alienated family members, who'd made a pact years earlier to stick together rather than sell out. Harold, suspecting that Molson and his son Bill were conspiring against him, was even more determined to buy back Junior's stake.

It was also a wake-up call for Molson. Clearly, the company could no longer try to subliminally beat Ballard into submission in the hope that he would eventually sell. Still determined to influence MLGL affairs, Molson overhauled its strategy. First, Seagram declared unequivocally that Molson wasn't interested in giving up its option; in fact, the company was going to seize the shares when they became available and use them to take a run at Harold's company. Almost overnight, Molson had changed from friend to foe, and that's when, according to Giffin, "the mud hit the fan."

And second, the company would employ the best weapon in its arsenal: cash. After two centuries of brewing beer, the Molson family is old Montreal money—wealthy Anglophones in a long line of descendants dating back to 1786 when twenty-three-year-old English orphan John Molson began making beer in Montreal. Indeed, the family-controlled company would be more than happy to bankroll Ballard's attempt to strengthen his own hold on the family business.

Molson's main objective was to stay friendly with Ballard and his children. That way, if the company snatched Harold's 308,029 preferred shares in HEBL, it wouldn't be fighting with the children over the holding company's common shares. Why? Because that's where the real power lay, thanks to changes in the Ontario Business Corporations Act in 1980, requiring the consent of two-thirds of the common shareholders to make any corporate changes. That change wreaked havoc on estate freezes, like Ballard's, across the country. The bottom line: Ballard's children had the real power in HEBL as custodians of the company's common shares. The new strategy for Molson was to neutralize the kids' shares now that their sibling pact had been shot out of the water by Mary Elizabeth. Molson dispatched Giffin to begin working on Harold Jr., and Seagram had already met twice with Michael Cohl, who represented the interests of the Ballard brothers, about buying their common shares.

Giffin got the ball rolling when he offered to buy the younger Ballard's shares. He repeated his earlier mistake and told his boss, Harold Sr., about the offer. Before long, Giffin was sidelined and the battle over Junior's shares came down to Bill and his father. Bill and his brother had apparently signed an agreement in late 1988 in which Junior agreed to sell his shares to a numbered company, 820099, controlled by Bill and Cohl. They formalized the deal in February 1989 with an agreement that granted 820099 the option to purchase all of Harold Jr.'s shares on or by June 30, 1989. That would have given Bill majority ownership of the outstanding common shares of HEBL. (Later, Bill would admit the plan was to either flip the shares to Molson or take control and spin off the arena.)

None of this was lost on his father. Harold Sr. worked his youngest son over pretty thoroughly; so did Crump and Giffin. Five months after taking out his daughter, Harold purchased Junior's thirty-four HEBL common shares on June 20, 1989. The total tab: $21 million, and this time, the line of credit came from the TD Bank. Said one Molson executive, "The one thing that became very, very clear was that for family reasons (that we really didn't understand), there was no way he would allow—if he could help it—the management, the ownership or control of the Gardens to flow to Bill. He would pay anything to avoid that." Thus, within a year of proclaiming to the world that he was erasing his children from his will, Ballard was one step away from eliminating them from the family business altogether. In doing so, he set the scene for the battle that would be waged after his death. And Bill Ballard would be front and centre.

Lost in the flurry of negotiations with his children was a two-page agreement Ballard signed after relentless badgering from his close friend. Giffin desperately wanted a token from Ballard, a reward for helping him arrange the financing that gave him back control of the company. Ballard signed an agreement on April 13, 1989, granting Giffin an option to purchase the thirty-four HEBL common shares formerly held by Mary Elizabeth after the $15.5-million loan was paid back to Molson. Ballard attached little importance to the gesture but for Giffin, it had enormous significance. For the next year, Giffin would clutch—even flaunt—the option as tangible evidence that he had truly become a player in the Gardens sweepstakes. His fellow executors and board members took notice too and, consequently, it would drive a wedge between them. How they attempted to even the score eventually started yet another battle for control of Maple Leaf Gardens.

CHAPTER THREE

Harold Ballard's Legacy

"There will be a lengthy court fight unless somebody rich steps up to the plate and pays everybody off." — ALAN EAGLESON

VERNON JACKSON RECEIVED A visitor from Toronto in his Cayman Island office on January 2, 1990. The vivacious, middle-aged blonde enquired whether Jackson, a local justice of the peace, would appear at a marriage scheduled for the following day. All the necessary paperwork was in order, she said, including a blank copy of a special marriage licence required by non-residents of the Caymans wishing to marry while on the islands. The only caveat: her groom-to-be was immobile. Would Jackson go to him?

The former high-ranking civil servant agreed, accompanying his visitor to condominium number 18 at the posh Colonial Club, to witness the signing of the marriage licence. When Jackson arrived, he found a sunburned Harold Ballard in a wheelchair seated in front of a table. The justice of the peace had no idea that the feeble-looking old man was a multi-millionaire hockey czar whom family and business associates, along with a pack of news reporters, were desperately searching to find. Nor, for that matter, did he know that his lady caller was Yolanda Babic-MacMillan-Ballard, who had secretly whisked the eighty-six-year-old away to the Caribbean three weeks earlier.

Even after their names appeared on the marriage application—a controversial document that would later be scrutinized by hand-writing specialists—Jackson remained blissfully unaware of the gathering storm around him. He left behind the completed marriage licence with Yolanda to process with the proper authorities.

The next day Jackson returned to Condo 18 to perform the civil wedding ceremony. Resplendent in off-white, Yolanda stood ready by Harold, who was dressed casually in Bermuda shorts and seated in his wheelchair. Denise Banks, a teenager who had worked as Yolanda's helper at the cottage and later became her full-time companion, would play bridesmaid.

Minutes before the ceremony was to begin, Jackson and Yolanda noticed that Ballard's sun-kissed skin could not disguise how pale and unwell he looked. Even Yolanda later said she was concerned about Ballard's pallor. When Jackson asked if he was ready to get married, a befuddled Ballard responded by saying *he* wasn't getting married.

Jackson figured Ballard was suffering from cold feet, not an uncommon occurrence in his line of work. With that, the justice of the peace said goodbye, leaving behind a subdued Yolanda with her dashed dreams on her fifty-seventh birthday. What happened next depends on whose story you believe.

Within hours of the aborted wedding ceremony, an unconscious Ballard was admitted into Cayman Island Government Hospital. Late the next day, on January 4, he was rushed by air ambulance to Baptist Hospital in Miami, where he was listed in critical condition with kidney failure brought on by diabetes and a heart condition. Dr. Vernon Sichewsky, a specialist in treating patients suffering from shock and trauma, was the attending physician on the airplane from the Caymans to Miami. He later told investigators that Ballard was in "bad shape" when he arrived at the Caymans hospital. "He was in very critical and unstable condition. He was close to dying."

Meanwhile, the battery of lawyers, friends and advisers back in Toronto were just finding out about the nuptials. When Ballard and Yolanda had first arrived in the Caymans on December 14, 1989, they checked into a beach-front condominium at the Casa Caribe on Grand Cayman. But two weeks later, for no apparent reason, they moved to the Colonial Club without telling anyone. Finally, contacts in the Caymans were able to track them down, despite strict orders from Yolanda to the hotel staff to advise anyone who called that she and Harold had gone to Hawaii.

Ballard's sudden disappearance was deeply suspicious. He'd been ill for weeks, in fact too weak to attend the annual National Hockey League Board of Governors' meeting in Palm Beach, Florida, in early December. And there were other puzzles: Yolanda sneaked Harold out of Maple Leaf Gardens without anyone knowing. In fact, Donald Crump found out they were gone only when a waiter from the Hot Stove Lounge called to complain about water dripping from the ceiling into the restaurant. Ballard's second-floor apartment was directly above the restaurant. After pounding on the door, Crump went looking for someone with a key to Ballard's apartment. Once inside, he found all the windows wide open and because it was so cold, the pipes had frozen, causing one to burst, seeping water into the floor. It wasn't until a few hours later that Ballard's hairdresser Joseph DeFrancesco told Ballard's associates that he, instead of the regular chauffeur, had driven the couple to the airport at Yolanda's request. Crump also noticed that the vault Harold had inside a column in the wall was open—and empty. Only the piece of paper with the safe's combination, which Ballard kept in a drawer of his desk, was left inside.

Worse, Ballard had been taken out of the country at a time when Yolanda knew his entourage would be scattered to distant parts. Rosanne Rocchi was scheduled to leave for a vacation in the Far East in early January, and Donald Giffin was already vacationing in the Caribbean with his wife, Patty. Only Donald Crump would be hanging around the arena, but Yolanda had little use for him anyway. She had thrown one of Harold's soiled diapers into Crump's hat a few months earlier.

The longer Ballard was away, the more alarmed Rocchi and Crump became about his lady friend's motives. Rocchi had become close to Ballard, so much that his associates viewed her as a surrogate daughter, even though she'd worked as a Gardens lawyer for two years before actually meeting Ballard. Born in Hamilton, Ontario, to Italian immigrants (her father was a tool and die maker), the thirty-nine-year-old Rocchi was the second of six children. She had earned three university degrees: a Bachelor of Arts in English Literature at the University of Toronto, a law degree at Osgoode Hall and later a Master's Degree in tax law. She began as an articling student at Tory Tory DesLauriers & Binnington but joined Miller Thomson in 1978 after she was called to the bar. Rocchi joined Sedgewick on the Gardens file a year later. After her senior legal mentor died in 1984, Rocchi toiled hard enough to keep the high-profile account with her firm and was rewarded by being named a partner. "I don't think he was particularly happy about having a young female lawyer but it was sort of novel and mischievous to have one around as a good little helper. Still it was another thing to rely on a woman's advice just because it wasn't the manly thing to do." The difference in their age, their background and even their gender would soon dissipate. "Every morning I would receive a call from Mr. Ballard announcing that he had the yellow pages in front of him and he was looking for a 'tough Jewish lawyer.' 'What have I done now?' He would reply, 'It's what you haven't done—get up here,'" Rocchi remembers. "If I was in the room when he was giving instructions to someone, he expected me to make sure they were carried out. When they were not, he would hold me responsible."

A chain-smoking stickler for detail, Rocchi began making headlines in 1989 during a trial that saw Bill Ballard convicted and fined $500 for allegedly assaulting Yolanda during another of their famous verbal brawls. As Harold's lawyer, Rocchi was given the task of defending her client's lady friend, and soon feminists hailed Rocchi as a defender of abused women. But the increasingly competitive directors on the Gardens board accused Ballard's lawyer of seeking publicity for herself. Harold was too frail to care.

Still, Rocchi and Crump knew that Ballard had offered his on-again-off-again companion his condominium at 130 Carlton Street (not in the Gardens) back in August before the disappearance if she would agree to get out of his life. In an internal memo, Rocchi recalled that Ballard had told her that he mistrusted Yolanda and wanted her gone.

A few weeks before Ballard's sudden disappearance, Giffin witnessed a disturbing scene in Ballard's apartment; he reported the details to Rocchi. On November 25, Giffin found Ballard huddled in a chair with blankets wrapped about him and a baseboard heater at his feet. Giffin had gone looking for "the chief" when he hadn't appeared in his bunker during the Saturday night hockey game. When Giffin asked Ballard why he wasn't watching the game, the old man asked his foot soldier to sit down. With Yolanda in the room, Ballard told Giffin that he was so upset "with that goddamn bitch" that he could not watch the game. He then said, "I have told that fucking Rosanne to get Yolanda out of this fucking building and she hasn't done a goddamn thing about it." At that point, according to the internal memo, Yolanda left the room, making some derogatory remarks. Ballard then continued with a litany of complaints, alleging that Yolanda was taking advantage of him, that she was isolating him from his family and friends and was monitoring his phone calls.

Moments later, Yolanda returned to the apartment, saying "that she was good enough to wipe his ass when he was in the hospital." To which Ballard replied "that she had never touched his ass." The bickering continued while a bemused Giffin tried to referee. When Giffin asked why the windows were all open, Yolanda accused Bill Ballard and Donald Crump of trying to kill her by pumping gas into the apartment. (She repeated these same words to Rocchi the next day.) Meanwhile, Donald Mazankowski, then minister of defence, sat waiting in the Directors' Lounge as a guest of Ballard.

The following week, Rocchi called to meet her client only to be told by Yolanda that he was on his way to see doctors at Toronto Hospital and that he would call her later. Hours passed and Ballard had not yet called. So Rocchi went to the hospital only to find Ballard and Yolanda fighting in the front lobby. When they returned to his apartment in the Gardens, Rocchi says Ballard repeated the same complaints he'd outlined to Giffin earlier. Ballard wanted space from Yolanda and he didn't want her administering his medication anymore. He dismissed Yolanda's complaints to the police about poison gas being pumped into his living quarters and chuckled at the thought of Donald Crump carrying a gas canister on his back. Ballard asked Rocchi to persuade Yolanda to accept the condo but Yolanda refused, crying that she'd devoted her life to Harold for years. Rocchi then suggested Yolanda take a two-week vacation in Florida as a trial separation.

Ballard was not alone in his suspicions. A few years earlier, Crump and Bill Cluff, the director of marketing who'd been around the Gardens for twenty-three years, had lunch with Norman Booth, a detective from Metro Toronto Police's 54 Division. Cluff had entered Harold's circle of friends through Bill in 1972, often driving to prison with the younger Ballard to visit his father. The bachelor with the raspy voice was one of the very few who was never relegated to Harold's doghouse because of his loyalty and genuine concern for the increasingly sick man. Cluff and Crump told Booth they "had a woman who was a problem" and they wanted her checked out, recalls Booth.

When Yolanda had showed up outside Ballard's door back in 1984, she was still on parole for her will forgery conviction two years earlier. Booth, who watched a few team practices while drinking coffee with Ballard in the red seats, said that Yolanda had previously given 60 Carlton Street as her home address to the Ontario Parole Board. In fact, when she first left the Prison for Women at Kingston Penitentiary in mid-1982, Yolanda headed straight for the office of millionaire businessman and fellow Slovak Stephen Roman, who she said was a close family friend. She eventually wound up on Ballard's doorstep. Booth passed along the information to Cluff and Crump, and included a stinging indictment from her parole officer. "The offender is a remarkable woman of determination and ambition," he concluded in his report. "She is both manipulative and persistent and able to employ an assortment of tactics including domination and flattery as the situation dictates."

The police detective offered to solve their problem by arresting Yolanda for listing a false home address. Booth recalls telling them not only would she likely be banished from the Gardens, she could also be thrown back into the slammer. Cluff and Crump said they'd get back to him—but they never did. Later, when Booth enquired, Crump told him they couldn't risk the publicity. The former police detective remembers telling Crump, "You can take it now or you can take it later."

Those words would come back to haunt them years later. When they had disappeared to the Caymans, Rocchi feared a death-bed marriage, so she hired a local law firm to check all newly issued marriage licences in the Caymans. The day before she was to leave on her vacation, Ballard's lawyer received a long-distance call at home confirming that a marriage licence had indeed been issued in her client's name that same day.

While she scrambled to get a flight out to the Caymans, Rocchi, Crump and Ballard's daughter, Mary Elizabeth, tried in vain to get through to Harold by telephone. In the meantime, they were leaving desperate messages for Giffin, who was staying on one of the Lieford Islands, just off the Bahamas. As well as being a close friend of Ballard, Giffin was one of the few who was on speaking terms with Yolanda. The problem was that Giffin's Caribbean hideaway didn't have a telephone; messages had to be delivered by staff at the local general store.

Finally, everything came together. Giffin called Condo 18 and after some prodding, Yolanda eventually spoke to him. According to media reports, she denied the wedding rumours outright, saying, "As the best man, you would be the first to know if such a happy event were taking place." Still, she refused to let Giffin speak directly with Harold.

Later the telephone in the condo was unplugged, effectively cutting off all outside contact with Harold. Desperate, Rocchi faxed a five-paragraph letter to the Colonial Club addressed to Ballard. "You should know if you marry her, your Will will be revoked should you die before returning to Toronto," she wrote. "Your children will receive two-thirds of the estate. They will end up controlling the Leafs or fighting over control. This is something you never wanted." Harold Ballard was handed the letter as the ambulance was leaving for Cayman Island Government Hospital.

Later that day, when Crump telephoned Condo 18, a hysterical woman answered the phone. "There's blood all over the place," Crump remembers the maid saying. "When I asked, 'Where's Harold?' she said, 'I don't know.'" It was all too much for Crump to handle any longer. His tenure at the Gardens had begun in 1971 just days before the RCMP took Ballard and Smythe (the man who'd hired him) away in handcuffs. The chartered accountant had lived through Ballard's eccentricities, his fights with his children, a hockey team whose fortunes were sinking embarrassingly low and now Yolanda. Crump picked up the phone and sealed his escape by accepting a job offer somewhere else.

In the meantime, Rocchi and Norman Bosworth, a Gardens director, were dispatched by the board of directors to fly down to the Caymans to fetch "the Boss." While Rocchi waited for the airport limousine at her downtown Toronto office, the Gardens chief financial officer called to say he wanted to personally deliver the petty cash she and Bosworth would need for the trip. Once there, Crump told her that after nineteen years at Maple Leaf Gardens, he was resigning his post to become commissioner of the Canadian Football League. Rocchi was speechless. The man everyone automatically expected would run the business in Ballard's absence was abandoning ship. She was at a loss for words again several hours later when she arrived in the Cayman Islands only to learn that a comatose Ballard had been flown to Miami.

As Yolanda and Denise Banks set up camp in her one-bedroom, $200-a-night suite at the Miami Marriott hotel, the Gardens board of directors back in Toronto were rankled by what they concluded was Yolanda's botched power play. The emaciated board—Donald Giffin; Steve Stavro; Edward Lawrence, a financial consultant; Norman Bosworth, retired head of Canada Dry; John (Jake) Dunlap, an Ottawa lawyer and former part owner of the CFL's Ottawa Rough Riders; and Paul McNamara—were all hand-picked by Ballard not necessarily for their business prowess but for their utility to him. Harold's board knew its place—and that was in the Directors' Lounge with free food and booze during the hockey games. Each director firmly clutched his two gold season's tickets, enjoying limitless alcoholic beverages listed on the wall in the lounge's bar. Every year, they were allowed to travel with the hockey team on one road game during the playoffs. Harold would ride in the bus with the players and his directors and their wives would follow behind in rented limousines. But they feared Yolanda almost as much as they dreaded Ballard's wrath. Harold guarded his power jealously and in the past, whenever his failing health had incapacitated him, Ballard would rise like Lazarus and exact his vengeance against those who dared to step into his shoes.

The board's longest-serving director knew that better than the rest. When Ballard suffered his heart attack at Stavro's home in early 1988—just after publicly announcing he would cut his kids out of the will—chairman of the board Paul McNamara distributed a seventeen-page manifesto to his fellow board members. While he acknowledged the unfortunate state of Ballard's health, he nonetheless urged the directors to quickly move from "one-man rule" (referring to Ballard as a "revolving cyclone") to a "more acceptable corporate structure. The old order has died. Pax Tecum." He suggested the immediate appointment of a chief executive officer (Ballard's title) and a chief operating officer or executive committee to stabilize the company and, incredibly, to "prevent any chaos from creeping into the operation...."

McNamara's frank offering urged a wide-ranging overview of operations, leaving no department unscathed. His main priority was returning the hockey team to the pride and tradition of the Conn Smythe years. To that end, the scouting ranks should be overhauled and a new general manager hired. The arena personnel, which McNamara described as "Alcoholics Disneyworld," needed improvements: switchboard operators should answer phones more promptly; bring in a small band of boys dressed in Leaf jerseys to replace the organist; too many of the ushers were over seventy years of age and "sloppy, drinking and rude...." The chairman declared, "I would change all this." His litany of suggestions also included primping the Directors' Lounge in "basic blue and white with shots of coral and pink" with a hostess "in an evening dress to keep the place organized" and creating a Maple Leaf Gardens Old Boys' club to honour alumni with lifetime passes to the Directors' Lounge.

Most importantly, he called for an investigation of the public company's internal operations. Everything from complete lists of employees on the payroll, company vehicles, credit cards and expense accounts to the disorganized distribution of free tickets and parking passes. Although his comments appeared to be a direct attack on Ballard's reign, they were also an indictment of Donald Crump, the man responsible for the Gardens' day-to-day operations and the lieutenant who carried out Ballard's commands. Not surprisingly, none of his fellow directors would heed the chairman of the board's call to arms, and when Harold's health improved weeks later, McNamara was permanently relegated to the owner's doghouse. Still, his bold proclamation set the stage for a similar probe after Ballard's death.

But in early 1990, the complications from years of neglected diabetes had truly placed Ballard in seriously critical condition. At least that's what Rocchi and Bosworth were saying with their daily updates from the ailing chief executive's bedside in Florida. As the death watch continued for weeks, the directors slowly began to believe that Harold was mortal after all. McNamara sought the opinions of three doctors who were familiar with Ballard's condition. "I for one knew he was a dead man," he wrote in a letter in early 1990. Emboldened, the other directors soon began acting as if the boss was never coming back.

That's when the jockeying began. While the autocrat who had operated the public company like a banana republic lay in a deep coma 1,600 miles away, the battle for control of his fiefdom began moving from the backrooms—where it had quietly festered for years—and out into the public arena. Ironically, Ballard's loyal soldier who had already put one foot out the door would eventually end up playing king maker.

Everyone had a theory about what was going to happen. Would Harold recover? Would his children re-emerge on the scene and battle it out among themselves? Was Harold leaving everything to Yolanda? Ultimately, the prospect of Maple Leaf Gardens without Ballard seemed inconceivable, giddily so. The stock price reacted favourably to that possibility—its trading value spiking by several dollars—as it did every time Ballard so much as coughed.

Alan Eagleson, back then still the undisputed godfather of hockey as executive director of the NHL Players' Association, predicted the ensuing battle with uncanny foresight. "There will be a lengthy court fight unless somebody rich steps up to the plate and pays everybody off," Ballard's long-time friend told *Maclean's* magazine. Indeed.

On January 5, 1990—the day after Ballard entered Baptist Hospital in Miami—Maple Leaf Gardens' board of directors took temporary control of the public company after an emergency meeting. Chaired by Paul McNamara, five of the six directors (Giffin was en route to Miami from the Caribbean) exercised their right under the Ontario Business Corporations Act, which gave them the power to assume control if Ballard was judged to be incapacitated. Just days before he was whisked off to the Caymans, Ballard had left instructions with the Gardens lawyer to determine whether he could force some of the directors to buy shares in the company. At the time, apart from Ballard, Giffin owned the most with sixty thousand shares, Stavro and Bosworth each had five hundred, McNamara owned fifty, while both Ed Lawrence, who joined the board in 1971, and Dunlap, who was appointed in 1983, saw fit not to invest their own money in the Gardens.

After a rancorous meeting, punctuated by outbursts from the usually sedate Steve Stavro, the group decided it would act as a six-man chief executive. Rule by committee was necessary for two reasons: one, the directors could share the blame if Ballard returned, and two, not many on this board were actually equipped to manage the day-to-day operations of Maple Leaf Gardens—a shortcoming that would become painfully evident in the months ahead.

The division of power was finally approved after a tense gathering in the Directors' Lounge on the main floor of the Gardens. Accustomed to being manipulated like pawns in a chess game, they all spoke tentatively, especially since every one of them nurtured dreams of one day taking the reins from Ballard. Nerves were raw and paranoia ruled so much that Giffin's stopover in Miami was viewed suspiciously by some at the meeting, since Giffin was known to be the only board member or officer of the company who had a cordial relationship with Yolanda. And of course, it was common knowledge that Giffin had coveted the hockey team in his every waking moment. According to the outlandish conspiracy theory swirling around the T-shaped conference table, the dying man's girlfriend and his trusted friend might have been planning a coup together all along.

Crump was there too, even though he was not a member of the Gardens board and technically was no longer on the company's payroll. A litigator from Miller Thomson (Sedgewick's old firm) named John Chapman sat in for part of the meeting on behalf of both Ballard's estate and the Gardens. Discussions centred on a draft press release Chapman had prepared for the board's consideration. During the meeting, Stavro hurled derisive verbal volleys about too many "fucking lawyers" being involved in handling the situation. A tough businessman who was not afraid to express his opinions, he made minor changes to the draft and then insisted the board—not the hired legal help—issue the announcement. Chapman had never met Stavro before the meeting, so he wasn't aware that the wealthy merchant had become increasingly jittery of late, confiding to his Gardens associates that he believed Ballard had frozen him out of his inner circle, although he suspected it was Yolanda's doing.

"They all knew that I was close with Harold," Stavro recalls of that time. "Certain directors didn't like that sort of thing. But they knew that as long as I was there, there was that [close] relationship. I was coming around the Gardens more. I knew what was going on so in a nice way, I'd drop in and bring Harold something and at the same time see what the hell was going on. I was trying to keep an eye on him and I didn't want to overpower everything, I just made sure I dropped in every three or four days.

"I don't want to say that they acted different, but we had a problem. We had a serious problem with the banks, with the team...with the press...there was complete chaos. He was not well. Everybody had a pass in the building, the building had been let go, there was chaos with the staff, chaos with running the place." Privately, his fellow board members were stunned by his disconcerting similarities to Alexander Haig. In fact, that first directors' meeting was later viewed by some as Stavro's coming-out party, when the wallflower turned into the *Mayflower*. Publicly, though, Stavro was emerging from the group as, one director told a newspaper reporter, the one who had the "kind of business experience one might need to operate the company."

Having settled the division of power, the newly empowered six-man executive did not turn its attention to spreadsheets, marketing plans or collecting long-overdue accounts receivable. Instead, fortified by their coalescing suspicions about one another and specifically Yolanda, they delved mercilessly into minutiae. While Bill Cluff, the Gardens marketing director, was appearing before the board to report on the plans to build a new kitchen in one of the private boxes, the directors took aim at Yolanda. First, they banned her two children, Anastasia and William (who had gained notoriety for their expenses, namely birth control pills and dry cleaning, paid for courtesy of Maple Leaf Gardens), from the Directors' Lounge, where all the rink rats converged for free food and drink during game intermissions. Next, they extended that prohibition to the Hot Stove Lounge. No more free steaks and chocolate cakes for the cottage.

Each decision was intended as a shot across the bow of their collective enemy, Yolanda. By now, Madame Queen, as Ballard called her, was terrifying Gardens staff several times a day with telephone calls from her bedside vigil, demanding updates on what "plots and schemes are brewing in the hearts of evil men and women."

Yolanda was increasingly out of sorts. A family reconciliation was already unfolding in Ballard's Miami hospital room between estranged father and two of his children. Mary Elizabeth flew down at Rocchi's request and immediately erased any power of liaison Yolanda had with the hospital medical staff. Bill arrived from a family vacation in the Barbados only to continue tormenting Yolanda with his presence. Harold Jr., however, couldn't make the trip because his bail conditions would not allow him to leave Canada. (Junior was convicted in 1989 by the Ontario Provincial Court for unlawfully breaking into his father's Montgomery Road home in Etobicoke and stealing $18,000 worth of furniture and sports memorabilia. The official excuse for Junior's absence at the time was that he was suffering from the Shanghai flu.)

Every day, Yolanda could feel her power over Ballard slipping—fast. By the middle of January, she had lost the first battle against the children to name Miami lawyer Paul Cowan as Harold's official guardian. The Dade County court in Florida ruled the guardianship would last thirty days while Ballard's children negotiated his return to Canada, health permitting. Yolanda reacted predictably by cursing, complaining, even trying to force-feed Harold. Actually, the Ballard circus had merely changed venues, this time enthralling American audiences who were lapping it up on the U.S. tabloid shows. Among the cameo appearances were Stavro, Wendel Clark, one of Ballard's favourite Leafs, and Allan "Lampy" Lamport, the ninety-year-old former mayor of Toronto and current president of the Hot Stove Lounge League.

By the time Yolanda flew back to Toronto in early February to beg a District Court judge to appoint her as Ballard's personal guardian, she didn't even have a change of clothes. The locks to the second-floor apartment she claimed to have shared with Harold had been changed. Yolanda was entitled to retrieve only her personal belongings, but instead, she took a pair of Harold's pyjamas.

Meanwhile, Ballard's estate lawyers had already retained private detectives to verify whether the signature on the Cayman Islands marriage licence was truly Ballard's or a forgery.

On Valentine's Day, 1990, Harold Jr. and Mary Elizabeth appeared before Judge Donna Haley in Surrogate Court to ask that she declare their father mentally incompetent. In an emotional plea, they requested the Ontario judge to appoint retired Supreme Court of Canada Judge Willard "Bud" Estey to act as Ballard's personal guardian if Harold, who had only weeks to live, was permitted to return home from Miami. The Saskatchewan-born Estey knew Ballard well and ingratiated himself even more when he declared during the hearing that he'd refuse the responsibility if Yolanda's request to share the task was granted by the court. Six years later, Estey would be called upon again to ensure that Ballard's last instructions were honoured.

The former judge was one name on a list of potential candidates compiled by Ballard's children. Among the others were former Liberal prime minister John Turner, now a senior partner at Miller Thomson, and former Ontario Conservative premier William Davis, who was a partner at Tory Tory DesLauriers & Binnington. Both men had conflicts because their blue-ribbon law firms were already involved in other Ballard matters. It was amazing how well the Ballards knew how to play all the angles.

Three days later, on February 17, 1990, Yolanda appeared to have finally lost the war over Harold. Justice Haley appointed Estey as the sole guardian of Ballard's personal affairs, which meant essentially looking after his medical care and limiting Yolanda's access to the dying man to fifteen minutes at the beginning of every visiting hour.

At the same time, Judge Haley also named Harold's three executors—Stavro, Crump and Giffin—as guardians of his purse strings. Together, the grocer, the accountant and the sheet-metal contractor were to form a committee, entrusted to "preserve and administer" the one thing in life that mattered most to Harold Ballard—his hockey team and the financial empire it made possible.

Donald Philip Giffin operated in Harold Ballard's shadow. "There was only one captain [Ballard] and it was aye-aye sir," he had told a *Toronto Star* newspaper reporter years ago. Now seventy-five years old, he'd met Ballard in 1950, the year after he began his sheet-metal business after arriving in Toronto from his hometown of Brockville, Ontario. The man Ballard nicknamed "Bulldog" for his tenacity was also sensitive, good-natured, and described as "straight as an arrow" by one of his colleagues. He was the kind of old-fashioned gentleman who would offer his chair when someone entered the room. He shared a tragic bond with Harold: Giffin's first wife, Jean, had died of cancer, like Harold's Dorothy, and the two women were buried in the same cemetery. Giffin's family was the kind straight out of a prime-time television series entitled "Yours, Mine and Ours." He had seven children: three boys and a daughter from his first marriage, another son he inherited from his marriage to his second wife, Patricia, and together they had two sons. What struck people most, including Ballard, was the respect and affection Giffin received from his children. In fact, nobody disliked Don Giffin.

Giffin loved hockey and the Toronto Maple Leafs. He soaked up the tradition and the lore and yearned for the power it afforded "the boss." He was the man with the dark tan who was always calling Gordon Stellick (the thirty-something who had been Punch Imlach's assistant in 1980 and eight years later became the Leafs' general manager) for spare hockey tickets and always "in a very nice way." Giffin was the board's spokesman, afforded the elder statesman role by the others because of his pivotal role in helping Ballard gain control of the Gardens.

Even so, he was one of the directors who had sat silently on the board and watched Ballard wreak havoc on the fabled hockey franchise. Nonetheless, Giffin had done little to conceal his burning ambition to follow in the footsteps of Conn Smythe and Ballard. But that self-ascribed rite of passage had to wait until Harold's death. In the meantime, during the next four decades, Giffin had built a lucrative family contracting business. He had even served as president of the Canadian Construction Association, where he forged alliances that further entrenched him as a member of the Old Boys' club. At the same time, he made himself useful to Pal Hal primarily by acting as a broker: he helped the financially strapped owner arrange loans; he developed good relations with

Ballard's children; and he was astute enough not to waste his time fighting the multi-talented Yolanda. He played the same role in the company's boardroom, all the while buying enough stock in the company to become the second largest shareholder in Maple Leaf Gardens after Harold. That was Giffin's contradiction: it was hard to figure out whether he was acting out of blind loyalty to Ballard or in pursuit of his personal ambitions.

John Donald Crump's motivations were much clearer: he acted mostly out of fear of and loyalty to Harold. "I had served Harold reasonably well and he trusted me," Crump explained. "I probably made him mad a few times by not doing what he wanted but probably it was to his advantage in the long run." An accountant by training, he had joined Maple Leaf Gardens as treasurer in 1971 after working at the Department of National Revenue, Peat, Marwick, Mitchell & Co. and at Famous Players Canadian Corp. Ltd. A self-described loner (he was an only child) and carpenter (he built furniture in his spare time), Crump worked long and hard to keep his boss happy and for that he earned the second highest salary in the company. Still, in return, he received little respect and plenty of abuse from an employer who treated him like a lackey, often telling him "to leave the working people alone," whenever Crump poked his head into the hockey operations. Others were more cynical. "Don acted in his best interests of staying in the will," mused a former Gardens employee. In fact, Crump's name was the only one that had consistently appeared on all four versions of Ballard's will.

The dour-looking Crump was actually very affable, a Walter Mitty type who loved his job because it gave him the chance to spend time with his wife (who was recovering from breast cancer) and two daughters, often taking them to hockey games and ice-skating shows.

Hockey operations were completely off limits to Crump. In 1978 the former high-school quarterback got his chance to run a sports franchise when Ballard purchased the CFL's struggling Hamilton Tiger-Cats football team for $1.3 million. During the course of the next decade, the team won a Grey Cup championship under Crump's tutelage, but gained notoriety for bleeding $20 million from the Gardens' balance sheet by the time it was sold for $350,000 in 1989. Davis Printing Division was another Crump initiative that proved financially disastrous and was eventually unloaded for $470,000 in 1990.

Crump and Giffin were close but the Gardens accountant didn't really forge a friendship with Stavro (who spent most of his time attending to his grocery business) until later. For her part, Yolanda found it hard to say anything nice about the bean counter. The two were combatants vying for Harold's attention every day. "I had a great deal of respect for Harold as a human being," Crump explained rather diplomatically. "He needed a great deal of help and my job was to keep him out of trouble." Crump's modest expectations relayed an important message that was not lost on Ballard's entourage: he wasn't interested in taking a run at controlling the Gardens—ever. "I wasn't going to incur all kinds of debt to satisfy some little part of my ego." In fact, his co-executors knew that Crump had neither the money nor the network necessary to take a serious shot at the Gardens. That meant as one of three executors, he would play an equally important role in determining the company's post-Ballard fate by using his swing vote to break a deadlock.

In the end, of course, Crump bailed out of the circus where he'd worked for most of his adult life. On the third day of January 1990, he accepted the $150,000-a-year job as commissioner of the CFL while Ballard lay unconscious in his Miami hospital bed.

The third man in the troika was Steve Stavro. As a young man, Manoli (Emmanuel) Stavroff Sholdas used to travel from the east end of Toronto on a streetcar to line up to buy hockey tickets at Maple Leaf Gardens. Helping his father Anatas run a small grocery store on Queen Street East, Steve (an elementary school teacher abbreviated his name) would sell produce to patrons on the streetcar that passed in front of his family's store. He arrived in Canada from Gabresh, a tiny town in Greek Macedonia, with his mother and brother Christo in 1934 when he was seven years old. By the time the three were fetched from Union Station in Toronto, his father had bought a corner store with the savings he'd squirrelled away working as a delivery boy in the butcher shop owned by a relative of his wife's.

Steve had a keen eye for numbers, unlike his brother Christo, who preferred words, and he liked to draw. Thus began a personal interest in display advertisements and marketing for the store, an interest still evident in his vast grocery empire today. And he loved sports—bantam hockey, soccer, speedskating and handball.

In 1953, the twenty-seven-year-old became a shareholder in his father's store and opened his own, called Knob Hill Farms, a name he picked off a case of carrots while on a buying trip in San Francisco. Four years later, he spent $300 to sponsor a Macedonian soccer team in the Toronto City Soccer League and in the sixties he became one of the co-founders of the Eastern Canadian Professional Soccer League. That's how he met Harold Ballard, during dinner at the Gas Light restaurant with sports columnist George Gross and a group of others who had gathered to ask Ballard if he would act as president of the infant soccer league. Ballard accepted, and although the league faded by the end of the decade (costing Stavro an estimated $250,000), the two men remained friends for the next thirty years. Ballard became a father figure for Stavro, who had lost his own father in 1960. "Harold fit into the slot. He was a quiet, good guy really," Stavro reminisced. "He was a different person publicly than he was privately." The same words could be used to describe the man many viewed as the Greta Garbo of the Gardens.

Stavro did little things for Ballard that added up to a lot for a man who'd become estranged from his own children. Stavro would send bushels of Knob Hill Farm flowers and sheep manure up to the Georgian Bay cottage. The two would spend hours driving around in a pickup truck looking for river rocks for Ballard's garden. Stavro and his wife, Sally, entertained Ballard (and sometimes Yolanda) at their homes in Toronto and Palm Beach, Florida, and Harold even spent a Kentucky Derby weekend at Stavro's 272-acre thoroughbred farm, which boasted forty horses. (Stavro's love of horses began when he was a child delivering groceries to Greenwood race track.)

Ballard appointed Stavro to the board of Maple Leaf Gardens in 1981 to replace the late Lorne Duguid. "I've known Steve for twenty-five years and I can't say enough good things about the man," Ballard said at the time. "I guess he'll have to buy a share in the place now." Soon, his fellow directors would jealously label Stavro "Harold's man" and Stavro concedes some of his fellow directors didn't like the fact that he was close to Ballard. In fact,

Stavro was perhaps the only director who enjoyed unrestricted access to Ballard's private domain—the bunker—usually stopping by before leaving the hockey game by the end of the second period. Stavro still wakes up every morning at 4:30 to make the rounds of his stores.

Right from the start, Stavro was not like the others. He was not obtrusive, never forced himself on Ballard and never called the Gardens for freebies. In fact, he had taken a page out of the late Bob Sedgewick's book and replaced Ballard's friend and lawyer as one of his trusted confidants. Harold respected Stavro and it wasn't because of his immense wealth. Soon, the common buzz around the Gardens was that Stavro would ultimately run the company. It wasn't talked about much; rather, it was assumed. The fact that he had created a mystique about himself only helped feed that image. Stavro played Howard Hughes to Giffin's Elmer Fudd. "By then, Harold had no use for Giffin," Gord Stellick remembers. "Steve was much younger and more vital." And like Harold, control was important to him.

The memorial dinner for the late King Clancy, the former Leaf defenseman and Harold's closest friend, provides a good example of Stavro's dedication. Clancy died in November 1986, creating a vacuum that attracted no shortage of people who rushed in to fill the void. For months after Clancy's death, Ballard became obsessed with arranging a ceremonial evening in his name with the proceeds going to Clancy's favourite charities. While the other Gardens directors rearranged the seating plans to move their friends and family closer to the head table, Stavro and his wife, Sally, rolled up their sleeves, buying and arranging the huge floral arrangements on the tables while kicking in another $3,000 to buy a full-page advertisement in the evening's program. "He scored a ton of points for that evening," quipped a Gardens inhabitant. "Steve would be one of the few guys Harold didn't use the prefix 'fucking' before saying his name."

It was years from the days of the small storefront on Queen Street to his nine giant no-frills food terminals. In 1991, he opened an eight-acre outlet (the world's largest) in Cambridge, Ontario. Naturally, his personal wealth multiplied and fed his extravagant tastes. Two stone gargoyles greet visitors as they enter through wrought-iron gates the horse-shoe–shaped driveway of his north Toronto mansion, which overlooks the eighteenth hole of the Rosedale Golf and Country Club (although Stavro is not a member). Inside it looks like an elegant English country home furnished in Chippendale, Sheraton and Hepplewhite. Sally Stavro (née Saunders, the daughter of a Macedonian who owned a local tavern) searches all over the world for antique porcelain to add to her already impressive collection. They have four daughters—two work with Steve in the family business—nine grandchildren and homes in West Palm Beach, Lexington, Kentucky, and a manor house on a hundred acres in Campbellford, just south of Peterborough. Stavro has shared the spoils too. He's a well-known but discreet philanthropist, and his generosity would help his cause years later.

Much like Giffin, Steve had the common man's touch. But that's where their similarities ended, except of course, for their consuming ambition to control Maple Leaf Gardens.

The ever crafty Ballard was aware of these unspoken desires, mischievously throwing together his combustible trio of executors to wield his big stick—all 80.3 percent of it—over Maple Leaf Gardens. Primarily, their duties were supposed to include the day-to-day operations of the hockey arena and the team, as well as paying for the owner's medical bills. The committee, however, could not sell anything without a judge's approval. To keep them honest, Judge Haley ordered the group to post a $2-million bond while a complete accounting of Ballard's finances was filed with the court. After Ballard died, of course, his will would dictate how his executors would manage his financial assets.

The trio was also required to openly declare any possible conflicts of interest. That routine request would irreparably poison the relationship between Crump, Giffin and Stavro, threatening to lead them to the foot of the stairs of the Supreme Court of Canada.

Donald Giffin had to come clean; he had an advantage over his co-guardians. He told Justice Haley about the option he had quietly secured on the shares held in the registered company called 810757 Ontario Ltd., set up by Ballard in 1989 to hold the thirty-four common shares in HEBL that he had bought from his daughter in January of that year. The shares were pledged as security on the

$15.5-million loan Molson extended to Ballard to buy back the shares. Giffin claimed that he had successfully badgered Ballard into giving him the right of first refusal on those shares in June 1989. By this time Giffin knew he was an executor and more importantly, he was aware of the clause in Ballard's will allowing the executors to buy the shares in his estate after he died.

The court decided that Giffin could keep his beloved option but he couldn't exercise it as a member of the committee. But the damage had been done. Stavro was broadsided by the admission while Crump, who had known all along, became increasingly suspicious of Giffin's motives. That distrust combined with Stavro's anger would turn into revenge as Giffin's co-executors became obsessed with levelling the playing field. In the end, Mary Elizabeth's thirty-four HEBL shares were pivotal in the protracted battle to control her father's company.

The first order of business while Ballard was unconscious and his reins had been completely snipped was naming his replacement on the board of directors as well as choosing a new president of the company. The board met on February 28, 1990, to consider Crump's appointment to the group. Jake Dunlap wanted to delay the vote until Norman Bosworth returned from a fishing trip in Florida. But after numerous hesitations—the board had not forgotten how Crump had scrupulously followed Ballard's orders "to tell those goddamn directors nothing"—the group finally agreed to appoint him as a director and secretary. At the same meeting, Stavro was named vice-president and Giffin would leave his post at the family business to become president of Maple Leaf Gardens.

But making that decision was the first of many internal battles among Ballard's executors. They had gathered to discuss the division of power at Stavro's house before meeting with the rest of the Gardens board. Stavro was already seeing conspiracies in the making. "It was sort of quiet but they already had discussed this matter [among themselves]," Stavro remembers. "Giffin spoke up and said, 'Well, I can manage. I'd like to take Harold's position.' I said, 'Well, you're not a hockey person, you're a sheet-metal man and I'm a food man.' I said we should get a hockey person to run it. Well, with that, we discussed it for a while. Should I mention what he wanted financially? He wanted the same as Harold, around $500,000 [Ballard also received $450,000 a year in bonuses]. I said, 'there's no way you're gonna get $500,000. I'll agree to one thing, you know $250,000 and I went up to $300,000. And I said it was only part time…that could be six months, three or a year but we have to look for a person to concentrate on MLG and the team."

Once the court approved, Giffin waited anxiously for the press release to be issued at 10:00 P.M. on March 1. He could hardly contain his excitement. For Giffin, it was the fulfilment of a lifelong dream; he was actually going to assume the mantle of one of the highest positions in Canadian sport. And maybe it was just the first step down the road to owning it all. At least that's what he hoped.

Steve Stavro wasn't around for the big announcement. He flew down to Florida before it all became public to watch one of his thoroughbred horses race. The official line out of the Gardens was that Giffin would "work closely with another Ballard friend, Steve Stavro."

To no one's surprise, one of the Ballards complained. This time it was Bill. Ironically, his choice for president was Stavro. At the time, Giffin was in Bill's bad books; the young Ballard felt double-crossed by the man he'd leaned on for years to smooth things over when life got tough with his dad. His feeling dated back to the sale of Harold Jr.'s shares. Bill claimed that he had an arrangement with his brother to buy Harold Jr.'s thirty-four HEBL shares through a numbered company with his partner, Michael Cohl. Instead, his father wound up snatching up the shares for $21 million in June 1989. Bill launched a $70-million lawsuit against his father, Giffin and Crump, who were also directors of HEBL, on August 2, 1989.

However, the next time the group would appear in court—and with the feuding Ballards there was always a next time—Bill and Giffin would be fighting on the same side against Steve Stavro and Donald Crump.

Harold Ballard returned home to Toronto on the Ides of March in 1990. Unconscious most of the time, he was oblivious to the events unfolding around him. That was just as well, considering how the triumvirate he had trusted was planning to take control. Still, the media circus that greeted his arrival would have pleased Pal Hal. It was exactly the kind of attention he had craved all his life.

For the next month, Ballard played out his final days in the intensive care unit in Toronto's Wellesley Hospital with Dorothy's graduation picture on the night table by his bed. The hospital, which provides the Leafs' medical care during the season, has a long history in the Ballard family. Dorothy had also worked there as a nurse.

A stream of visitors and business associates paraded through his room just as they had in Miami. However, Ballard's health never improved. By early April, he'd all but slipped into a coma, clinging to life with the help of a ventilator. Just before three o'clock in the afternoon on April 11, 1990, Harold Ballard died. While his body lay in state in the Directors' Lounge, the responses were predictable. The obituaries covered the spectrum from saint to sinner. Meanwhile, the atmosphere at the Gardens became more bizarre. Take the hidden camera located in a corner at the back of the Directors' Lounge. Crump had it installed to film the unwitting visitors who stopped by to pay their last respects. Every sob, every smile, every wisecrack was taped. Actually, Crump was keeping tabs on the unpredictable Yolanda, who he was convinced was capable of anything when she thought no one was watching. Better than a policeman standing guard, the camera caught three tapes' worth for the archives.

Ballard was buried in a private family ceremony next to Dorothy. A week later, his legacy would become public. The appointment of the executors and their tasks were outlined: Stavro, Giffin and Crump were to transfer Ballard's 80-percent controlling block of Maple Leaf Gardens shares into a trust. And his secret would be made public: as many already knew, the trust designated eight beneficiaries—the Charlie Conacher Throat Cancer Fund, Wellesley Hospital, Princess Margaret Hospital, Hockey Canada, the Hugh MacMillan Rehabilitation Centre (formerly the Ontario Crippled Children's Centre), Centre for Canadian Living (previously known as the Centre for the Mentally Retarded), the Salvation Army and a special scholarship fund to assist the children of former Gardens employees—who were to receive annual donations from the dividends earned on the MLGL shares held in the trust. Although Ballard named the beneficiaries, he gave his executors full discretion over how much each would receive.

The will, as we've seen, also stated that Harold's shares in the trust were to be sold off within twenty-one years. When that happened, all the estate's debts were to be paid and whatever remained was to be transferred to the Harold E. Ballard Foundation, an organization Ballard set up in June 1984 to make charitable donations and associate Ballard's name with philanthropic endeavours for years after his death. The three executors were also directors of the foundation and again had the authority to choose which charities would benefit.

The most controversial clause in the will was one added in 1987, allowing the executors to buy the shares for themselves at "fair market value supported by two independent appraisals." The contentious clause was included, Rosanne Rocchi explains, to level the playing field among the three executors. For years, Harold had known that Giffin and Stavro were capable of taking a run at the company. The strained family relations with his children had ruled them out entirely. Thus Ballard didn't want to prevent the friends to whom he'd entrusted his fortune from possibly buying the Gardens because the law would normally forbid them buying assets they were supposed to be guarding as executors. Stafford Smythe had the same provision in his 1972 last testament; that was how Ballard had secured control in the first place. "The inclusion of that clause was to place the executors on a level playing field—nothing more," is how Rocchi explains her client's intentions at the time. "If he had wanted to give them an advantage, he would have told me. He never did. There was no heir apparent and no passing of the torch." By explicitly stating that he would permit his executors to purchase his estate, Ballard had laid the groundwork for the battle that began even before his death.

The prevailing wisdom at the time was that Ballard was worth over $100 million. By late April, the executors had figured out just how much those claims had been exaggerated.

When he died, Ballard's financial affairs were a hodge-podge of unpaid debts. His estate included $1.5 million in cash, the value of his preferred HEBL shares were valued at $3 million, his thirty-nine common shares in HEBL another $10 million, for a total of $14.5 million. On the other side of the ledger was $4 million the court had ordered him to pay National Bank over the Michael Gobuty fiasco. Yolanda weighed in by launching a $10-million suit, claiming that she was Harold's common-law wife.

All considered, that left about $500,000 to work with, enough to cover only the probate fees. Where the executors were going to get the $4 million owed in taxes to Revenue Canada and the $20 million to repay Molson by the end of 1990 was anybody's guess.

The strategy was obvious: the executors knew they had to clean up the shop, rebuild the hockey team into a contender (the big money comes in during the playoffs) and watch the value of MLGL shares rise. After that, they didn't agree on much else. They began talking about shrinking the size of MLGL's board from seven to five directors, but that would be a problem because there wouldn't be enough independent members to create an audit committee required by the Ontario Business Corporations Act. After Crump and Stavro sought and received a legal opinion confirming this, they set their sights on purging the board entirely.

Around this time, in late May 1990, McNamara wrote a letter to Giffin asking the board to investigate the legal fees charged by Miller Thomson from 1987 to 1989, which had totalled about half a million dollars a year. In his note, McNamara seriously questioned Miller Thomson's fees, especially since he'd been musing out loud about the law firm's many roles with Maple Leaf Gardens. In an attempt to pare costs, McNamara suggested taking the matter to John Ziegler, or possibly pooling legal costs with another Canadian team, say the Winnipeg Jets.

McNamara appeared to be aiming at Rocchi. She had been named by Ballard as the Leafs' alternate governor to the NHL in 1989 (you'll remember McNamara had asked for the job years earlier but was denied), and like many of his colleagues on the Gardens board, he increasingly viewed her with suspicion. Months earlier, in the fall of 1989, McNamara had written a letter to Ballard (which he asked Rocchi to deliver) thanking him for the "second right of refusal on your control block of MLG stock," all the while thinking that Ballard had assigned the first right to Giffin. "After all the years with you at the Gardens," he wrote, "I would hate to see control go to some purely financial wizards of flip mergers." He ploughed on: "It would be nice to know that when you sell or in the event of your death that friendly hands are in the driver's seat."

Rocchi never delivered the letter but she did brief her client about its contents. "When are you going to fire Paul McNamara?" she says was Ballard's response. Having received no answer, McNamara later wrote directly to Rocchi that "if the possibility comes up, I would be willing to enter into an option agreement with Harold to purchase the Gardens."

With Harold gone, Rocchi appeared vulnerable. McNamara was persistent in his demand for a review of the company's legal expenses. Giffin fended him off, defending Rocchi as having done "a fine job keeping MLG and the board out of trouble." And the company's auditors, Peat Marwick Thorne, conducted a review that revealed the hourly rate of $225 charged by Miller Thomson was about $40 an hour less than that of most Bay Street firms and those retained by other NHL teams.

In the end, four MLGL directors—all Ballard cronies—were sacrificed to signal the new business era at the Gardens. A few weeks after the will was read, Stavro, Crump, Giffin, Rocchi and William McKinnon, the Gardens accountant from Peat Marwick Thorne, met to choose replacements for Jake Dunlap, Norman Bosworth, Paul McNamara and Ed Lawrence, who volunteered his resignation.

McKinnon suggested cable czar Edward Samuel "Ted" Rogers, the chairman of Rogers Communications Inc., as a possible candidate because of his expertise in communications and because he was also a client of the accounting firm. Crump balked and Giffin did what he always did; he called for someone else's opinion. This time it was Richard Thomson, chairman of the Toronto Dominion Bank, who told Giffin he'd prefer that Rogers stick to his own knitting and worry about his cable company's ailing balance sheet. (TD Bank is a major creditor of Rogers.) Nonetheless, Rogers still accepted the appointment.

However, the bank did get one of its own on MLGL's board with the nomination of Frederick McDowell, a former TD vice-chairman. McDowell grew up on a farm in Mossbank, Saskatchewan, about forty miles south of Moose Jaw, in the thrall of recession where farmers lived off the relief trains that pulled in every month bringing smoked cod, GWG jean overalls, dried fruits and bales of hay for the cows from the East. Radio was the window on an entirely different world and every Saturday as a boy McDowell and his family would feverishly finish their chores in time to listen to Foster Hewitt give the radio play-by-play of the Leafs. In fact, the first time the career banker visited the Gardens in 1959, he went looking for the catwalk Hewitt travelled to reach his famous gondola.

The third nominee, the thinking went, would bring retail experience for the company's new marketing strategies. An Eaton would be nice, even though the selection committee knew that one of Ballard's commandments was never to appoint an Eaton, a Bassett, a brewer or any of those establishment types to his company's board. Fredrik Eaton, the president of Eaton's of Canada Ltd., was the group's first choice. But the giant retailing family likes to divide up board memberships among the siblings. The youngest, Thor Edgar, was next in line. And that was swell with Stavro because although he was better acquainted with the eldest sibling, John Craig (chairman of Eaton's), he knew Thor from horse-racing circles.

With the new slate of candidates set for the annual meeting in August, the group turned their attention to tightening up the Gardens' sloppy and lax internal business operations. An internal audit was conducted, and the result of that review would end up costing the company hundreds of thousands of dollars in special forensic audits and prove a major embarrassment for the man who kept the books for Harold.

There was an old saying about Maple Leaf Gardens: employees got paid minimum wage plus as much as they could steal—and that included the boss. In Harold Ballard's company, there was plenty of opportunity to play the margins. There were no cash registers at the concession stands, thus no official receipts. Little wonder why, back then, Toronto had the lowest per capita concession consumption in the NHL—$2.40 a person—even lower than the Quebec Nordiques!

Employees operated the concessions during concerts and took home the so-called profits. Even souvenirs should have been a veritable cash cow for the most popular team in English Canada. Instead, vendors had cut a deal that allowed them to pay the Gardens a percentage of their sales, even though no one ever knew exactly what those numbers were because no official receipts existed and no inventories were ever done.

Harold took advantage of the system too. About a month before the owner's death, details of his pillaging started to surface. The first casualty on the hockey side was head trainer Guy Kinnear, who, before leaving, tossed a grenade that set off the expensive internal review that infuriated Stavro and rattled Crump.

Kinnear, who had long been considered Ballard's spy among the players and coaches since his arrival back in 1967, asked general manager Floyd Smith to arrange a meeting with Rocchi. On March 15, the same day Harold returned to Toronto from Miami in an air ambulance, Kinnear informed Rocchi and Smith that he'd been selling game-worn gear for years and depositing the proceeds into a joint account at the Canadian Imperial Bank of Commerce registered in Ballard's name. Kinnear would gather used hockey sticks and jerseys at the end of the games, get them autographed and sell them through the Hot Stove Lounge and Olympia Sports in Midland, Ontario. Essentially, Kinnear had created a $150,000 market for the goods (which ordinarily were donated to charity) over the course of a decade. The problem was that the sticks were a corporate asset that Ballard and Kinnear were benefiting from personally.

Ticket scalping was another under-the-table windfall for Ballard. Each director automatically received two complimentary gold season's tickets, including Harold, even though he sat in his bunker every game. Although no one dared to ask him while he was alive, it turned out Ballard had been pocketing the proceeds from selling those tickets. For a number of years, Ballard had received six red tickets and two golds; the latter he received as a board member and, thus, the seats were located in the directors' box. Ballard swapped those two gold tickets with an elderly female sports fan, who owned two gold tickets in another part of the arena. While she sat with the directors in the box, Harold flipped the tickets she'd given him to other buyers and pocketed the money. Of his six red seats, Ballard sold four at a discount to a contractor in Midland, Ontario, who supplied building materials to Ballard's Georgian Bay cottage. The other two reds were often given to the Canada Customs officer at Pearson International Airport who spotted Yolanda and Harold on their way to the Cayman Islands.

Then there was the matter of the boat. Kinnear told Rocchi that Ballard had bought a boat for $20,000 from Paul McNamara, registered under the British Registry as *Pius II*. Ballard didn't like the name much and wanted to rename it *Slapshot*. Although the necessary paperwork to transfer the ownership and change the name was prepared, they were never filed. The boat was harboured at the Wye Heritage Marina in Georgian Bay and was used mostly by Kinnear. However, its roof was in need of repair and the outgoing trainer asked if the Gardens maintenance people could fix it.

There was also the Bronco supplied to the Gardens under the terms of its advertising agreement with General Motors, which Yolanda had used to drive to Ballard's cottage. And there was a mysterious van that had arrived from Cincinnati.

Rocchi and Smith went to Giffin's office after the meeting with Kinnear and a letter immediately went out to the company's auditors. Stavro and Crump learned of Kinnear's confession—and the subsequent internal investigation—the following week. Stavro was furious because "they were trying to smear Harold's integrity," he says, but agreed to the audit in the hopes of clearing his old friend's name. More importantly, Stavro thought it was another example of the undercurrents at work; how he was being kept out of the decision-making loop by Giffin and how the "czar" Rocchi was indirectly pulling the strings. "My view is that she was a paid employee but her influence went beyond that," Stavro says. "I didn't know about a lot of things she did, but if I did, I wouldn't have stood in the way."

Finally, after months of interviewing Gardens staff and painstakingly poring over the company's financial books, Peat Marwick concluded that Ballard's estate had to reimburse the public company $275,000 ($150,000 for the used equipment, $70,000 for the sale of complimentary hockey tickets and a charge of $55,000 for the Gardens portion of the special audit). Stavro was relieved. Ballard's activities were minor misdemeanours, he thought, certainly no worse than what goes on among the owners of other NHL teams (although most don't operate public companies). Still, Stavro was angered by what he saw as a supreme act of disloyalty to Ballard's memory. And worse, it was expensive. "When Peat Marwick said they wanted to be paid $250,000, I said no way," he recalls. "If they'd been doing their job as accountants they would have found all this stuff and raised it years ago." Indeed, Stavro insisted that only the executors could approve all expenses resulting from the audit.

Other Ballard supporters, like Gord Stellick, were more direct in their criticism. "They went after the weakest guy—the trainer—instead of the one trained to provide the proper accounting. They all turned a blind eye to what was going on and now they wanted to act like big shots and go after the stick guy."

However, Peat Marwick's sixty-six-page report was potentially troublesome for Crump. Although it never suggested any impropriety on his part, the audit portrayed a company in disarray and, by extension, an unflattering image of Crump's managerial and professional skills. Ballard may have made all the major decisions, but Crump orchestrated the day-to-day operations of the company. Ultimately, the special audit depicted a company with weak internal controls that was being operated as a small, parochial operation rather than a multi-million-dollar entertainment enterprise. According to the controversial report, there was no official budget for hockey equipment; employees who had authority to purchase supplies on behalf of the company, such as food and beverages for the concession stands, building supplies, even toilet paper, didn't have prescribed spending limits. "Orders appeared to be filled out and copies retained on a haphazard basis dependent upon the personal preferences of the manager in the relevant area of operation," the report said. The accounting firm even provided a basic explanation of how employees should fill out and file copies of their orders.

Quotations received for all major contracts put out for tender "are not documented," the report continued. That meant no one really knew if the maintenance work was actually cost-efficient. As well, not only were staff manually counting the hot dogs at the end of each event to determine how many had been sold, cash receipts were deposited directly by the concession employees instead of the cashiers' department. In the end, Peat Marwick concluded that "no system of central reporting and responsibility exists.... Without any measure by which the performance of each department can be assessed, managers have no incentive to improve the efficiency of their operations and no yardstick to gauge the success of any actions which they may take." The accounting firm recommended Gardens management create a number of profit centres to be used primarily to help monitor budget targets.

The implication was that Ballard hadn't been the only Gardens employee on the take. "Harold Ballard had no difficulty ripping off the shareholders, ripping off the customer or ripping off the government," muses a business associate. "That was all part of the game." However, he says, the game didn't include ripping off Harold.

On the heels of the Peat Marwick tome came the mysterious chocolate bar box that Yolanda kept obsessing about to Giffin. A few weeks after Ballard died, Yolanda began asking if Giffin had found the candy box containing alleged kickbacks from concession stands and travel money in the form of per diems that Harold had stashed away over the years.

Gardens staff denied any knowledge of the box. But so vivid was her memory in detailing its contents that Giffin began taking her seriously. He eventually found it in Ballard's apartment and called McKinnon, who met with him in the Directors' Lounge. Inside, they found about $150,000 worth of Englehard fine gold bars that had been purchased by an accountant who kept the books for the Hot Stove Lounge, and about $74,000 in cash (most of it in U.S. currency). Later, they learned of about $700,000 in Canadian and U.S. funds that Ballard had sitting in a Bank of Nova Scotia account in the Cayman Islands. Rocchi had to inform Revenue Canada and hope that by making a voluntary disclosure the Gardens would be spared a full-blown audit.

By the time the annual meeting rolled around on August 31, 1990, most of the post-Ballard clean-up operation was completed—with one exception. In two months, Molson would exercise its option on 20 percent of Ballard's MLGL stock. That would reduce the estate's holdings in MLGL to 60.3 percent from just over 80 percent. The more pressing concern was trying to figure out what the brewery was planning to do with its sizeable chunk of stock.

Still, the new board would have to deal with a more immediate problem. On July 16, in one of its last moves before being overhauled, the company's outgoing board of directors voted in favour of a $2.75 special dividend. However, company officials waited three days before issuing a statement. That alone was enough to get them into trouble with the Ontario Securities Commission (OSC) and the Toronto Stock Exchange for breaching timely disclosure rules. But it got worse.

Before the release was sent out, a Gardens secretary acted on the information after reading a draft copy of the news release she had been instructed to fax to the company's auditors. Twenty minutes before trading started, she called her broker at CIBC Wood Gundy and ordered him to buy $25,000 worth of MLGL shares. The TSE didn't learn of the special dividend until half an hour later, when it halted trading in the stock. By December 1990, the OSC announced it was holding hearings into the matter. Not an auspicious start for the so-called new era at the Gardens.

The NHL governors were scheduled to meet in Toronto three weeks after the Gardens annual meeting in August. One of the items on the official agenda was coming to terms with Molson's option. For five months, Rocchi was huddling with Norman Seagram and Hershell Ezrin, executive assistant to Cohen, to devise a reasonable solution.

One thing was clear: the NHL governors were demanding that Molson unload the shares. The only issue up for discussion was figuring out how. At the time, everyone feared a fire sale of a magnitude that would depress the stock price dramatically.

Ezrin and Seagram wanted a corporate restructuring much like the one that was floated in Molson's fourteen-page proposal back in April 1988. The plan was to divide Maple Leaf Gardens into two separate entities: Team Co. would be the operations of the hockey team, and the rest of the company's assets, such as the real estate, would be housed in Arena Co. Molson wanted the arena in order to protect its sponsorship and marketing rights and control the concessions for the all-important beer sales. Even if Labatt bought the hockey team, it would still have to play in a building owned by Molson. This was the "butterfly" reorganization that would ultimately provide a tax shelter to Molson. A presentation was scheduled before HEBL's directors for July 31. It never happened.

That's because during a meeting with Seagram and Ezrin in July, the three executors told them the idea wouldn't fly. It was considered inappropriate for a number of reasons: this kind of reorganization would create a cumbersome and expensive corporate structure; it did nothing to enhance the value of the public shares; the Leafs wouldn't control their venue and for the first time, the team would have to pay rent. The bottom line: Molson and no one else would come out the big winner.

NHL president John Ziegler wrote to both sides a month later giving the thumbs down to the butterfly reorganization. Molson also floated the idea that the Gardens could buy back the 20-percent block but no money would actually be exchanged until the team moved into a new arena as a tenant or as an equity partner with Molson. Although there weren't any definitive plans to build a new facility, Molson was still keeping all its options open.

Finally, an idea was presented that did fly. In a letter to Ziegler dated September 10, Seagram suggested parking the shares in a blind trust, although he hadn't told anyone at the Gardens about it. Rocchi didn't find out about it until days before the NHL governors convened at the Four Seasons Hotel in Toronto. She fired off her own letter to Ziegler, which was circulated at the governors' meeting on September 24, asking if the trust would protect Molson's passive stake holdings or its financial investment as a sponsor of "Hockey Night in Canada." Worse, she complained that the trust didn't deal with divestiture.

In the end, nineteen clubs voted in favour of the resolution— one against and two (Toronto and Montreal) abstained—that would create a so-called blind trust to be administered for one year by a trustee nominated by the league. The deadline for its creation was December 12, 1990, the night the Leafs and Canadiens played. Molson would waive any voting rights as a shareholder, although the company continued to collect dividends on its shares. The brewery was also prohibited from acquiring more MLGL stock while owning the Montreal Canadiens. And lastly, the league reserved the right to approve any purchaser who acquired more than 9 percent of Molson's block. This would be tested the following year.

On November 1, Doug Love, Molson's in-house lawyer, called the Toronto Stock Exchange's Market Surveillance section informing them that Molson would exercise its option on the MLGL shares. A press release would be forthcoming from Molson and the NHL. As a courtesy, the TSE called Rocchi (she was lawyer for the executors who controlled HEBL and, for now, Molson's option) to notify her of the exchange's plan to halt trading pending Molson's announcement. It was obvious she hadn't a clue.

Moments later, she was back burning up the phone lines to

Ziegler in New York, who casually dropped another bomb. It seemed that Molson had changed its mind; now the company wanted two years to unload its MLGL shares and three trustees to act as custodians. Also, the brewery didn't want to seek NHL approval of any purchaser even though the league's own by-laws required that. Rocchi was stunned that Ziegler had agreed. For his part, the beleaguered league president meekly admitted he had been led to believe that Rocchi had participated in the new arrangements all along.

Having put down the phone with Ziegler, Rocchi wrote a letter to Stavro, Crump and Giffin summarizing the morning's telephone conversations with the TSE and Ziegler. For the rest of the month, leading up to the governors' meeting at the Breakers' Hotel in West Palm Beach, Florida, the Molson option would dominate the league's agenda.

Rocchi and Seagram both made presentations to the NHL board on December 8. The governors—including Molson—finally agreed on the creation of a blind trust to be administered over one year by three trustees. The league chose Arden Haynes, the former president of Imperial Oil Canada, while Molson selected former Ontario premier David Peterson, who had just lost the provincial election (Hershell Ezrin had been Peterson's executive assistant), and Conservative senator Michael Meighen, who was married to a member of the Molson family in Montreal. The senator was a big hit with the American owners.

The chaos and confusion of the Molson débâcle only exacerbated the tension back in Maple Leaf Gardens. It had already been a messy year for the public company, Ballard's estate and his executors. Having resolved one dispute with Molson, the executors and the board of directors would be faced with another, more complicated conundrum looming on the horizon. One that would see some heads roll.

CHAPTER FOUR

Drawing the Battle Lines

"I'm telling you that what you're doing is wrong." — ROSANNE ROCCHI

"**C**UE TO MUSIC...BLUE,** standby...fade to yellow...roll yellow... ready blue, music, roll blue...C'mon Ronnie!...Guys, I'm coming upstairs to you...'Let's go up to the broadcast booth to Bob Cole and Harry Neale.'...Have a good game, everyone!"

The sounds of preparations for our collective Saturday night ritual just seconds before airtime emanate from a large mobile truck parked behind the north end of Maple Leaf Gardens. Inside the transportable control room, there is a symphony of television monitors—all colour-coded—depicting raw images being filtered through cameras strategically positioned inside the arena.

Mercurial John Shannon is the latest in a growing line of hockey programmers. As the show's executive producer, he's ultimately responsible for making sure that every goal, every body-check, and every grunt, spit and drop of sweat is captured for the 1.5 million viewers the show commands religiously every Saturday night.

"Hockey Night in Canada" is a Canadian institution that has made household names of play-by-play announcers and colour commentators who defy the odds weekly by finding new ways to describe grown men on skates chasing after a frozen puck. But the franchise is more than prestige, it's big money. Hockey is a booming business, albeit a little late joining the ranks of other multi-million-dollar professional sports. For the Canadian Broadcasting Corporation, "Hockey Night in Canada" is the breadwinner that fills the coffers, charging up to $20,000 for a thirty-second spot—and that's during the long regular season. For its growing list of corporate sponsors, hockey is the proven way to sell their product across the wide swath of the consuming public the sport has always attracted.

Indeed, it's a long way from the handshake that created the holy trinity of public broadcaster, hockey and corporate sponsor. In his book *The Boys of Saturday Night**, sports writer and broadcaster Scott Young describes how the history of live radio and television broadcasts from Maple Leaf Gardens began with a handshake on the fairway of the 15th hole of the Orchard Beach golf course on Lake Simcoe back in 1929 between Conn Smythe and Jack MacLaren, head of the Canadian arm of a Detroit-based advertising agency called Campbell-Ewald Ltd.

At the time, the Leafs were still playing out of the 8,000-seat Arena on Mutual Street. The two men, who rented cottages near each other during most summers, would shake hands on a deal that would see the Toronto Maple Leafs broadcast their home games with MacLaren serving up General Motors as the sponsor. What would later be known as the "General Motors Hockey Broadcast"—and the forerunner to "Hockey Night in Canada"—would not take effect until two years later when Smythe's world-famous hockey shrine would be completed.

Even with the advent of television broadcasts in the 1952–53 hockey season, the sponsorship rights which began at $100 per game were not assignable. The bottom line: whenever there were any changes in sponsorship, the rights reverted to the original handshake on the Orchard Beach golf course.

In 1933, a new American president sent up to run GM in Canada decided not to renew his company's five-year contract, even though by now the games were being broadcast from coast to coast. Imperial Oil took over when GM's contract expired in 1936—fetch-

---

* Young, Scott, *The Boys of Saturday Night: Inside Hockey Night in Canada.* Macmillan of Canada, Toronto, Ontario. 1990.

ing it for less than $100,000—beginning the oil company's esteemed forty-year affiliation with Canadian hockey.

The sponsorship torch was again passed, this time to Canada's largest brewery, when in 1976 Imperial Oil bailed out of hockey telecasts. By then, Maple Leaf Gardens was receiving about $1.5 million annually for selling its broadcast rights, but when Molson took over, the Gardens signed a new nine-year deal that provided $2.3 million a year, rising to $3 million in 1984–85. But midway through its contract Molson had a change of plans, which would ultimately transform the brewery into the most powerful name in hockey.

In 1980, Morgan McCamus, chairman of Molson Breweries, wanted two things: a legacy and a guarantee to keep the enemy out. With five years remaining on its current broadcast contract, McCamus set his sights on a long-term deal with Maple Leaf Gardens that would entrench Molson in the Gardens and keep Labatt out for a very long time. He pressed Ted Hough, who was head of the Canadian Sports Network (MacLaren Advertising Ltd.'s subsidiary that was still running "Hockey Night" from the early 1960s to the late 1980s), to see what he could put together. Hough was good friends with Harold Ballard and his trusted legal sidekick, Robert Sedgewick. In fact, Hough was the Gardens representative at the NHL's broadcast meetings. And back then, Ballard trusted the folks at Molson.

After a few weeks of "friendly" discussions—gyrating around pay TV, pay per channel, pay per view and whether government regulations would prohibit breweries from advertising on television—the Gardens and MacLaren Advertising Ltd. inked a fifteen-year deal dated November 25, 1980. The new contract would replace the existing one and in effect saw Maple Leaf Gardens deed away all its television matters to MacLaren, giving the advertising company exclusive rights to televise and broadcast (including radio) all Leaf games (home, road, regular season and playoff) starting at an annual rate of $2.5 million in 1980; every three years after that, the amount would be increased by $250,000 to a total annual rate of $4 million by the time the contract expired in 1995.

Numerous stipulations were also listed in the 1980 agreement, including black-out rights (which allowed Molson the right to

broadcast into Leafs' home territory when the team was not playing at home) and a provision for some minor adjustment in values
during three-year plateaus, which were tied to changes in the
advertising rates of "Hockey Night in Canada."

The most controversial clauses—numbers 10 and 11—could
significantly adjust payments and profoundly affect the amount
MLGL might collect for its broadcasts. Known as the "escalator" and
"enhancement" clauses, they allowed that if during the life of the fifteen-year agreement, the value of the broadcast rights were either
significantly diminished or enhanced by events not contemplated at
the time of signing in 1980, the annual payments to MLGL would be
adjusted accordingly. In other words, MLGL could receive less or
more depending on the circumstances. According to the contract,
the relationship between the two parties would be "governed by
mutual understanding and goodwill whenever differences arise."

In fact, Donald Crump remembers that clause 10 (the so-called
escalator) was built in for Molson as protection against the notoriously fickle Ballard. "Harold would go on them every now and
then. If he wanted something, he would say give me this or I'll take
this goddamn axe and I'll cut this bloody cable," Crump recalls. He
claims the enhancement clause (number 11) was added for MLGL's
benefit by ensuring that if economic conditions caused broadcast
rates to increase, Maple Leaf Gardens would benefit from those
changes. However, he says he never believed that either side had a
legal leg to stand on to enforce their respective clauses.

The beer barons had also snared exclusive promotional rights
at the Gardens, including advertising in programs and on the
backs of tickets; the arena would sell and serve only Molson products at Leaf functions and during hockey games; the company
automatically received fifty season tickets and a private box; and
finally, the brewery was entitled to select the Molson three stars of
each Leaf home game.

In 1984, four years into the agreement with McLaren, the contract was assigned to Molson, which had already secured its option
on 20 percent of Gardens stock and right of first refusal on the rest
of Ballard's controlling block. In effect, Ballard had cut a deal for a
public company that he controlled with another to whom he was
indebted through his own holding company.

That interconnected relationship would pose a tricky problem for the executors after Ballard's death. The month following Ballard's death in April 1990, Rosanne Rocchi and the lawyers at Miller Thomson began scrutinizing the 1980 television deal more closely. Rocchi, named the Leafs' alternate governor by Ballard in late 1989, began participating at the league level with the powerful governors while also attending the NHL broadcast committee hearings. It was during this time that Rocchi figured out how those all-important broadcast revenues flowed from the League to the teams.

Two things struck her: one, how remiss the Gardens had been in collecting their TV money from Molson. In fact, the payments, which she described as a "nice piece of change," were on average two months overdue and that was significant when you consider the interest rate at the time of the signing in 1980 was in the 22-percent range. "It really concerned me that no one knew the payments weren't coming in," she recalls.

The second, more disturbing issue, was that in her opinion, the Gardens should have triggered its enhancement clause way back in 1985—after the first five years of the contract. Yet, again, no one at the Gardens had pressed the brewery on that matter either. Keep in mind, the agreement with Molson had been made during an era of partnership and goodwill, so much so that Ballard agreed to let Molson monitor whether the situation changed enough for the clauses to take effect. That also meant that Molson would control access to the numbers MLGL needed to make a claim on the two clauses.

Robert Stellick, the thirty-year-old rink rat who'd replaced Stan Obodiac as the Gardens' public relations director after Obodiac's death in 1984 and who now held the lofty title of director of business operations and communications, was asked by Rocchi to check rate card statistics that would allow the lawyers to calculate how much more was owed by Molson to the Gardens. (Stellick had come to the Gardens from central scouting with the NHL's Toronto office. His older brother, Gordon, had a short stint as general manager of the Leafs before being unceremoniously fired by Ballard.)

Crump and Ian Clarke, the accountant from Peat Marwick who later filled in as controller on a temporary basis when Crump went to the CFL, were affronted by Rocchi's actions. While they fumed, Rocchi took charge, becoming a quasi chief financial officer, creating a tickler system for scheduling receivables, including the TV monies already in arrears and those to be collected in the future. She rifled off letter after letter, urging Clarke and later Stellick to get after Molson to write the cheques.

In the meantime, Rocchi wrote a letter to Norman Seagram giving notice that the Gardens board of directors was seriously examining its rights under the 1980 broadcast deal. Molson countered by dispatching Ronald Simpson, the brewery's vice-president of sports, to scrap the old contract (which expired in 1995) and renegotiate a brand-new one to the year 2000. To make "Hockey Night in Canada" work as a network, Molson needed Toronto. "This was Canada's national sport. 'Hockey Night in Canada' out of Toronto and Montreal are the two most watched spectacles and have exclusivity of advertising in category, which gave you an enormous amount of prestige and impact in the marketplace," explained a former brewery official.

All this wasn't just about serving up beer drinkers. Molson made money from its exclusive marketing and promotional rights at the Gardens by selling them—often at a huge premium—to other companies, such as the Ford Motor Co., Royal Bank of Canada and Canadian Tire Corp. These advertisers demanded an audience with the greatest collective purchasing power and those viewers happened to live mostly in southwestern Ontario. Molson was also concerned about protecting itself against Labatt, which had emerged as a formidable force in beer marketing, especially through the brewery's affiliation with the Toronto Blue Jays. No doubt because Molson was being forced by the NHL to relinquish its 20-percent stake in MLGL at the time, the brewery preferred to bargain from the stronger position that stake afforded the company. Indeed, Molson was mixing the private estate business with the public company's affairs. When Ronald Simpson called Rocchi to set up a meeting to fast-track the negotiations between Molson and the Gardens, Rocchi agreed to meet, but told him, "bring your chequebook because you owe us money."

In early June 1990, the executors met with Seagram and Hershell Ezrin (who was Cohen's newly minted executive assistant) to discuss proposals for Molson's divestiture. After all, Molson owned its MLGL shares indirectly through HEBL, which was controlled by the estate. "At the meeting, we agreed that the divestiture and the renegotiation of broadcast rights would be difficult in that there were different corporate entities on each side of the equation and it would be necessary to ensure that scrupulous efforts be made to ensure that there could be no issue of benefit to one party at the expense of another," explains a letter summarizing the meeting.

At the same time, the executors had been talking to Molson about another matter. The clock was winding down on the repayment of the $15.5 million Harold had borrowed from Molson to buy his daughter's shares in early 1989. The loan was coming due at the end of 1990, and the executors were acutely aware that Ballard's estate couldn't finance the repayment. About three weeks after Ballard's death, the executors and Rocchi visited the estate's bankers. Ostensibly, the Toronto Dominion Bank wanted to introduce one of its lucrative customers to the bank's new main branch manager—Tasker Kelsey, who'd just arrived from Calgary. Over coffee served in fine china, Kelsey got down to business. The bank wanted to know if the estate was going to continue guaranteeing the loan Ballard had signed off in 1989. An account manager had sent a letter to Rocchi about this even before Ballard's body was cold. Rocchi and the executors asked the TD if the bank was willing to consider taking an equity position in the Gardens. The opportunity would be available when Molson's option came due in November 1990. Kelsey declined but requested that TD Capital—the bank's investment arm—be given the contract to broker a deal. A bank memo dated April 1990 said, "The executors believe that Molson is not interested in the team but rather the real estate. What they really want is a long-term advertising and sponsorship arrangement and there is room for negotiation." That became clearer when Molson and the executors began talking.

Meanwhile, back at the Gardens Rocchi was hanging tough with MLGL's board of directors, urging them to resist pressure from the brewery and keep the old deal to preserve any rights of enhancement—and the millions owed as a result to Maple Leaf Gardens. So long as Molson was a shareholder in MLGL, it had a right of first refusal. Rocchi said Molson had perceived this right as giving the company leverage in its contractual relations with the Gardens. The most material contract Maple Leaf Gardens had was its broadcast rights.

Not only that, Rocchi took the matter straight to the league's head office in New York. Joel Nixon, the vice-president of broadcasting at the NHL, recommended the Gardens obtain an expert's assessment of the 1980 broadcast deal and, more specifically, whether the clauses at issue were affected by the changing market for those TV revenues. Ralph Mellanby, the former executive producer of "Hockey Night in Canada," was selected from three candidates to produce a report for MLGL's board of directors by the end of the year.

The Essex, Ontario, native had been the first executive producer hired by the Canadian Sports Network, in 1966. A five-time Emmy Award winner, Mellanby pioneered much of the modern-day hockey telecasts, including the rise of Don Cherry's star on the current weekly telecasts. After eighteen years in hockey with the CBC and MacLaren, the ambitious Mellanby left the public broadcaster to produce the television coverage of the Calgary Winter Olympics and the Summer Olympics in Seoul, Korea, for rival network CTV in 1988.

Always a controversial figure, Mellanby produced a thirty-seven-page opus for a $50,000 retainer. Written with the help of attorney John Chapman, the report fell into the laps of the Gardens' first post-Ballard board of directors in early December 1990. Six years later, it would become an important prong in the Public Trustee's legal case against Steve Stavro and his co-executors.

Needless to say, in less than a decade, gone was the cordial atmosphere of partnership. In a memo later that year, one of Rocchi's law partners, John Chapman, captured the disintegrating relations between the once friendly parties. "...There has been a partial or complete breakdown in the partnership philosophy which permeated the dealings up to 1980. Sedgewick died in 1984. [Ted] Hough left HNIC ['Hockey Night in Canada'] around 1986. The personnel at Molson have changed. It is unknown as to whether Molson will be able or willing to recognize that the 1980 Broadcast Agreement was motivated and governed by an overall obligation to be fair. It is expected that both parties will rely more on legal opinions and less on a history of dealings and goodwill than was formerly the case."

In the spring of 1990, only a few weeks after Ballard's death, Crump, Giffin and Stavro were already operating in a whirlwind of seemingly conflicting roles. As caretakers of the estate, they were expected to be mindful of their fiduciary responsibilities. As directors of MLGL and the holding company HEBL, they owed certain duties to the shareholders. And as trustees of Ballard's trust and directors of his charitable foundation they were obligated to the beneficiaries of Ballard's estate. The tension created by wearing all of those hats often confused them and led them off on tangents.

While Rocchi and Bill McKinnon, the company's auditor from Peat Marwick, were attending to the corporate details, Crump, Stavro and Giffin occupied themselves with what could best be described as their own personal projects. "Rocchi was reduced to babysitting Maple Leaf Gardens," said an observer who saw what unfolded in the months following Ballard's death. "She paid the bills and kept records for them. Meanwhile, the executors were running around trying to take over the place." Others would dismiss her as a dilettante, someone who had never run a company and was now acting like a CEO. "Nobody was running the business, that's why Rosanne Rocchi was in there like flint," Bellmore later said. "That would have been a real trip for any lawyer. There's a lot of ego but lawyers aren't good at making business decisions."

At that time Crump, who was largely responsible for the untidy state of the company's financial books, had just joined the Canadian Football League and Stavro was busy operating his Knob Hill Farms grocery chain. Giffin was the only one of the three on the company payroll, earning $300,000 a year and driving a company car, as president. One of his first initiatives was convincing the board to declare the special dividend of $2.75 a share on July 16, 1990, which further ingratiated him with the company's largest shareholders, Harry Ornest and Jim Devellano. Of course, the estate fared well too, receiving $8.12 million, courtesy of its three-million-plus shares, which went straight to servicing the debt owed to the TD Bank.

Giffin's interests lay almost exclusively in the hockey operations: building a tunnel between the Gardens and the Hot Stove Lounge; installing private boxes; constructing a state-of-the-art dressing room. A private enclave for the players' wives was built (for which he hired an interior decorator), and even the tacky Directors' Lounge was spruced up by replacing the plastic ivy hanging from the plywood walls with dried flower arrangements.

Ushers and usherettes, arguably the oldest in the league (so said Paul McNamara), were gussied up with new uniforms, courtesy of Eaton's. Giffin and McNamara, before he was iced as chairman of the board, raised banners and retired sweaters in memory of the once-proud hockey tradition at Maple Leaf Gardens. They welcomed the Leaf old-timers, such as Mike "Shakey" Walton and former captain Frank Mahovlich, who had been publicly snubbed by Ballard, inviting them back to the Gardens to watch games in a newly created alumni box. Directors began travelling with the team on road trips and even popping their heads into the dressing room on occasion.

For himself, Giffin refurbished Conn Smythe's old office, which had been used primarily as a storage room during Ballard's reign. Even so, Stavro (who had vehemently opposed his co-executor's appointment as president) saw it as another example of Giffin's overreaching desire to permanently plant himself as the new Major of the Gardens. He was even more annoyed when he learned that Ballard's office had been scavenged by employees looking for memorabilia. "I wanted Harold's office to be preserved as a showpiece to raise money for charity," he said later.

True to his affable character, Giffin also employed an open-door policy that often created friction with his co-executors. Unlike the presidents of most major companies, Giffin simply refused to vet his visitors, preferring instead to operate the Gardens the way he did his family sheet-metal company. In doing so, Giffin became the recipient of all kinds of information, including gossip. The problem was that he'd hoard it, and that only exacerbated the already strained and increasingly suspicious relations with his co-executors.

It became so preposterous that Rocchi had to force Giffin to agree that each executor receive Giffin's own personal correspondence in every transaction or discussion and that he enforce the rule with Molson in particular. Stavro's lawyer would make a similar request a year later.

For his part, Stavro's attention was directed mostly at building operations. Quicker than you could say "time clock," Stavro had them installed inside the Gardens. All employees were forced to punch in and out when they came to work. That's what they do at Knob Hill Farms, except, of course, for Steve and his wife, Sally. And it's the same daily ritual that building operations personnel and unionized workers at the Gardens are still being subjected to today.

As well, the self-made millionaire wanted to replace the money-losing employee cafeteria, known as the Grill, with a Tim Horton's doughnut franchise. It was sold to Stavro's colleagues as a revenue-generating idea, but it wasn't quite what the homecoming Leaf fans—or Ron Joyce, chairman of the doughnut company—had in mind for the late Leaf all-star defenceman.

Like Giffin, Stavro wanted to give the place a face-lift. First, he hired real estate developer J.J. Barnicke to provide an evaluation of the real estate, which they estimated at $18 million. (A year earlier, Giffin had arranged for Ballard to meet with Angelo del Zotto of Tridel Corp. to appraise the property and prepare architectural drawings for possible redevelopment.) Next, Stavro enquired about how much it would cost to remove the grungy film on the exterior of the building. For that, he sought two estimates: one for sand-blasting, which was exorbitantly priced. The other was an interesting suggestion put forward by a small, family-owned business out-side Toronto. They offered to chemically treat the building at a much lower price than it would cost to sandblast. Although Stavro usually is sympathetic towards family-run enterprises, the idea was given a decisive thumbs down. The potential environmental hazard that could result when toxic chemicals dripped onto the sidewalk of one of the busiest corners in downtown Toronto was just too risky. The upshot: the art deco structure was sandblasted.

Crump, on the other hand, was enjoying his honeymoon as commissioner of the Canadian Football League. Although he didn't appear to have any desire to leave his own thumbprints all over the building where he'd worked since 1971, he was certainly tenacious about securing generous retirement allowances for some of its inhabitants, like Johnny Bower (the legendary Leaf goaltender who was now employed as a player scout for the team) and the late John Grinsky (who'd been at the Gardens for eight years and stepped into Crump's shoes as controller until Ian Clarke arrived). In fact, one of the first orders of business approved by Justice Donna Haley during the committee stage was a consulting contract for Crump. After his salary terminated at the Gardens at the end of February, the Gardens agreed to pay him $100 an hour, on top of the $12,000 he'd collect annually as a member of the company's board and the executor fees he'd be entitled to receive.

Weeks later, Crump requested a retirement allowance of $44,500 from the Gardens, which was the maximum allowable contribution to his Registered Retirement Savings Plan. The matter was debated for months and court approval was pending. By the middle of 1991, the lawyers were still shuffling paper around, leaving the matter unresolved. So Crump never resigned as secretary-treasurer of Maple Leaf Gardens.

Often, because the executors couldn't agree on almost anything, the conflicting issues kept coming to the boardroom table. For example, Stavro wanted all three executors to sign off on any cheques written totalling over $5,000. That idea would have crippled company operations because most of its accounts payable—from payroll to the electricity bill—exceeded that amount. Stavro insisted while the others resisted, so it was debated by the directors. Thus, instead of dealing with the big-picture strategies that most boards tackle, the executors would grind the meetings to a halt with all these minutiae.

The great divide between the executors began to build even before Ballard died with the disclosure of Giffin's option on the shares formerly held by Ballard's daughter. During the week of private discussions in Justice Haley's chambers in late February 1990, the judge had ruled that Giffin could keep the option as long as he didn't exercise it while Ballard was alive. That wasn't good enough for Stavro, who soon became obsessed with its very existence.

Days later, Stavro called Don Crump and asked him to arrange a meeting in his Gardens office with Don Giffin. The executors knew the contents of Ballard's will—and more importantly, were aware that it included a provision that allowed them to buy his controlling block of MLGL shares. These documents were filed with Judge Haley with all the others when Crump, Giffin and Stavro were appointed as committees. The executors began the March 1990 meeting with a few cursory comments about Ballard's ailing health. "The main issue was that we should work together for the best intentions of Harold's will," Stavro recalled of the meeting. He said they agreed not to be used by Labatt (a business partner of Bill Ballard) or Molson, which he knew had sway over Giffin. Finally, the discussion turned to purchasing the Gardens together. "If one was short of capital, then he had the right to bring in an outsider to finance his third." The three men shook hands in agreement. "We put our hands together like the three musketeers and we vowed that we wouldn't be used one against the other."

He explained the intention of the meeting was to establish an understanding between them—that is, he interpreted Ballard's intentions were that "definitely we should get something," and they should work together to fulfil that last wish. "That's why I ordered Brian [Bellmore] to get an agreement." Stavro knew that Molson had designs on the place. The handshake was to make sure that, heading into negotiations with Molson over the Mary Elizabeth loan, Ballard's three executors were on the same team. Not only that, Stavro claimed that he was being excluded in the decision-making process by Crump and Giffin. He was the third man out and he wanted them to proceed as equals.

On April 6, 1990, five days before Ballard died, the three executors gathered at Stavro's Teddington Park home. Brian Bellmore, Stavro's personal lawyer, produced a draft agreement for the executors to consider signing. The document was a throwback to the days of the Ballard-Smythe-Bassett troika in the early 1960s. The contract proposed that once Ballard died, all three men would agree to purchase the assets of the estate together—if at all—and having done that, when one of the executors died, his interests would automatically be assigned to his co-partners. In other words, Giffin, Stavro and Crump would agree not to pass their interests to their heirs; their estates had to offer them first to the other executors.

Giffin had the most to lose by scribbling his name on the document, which he claimed was presented to him for immediate signing even though his lawyer, Ronald Farano, had not been invited to the meeting. First of all, he was the oldest of the three by at least ten years and he would likely be the first to bequeath his interest in the Gardens to his seven children. (Several months later, Giffin discovered that he had inoperable cancer.) Stavro had four children and money to burn while Crump had two children and no financial means to seriously contend for control of the company. It wasn't hard to figure out that Stavro stood to gain the most from this arrangement.

Not only that, a clause in the document said, "The parties hereto agree that this agreement shall supersede any options or rights that they now have to purchase the shares of HEBL." Since Giffin was the only one of the three holding any options or rights on the shares, this exercise was designed to wipe out any perceived advantage Giffin might have had over the other two executors.

In an unusual display of foresight, Giffin refused to sign the document at Stavro's home, even though Farano later claimed in a letter to the Public Trustee that "Mr. Stavro became very exercised and insisted that the three members of the Committee sign the document then and there." Instead, Giffin called Rocchi after he left Stavro's mansion, relaying what had just happened but failing to mention the earlier meeting in his office that had ended with the handshake. Stunned, Ballard's lawyer warned him, "I'm telling you that what you're [the committee] doing is wrong," and advised him not to sign any agreements and to speak with his own attorney immediately. Bellmore and Stavro flatly deny Giffin's allegation that they were insisting Giffin sign the agreement, which Stavro maintains his co-executor had already agreed to in principle.

It's not clear whether Giffin had a sudden change of heart when he saw how his handshake translated onto paper or if he misunderstood Stavro's intention. Nonetheless, the spectre of court-appointed guardians carving up Ballard's treasure chest for themselves while he lay jerking back and forth in a hospital bed raised the question of whether they might have been breaching their fiduciary duties to a dying man. Besides, as members of the committee, they had no power of sale (that would come after Ballard died) so they couldn't just help themselves to his purse. In fact, they had to ask for Justice Haley's approval for almost everything they did, from paying Yolanda's hotel and dry-cleaning bills to drawing up the $300,000-a-year employment contract naming Giffin as president of Maple Leaf Gardens. Worse, by even contemplating such a cosy arrangement between them, they could have been accused of self-dealing, and if the court found a conflict of interest it could have resulted in their removal as executors of Ballard's estate or at the very least, a firm rebuke. The court, however, was never told. Details of the secret meeting would surface four years later when the Public Trustee sued Ballard's executors.

The architect of the Stavro proposal took issue with Rocchi's tough stance, especially since she'd never actually seen a copy of the document—and hasn't to this day. Brian Bellmore and Stavro had hooked up back in February 1990. Stavro had been impressed with Bellmore after watching him successfully argue on behalf of a group of Bulgarian Orthodox parishioners in East Toronto. The case, which went to the Ontario Court of Appeal, involved a controversial decision to allow the parish to parachute a Bulgarian priest into the community to replace the pastor who had just died. Stavro's father, Atanas, had been one of the church's original builders.

"When I got back to the office after the trial," recalls the fifty-four-year-old attorney, "Steve called to thank me. He never said that he was bankrolling these people, but whenever I submitted an invoice, it was paid within a week. I was surprised because these people didn't look well off." A few weeks later, Stavro called again to ask if Bellmore would represent him at the mental incompetency hearing in Judge Haley's chambers. It was the chance of a lifetime for the Toronto born and bred hockey aficionado. Bellmore had played varsity hockey and had attended the same school as many Leaf legends. Since then, Stavro and his Harvard-educated litigator have been almost inseparable socially and professionally.

Bellmore called Rocchi at her office to explain the plan tabled at his client's home, describing it, however, only in general terms. By this time, Ballard had died and the trio had officially become executors of his estate with all the powers associated. Bellmore figured they were now in the clear and Stavro's proposal was left on the table.

Although Rocchi and the three executors had met several times at Teddington Park to discuss estate matters, she and Stavro had never spoken directly about his proposal. In her mind, she had dismissed the fight over Giffin's option as a red herring because she'd always figured that it wasn't worth much. In any event,

Rocchi thought that if Stavro wanted Giffin to relinquish his option and level the playing field, then why did he have all these other terms in the proposal? In the end, she suspected that the agreement was intended to give the executors the opportunity to become brokers, middlemen who would charge a commission for flogging Maple Leaf Gardens to an outside buyer, like Labatt or Molson. The problem is, when you're an executor, your fiduciary responsibilities don't include playing agent.

In early May, Giffin asked Rocchi to join him and his wife, Patty, for dinner at a Chinese restaurant in Markham, Ontario. When they arrived, Donald Crump was already waiting in the parking lot. Crump and Giffin had previously agreed on the location because it was halfway between their homes—Giffin lived north of Toronto in Thornhill, and Crump resided east in Agincourt.

Once inside the restaurant, Giffin expressed grave concern that Stavro was still pushing ahead with his proposal. Rocchi was worried that he was showing signs of buckling under the pressure from Stavro. In an attempt to gird him to take a tougher stand, she alarmed Giffin with her dire predictions of what would happen to them if the court ever found out what they had done (and were still thinking of doing). Crump, on the other hand, didn't say much during the dinner, although later he would say that he began harbouring suspicions about the motives of his two dinner companions.

Rocchi wrote them both a blistering five-page letter on May 17, 1990, a week before leaving for a long-awaited vacation in Greece and Egypt. Her missive outlined why Stavro's plan would constitute "a serious conflict of interest and would, if discovered, be sufficient to provide grounds for removal of you as Executors of the Estate, such agreement being in breach of your fiduciary obligations."

Rocchi's letter was prescient, raising many of the fundamental issues that would surface in court years later. Although Ballard's will permitted an executor to purchase the assets, it allowed for only one because the sale had to be approved by an independent executor. If all three of them were contemplating buying the assets together, she reasoned, there would be no one left to give the necessary approval.

But in a contradictory note, Rocchi outlined clearly that if one of the executors wished to purchase the estate's assets, "an application would be made to Court to confirm the sale," because the court is the only jurisdiction that can confirm fair value. Although the beneficiaries of the will—and the trust—are charities, the Public Trustee doesn't have the authority to consent to a sale. Even though clause VII of the will—a document Rocchi wrote herself—clearly authorized any trustee of Ballard's will to purchase assets "without court authorization," she argued that only applied to items in the estate covered in the will. Those assets included only Ballard's Georgian Bay cottage, his house, condominiums, and sports memorabilia. His controlling block of MLGL shares was to be transferred into the Harold E. Ballard Trust and disposed of there, which meant the trustees were bound by a different set of fiduciary obligations that governed the trust. And because the beneficiaries of that trust were non-profit organizations and charities, Crump, Stavro and Giffin, as trustees, were obligated to get court approval before selling or buying the shares.

On May 20, four days before Rocchi left on her two-week vacation, the executors and their lawyer gathered at Stavro's home. During their meeting, Rocchi handed each a list of about forty tasks that were to be divided among them and completed in her absence. Stavro seemed eager, saying he wanted to tidy up all the outstanding items regarding the estate, such as paying Ballard's hospital bills, settling taxes owed and dealing with the litigation surrounding the Michael Gobuty fiasco. "Let's get ready to sell," Stavro apparently declared, asking if it could all be done before Rocchi boarded the airplane.

Meanwhile, Bellmore had been calling and writing the estate's lawyer frequently, asking for documents and information "that seemed to go far beyond what he needed to advise an executor in his personal capacity," Rocchi remembers. However, her firm handed the documents over out of professional courtesy.

Weeks of bickering and late-night telephone calls came to a head at a meeting in Giffin's lawyer's midtown Toronto law office on June 29, 1990. Farano, Bellmore, Rocchi, John Chapman and Don Champagne (a corporate lawyer retained by Bellmore) thrashed out their conflicting opinions on the proposal put forward by Stavro at his home in early April. Bellmore tested Rocchi's patience, demanding that she support her position—that executors and trustees couldn't purchase trust property—with detailed legal references and the appropriate case law.

Needless to say, none of these events unfolded in an orderly fashion. The circus atmosphere that prevailed during Harold Ballard's reign continued well after his death. And of course, Yolanda started the ball rolling with her legal claim against Ballard's estate, demanding a whopping $10 million in support—quite a jump from the $50,000 a year stipend Harold left her in his will. Even Denise Banks, the teenage companion of Yolanda, hired a lawyer to try squeezing something out of Ballard's estate, claiming she was a dependent. Finally, it all became too farcical when Mike Wassilyn, MLGL's scalper extraordinaire, publicly declared that he was Harold Ballard's illegitimate son.

In the midst of all this, Ballard's three executors continued bickering among themselves. During a lunch gathering across the street from the Gardens at the Westbury Hotel, Crump and Stavro confronted Giffin about his reluctance to step down as company president. When he had been appointed six months earlier—Stavro opposed the appointment, preferring instead to name his friend Provincial Court Judge Joe Kane—it had been viewed as a temporary measure until a new board could be assembled. "He didn't want to leave. He fell in love with the place," Crump explains. "He got the new board that just came in to extend his contract and make him chairman. We had a real knock 'em down drag 'em out fight over at the Westbury. I thought at times there were going to be blows thrown, but he still didn't want to leave his position."

In the minds of Giffin's co-executors, the three new independent directors (Rogers, Eaton and McDowell) were sympathetic to the "tin snip," the name Crump used to refer to Giffin behind his back. Thus, the more Giffin hung tough, the more Stavro and Crump began to see events unfolding with the view of Us against Them.

Meanwhile, Rocchi was going head to head with Seagram and Ezrin of Molson over how to unload the brewery's 20-percent option on the Gardens. And for that, she was getting nothing but grief from the middle-aged men at the Gardens, who resented her actions as that of a control fanatic. Back at 60 Carlton Street, a small group of forensic auditors from Peat Marwick were crawling all over the place investigating the alleged misappropriation of stick money, ticket scalping and box-office shenanigans. And everyone held their breath fearing a complete company audit by Revenue Canada.

It was all becoming too much for the diminutive Rocchi. After a year in which she saw Ballard die a slow and painful death on the heels of her own marital breakdown, Rocchi wanted out. During an emotional dinner at Cibo's, a tony restaurant in midtown Toronto, on September 12, 1990, Rocchi told Bill Cluff, Bob Stellick and Crump that she couldn't handle the day-to-day tasks she had been performing for the company. Through tears, Rocchi insisted that they hire a new chief operating officer immediately because Ian Clarke, who'd temporarily stepped in to fill the breach left by Crump, couldn't handle Giffin, who she thought was out of control.

On one of only a few occasions, Rocchi actually agreed with Stavro and Crump. Like them, she believed that Giffin was too clubby with the boys at Molson. Interestingly, Crump was convinced at the time that Rocchi had been conspiring with Giffin to deliver Maple Leaf Gardens into the hands of the brewery. Now, he couldn't quite believe he was hearing her complain about how she was running around trying to set up meetings with NHL governors to resolve the Molson option issue at the league meetings in Toronto later that month, and how Giffin was going off on tangents behind her back. She offered them this example: Rocchi said she'd been given letters describing discussions between John Ziegler, Norman Seagram, Bill Wirtz, the powerful owner of the Chicago Blackhawks (and one of the most influential NHL governors) and Giffin. Angry, she accused Giffin of deliberately keeping her in the dark and worse, she shocked her audience at Cibo's when she confided to them that she was convinced Giffin was about to sell out the Gardens to his friends at Molson.

Crump, for one, valued her loyalty to the Gardens and begged her to reconsider. No one else cared enough to take on all the responsibilities that she had assumed, he told her. "When all those things are happening, who do you talk to? Who's going to believe you?" he later explained.

Indeed, during the last years of Ballard's life, Rocchi had become the de facto mother hen of the Gardens, performing tasks most solicitors would never touch. Conscientious almost to a fault, the thirty-nine-year-old lawyer who had worked as a supermarket cashier and supply teacher to finance her university education felt so protective of Ballard as someone "quite vulnerable," that she couldn't quite figure out when to say no. So much so that she was the one person everyone called, at all hours of the day or night, whether it was to give legal advice on contracts (she kept enlarging the font size in her letters to accommodate Ballard's failing eyesight), preparing briefing binders for the directors or refereeing fights between Yolanda and Harold (often hiding him in the Leafs' dressing room, which she knew was one of the few places in the Gardens that was completely off limits to Yolanda) and the rest of the Gardens staff. On Saturday mornings, she would often stop by the Gardens on her way to work to deliver licorice and digestive cookies for the man "who gave [her] a chance to prove [her] mettle." In the end, Harold Ballard had been sick for so long, the lines of the defined roles became blurred and then almost entirely erased by the time he died. Rocchi's growing influence was not lost on Ballard's courtiers. Within days of the despot's hospitalization in early 1990, chairman of the board Paul McNamara began agitating for a change of lawyers.

Still, Rocchi's role seemed to expand during the transition period after Ballard's death. With the departure of Crump to the CFL, Rocchi was the only one who knew the place well. Despite their misgivings, she was hardly dispensable. In fact, it was Gardens management that enlisted her help in collecting large receivables (like the TV payments), negotiating labour agreements for employees, even assisting Mellanby with his report. For that, Miller Thomson was collecting half a million dollars a year in legal fees.

"Lawyers would not generally be so pro-active," Rocchi says, however, "the continued tensions within the troika made my job impossible. I didn't have enough fingers to stick in the holes of the dyke and they were busy raising banners."

Oddly enough, the tables would turn. Three months after her emotional plea in Cibo's, Rocchi would be fighting to keep her job as lawyer for Maple Leaf Gardens.

In the meantime, Rocchi delivered the lengthy brief on executors' duties that had been requested by Bellmore. In a twenty-two-page letter dated October 24, Rocchi took a not-so-subtle poke at the executors, pointing out that she had already painstakingly walked them through their duties on countless occasions. The letter appeared to do the trick, for the moment. Stavro's proposal disappeared (although it would resurface in another incarnation two months later).

The next day, Rocchi received a telephone call from Giffin about a letter Ted Rogers had sent him expressing concern about possible conflicts of interest that would arise from having the same lawyer act on behalf of the estate, the Gardens, and HEBL because their interests were often divergent. Rogers suggested that perhaps the independent board members should get their own legal counsel, say someone at McCarthy Tétrault, a law firm used by Rogers and Stavro and endorsed by Ted McDowell in another letter a week later on November 1. McDowell suggested lawyer Blair Cowper-Smith at McCarthy would be a good alternative. Of course, the issue of potential conflicts was just as true for three of the directors, including the president, who were also executors of Ballard's estate, which controlled the largest shareholder in the company.

Rocchi was unfazed, albeit tired of covering the same old ground. For one thing, the issue had been raised, debated and resolved four times already that year. As well, Rogers and McDowell had been openly critical of her, saying she was taking too hard a line during the fall negotiations with Molson, accusing her of jeopardizing MLGL's relationship with its largest sponsor. Rogers and Mickey Cohen both sat with McDowell at TD Bank board meetings. The two Teds argued that Molson's option was an estate problem, since the optioned shares were housed in Ballard's holding company and should not have been brought to the public company's board of directors, let alone handled by the company's lawyer. Stavro agreed with them.

"Ted Rogers made his opinion known that he was not interested in having Miller Thomson or Rocchi on as counsel for either the Gardens or the estate or Harold E. Ballard," Crump recalls. "I felt that I understood the conflict but I never really knew how big it was in the minds of some of those directors."

Another battle was shaping up in the courts. Bill Ballard was still fuming about his brother's betrayal by selling out to their father in

1989. Seventeen months later, in November 1990, the lawsuit he had begun against Harold Sr., when he was still alive, and his two cronies was about to play out before Justice James Farley.

Bill had two complaints: that his father, Crump and Don Giffin (who had replaced Bill as director of HEBL in late 1988 after the younger Ballard was convicted and fined $500 for assaulting Yolanda) had breached Harold Sr.'s deal with Junior. Two, that Giffin, Crump and Harold Sr. had "conspired" to mismanage the company, which existed merely to receive dividends from its shares in Maple Leaf Gardens, thus weakening Bill's stake in the holding company. He cited the $21 million HEBL borrowed from TD Bank to buy out Harold Jr., a debt that imposed a massive load on the company, and weakened its balance sheet, already staggering with a $38-million debt load. Bill Ballard wanted Crump and Giffin taken off HEBL's board and his brother's shares returned.

During the two-week trial, Bill and his lawyer, James Hodgson, also learned about deals that had taken place prior to his brother's buyout and just after he was turfed from HEBL's board. Around the time Bill and Harold Jr. were shaking hands on a deal in late 1988, Crump and Giffin transferred some of Harold Sr.'s personal properties—the Carlton Street condo, the house on Montgomery Road, the Georgian Bay cottage—to the holding company for about $900,000. Bill claimed they did that merely to extract money from the holding company for his father.

Crump testified that the asset swap in part resulted from his own suspicions about Yolanda and that the children would be happy that he was protecting Harold's possessions from the woman they all viewed as a gold digger. "I felt that in large measure she was concerned with her own financial self-interest," he said in a sworn affidavit. "As Harold Sr. became older and encountered health problems, and he spent more and more time with Yolanda to the exclusion of others, I became increasingly concerned that she would persuade Harold Sr. to convey assets to her or to her friends." He also said he hoped the holding company could generate rental income from the properties, even though they had no tenants at the time.

More importantly, he transferred the 350,320 common shares in the Gardens (which Ballard held directly) into the holding company. He did this for two reasons: to keep them away from Yolanda and because Molson had already admitted that it intended to seize the MLGL shares in HEBL. That would reduce HEBL's stake in Maple Leaf Gardens from 70.75 percent to 50.75 percent.

Crump dismissed Bill's lawsuit, saying it wasn't about broken contracts, but really stemmed "from his poor relationship with Harold Sr. and the antagonism between them."

Bill's lawyer countered that Crump and Giffin merely rubber-stamped Harold Sr.'s efforts to entrench his control of the family firm at a time when he was paranoid about losing the company to Molson or Labatt. On the witness stand, when Jim Hodgson asked Crump why he carried out Ballard's orders without questioning them first, he replied, "I am not sure I should have been concerned about [why] it mattered. It was what he wanted [that] I was concerned about." When Hodgson floated a similar question to Giffin, he elicited a litigator's dream answer. "I clicked my heels and saluted," came the response. Indeed. Giffin was Harold's man. That was how he viewed himself and also how he wanted others to see him. Judge Farley would have something to say about that months later when he made his ruling. Until then, the lawyers on both sides agreed that the shares in HEBL would not be touched without prior notice to Bill Ballard. That undertaking to the court would be an obstacle for the one executor who wasn't directly involved in Bill Ballard's suit.

Meanwhile, back in the Gardens boardroom another paper trail of memos and letters was being laid down. Rocchi and her boss, Judson Whiteside, were still trying to fend off the assault from Rogers and McDowell. They met with the Gardens directors to explain their firm's position on November 14. Two days later, Rocchi prepared to fire off a letter to each board member, but first faxed a draft copy to Giffin. In her defence, Rocchi wrote that since Miller Thomson had been performing quasi-management duties for years, it would be less disruptive and less expensive to maintain the status quo. "Based on our knowledge of MLGL's business operations, we have concerns that it lacks internal expertise on a number of aspects vital to its business (NHL relations and television)," she wrote.

The chairman of the board was incensed when he read that passage. He was quickly on the phone to Rocchi, accusing her of "taking shots" at him personally. He said his fellow board members agreed with his interpretation and "Stavro would be jumping for joy at those statements." Remarkably, Giffin was so insulted that he refused to speak to Rocchi for days after that, quite a display of anger for a man who was accustomed to calling the lawyer countless times a day. When he finally did ring her up on December 2, Rogers was waiting to be patched into a conference call. The cable czar berated Rocchi, ordering her not to attend the NHL Governors' meetings scheduled to begin the next day in West Palm Beach, Florida. Giffin and Rogers said they wanted MLGL to reposition its stance and abstain from any involvement in resolving the Molson option, which was still dragging on mercilessly.

Giffin also said, "The board has no objection to Molson remaining a participant in the arena or building," but they agreed the company could not remain a shareholder in the hockey team. Rocchi became suspicious, she later claimed, because it was a complete reversal of the decision made by the entire board earlier in the week. Worse, Giffin and Rogers sounded as if they were still considering the possibility of splitting MLGL into two companies, the same proposal forwarded by Molson and shot down months ago.

So Rocchi refused to take orders from Rogers and Giffin, arguing she hadn't been given instructions by the entire board. That defiance set up a showdown when she returned from Florida the following week.

While Rocchi was holed up in meetings at the Breakers' Hotel, she met with Bruce McNall, the former owner of the Los Angeles Kings, who would soon become one of her clients. McNall would purchase the CFL's Toronto Argonauts (with partners Wayne Gretzky and the actor John Candy) from Harry Ornest in 1991 and Rocchi would become one of the team's league alternate governors.

Back in Toronto, Mellanby tabled his report and much to the chagrin of Rocchi's growing list of detractors, Mellanby's numbers confirmed what Rocchi and her partners at Miller Thomson had long suspected. According to the study, Maple Leaf Gardens should have been earning roughly $12.25 million a year for its broadcast rights. (Remember, it was collecting just under $4 million annually at the time.) He suggested the Gardens should "attempt to secure revenues of approximately this level" for the remainder of the agreement. "Molson had the best TV sports deal ever made—and I mean in the world," Mellanby later recalled of the broadcast deal he reviewed for the Gardens board of directors. "It was a great deal for Molson and I was concerned that Molson would pressure the board into a new deal because they were the new kids on the block." Mellanby, who was also a shareholder in the Gardens, should have known that much. He had worked directly with the same brewery people who had snared the sweet deal from Ballard back in 1980. He cautioned the Gardens directors not to sign a new deal quickly for the sake of grabbing the increased revenues that he had outlined in his report.

That caution was tied to a strategy that had been plotted by the Gardens lawyers at Miller Thomson. John Chapman not only suggested the board seek the higher rates in its new contract deal as suggested by Mellanby, but more controversially, he argued that Maple Leaf Gardens should have been collecting as much since 1985 because the enhancement clause in its contract with Molson should have been triggered. Based on his calculations, the Gardens was owed at least $40 million in back pay alone. (Thoughts of pursuing millions in retroactive payments would dominate the agenda of the board of directors over the next year and a half. In March 1992, the board unanimously decided not to challenge Molson on the controversial enhancement of its television revenues after having been advised by their new lawyers that it would be "a gross waste of time with little or no realistic prospect of success.")

Suddenly, the estate was being forced to make what appeared to be an impossible choice—whether or not to take Molson to task over the broadcast money owing to MLGL at a time when the brewery was ready to pull the trigger on its $15.5-million loan for Mary Elizabeth's shares at the end of the month. Once again the private company's business was being mixed with the public.

As expected, Miller Thomson's Chapman wrote a lengthy opinion advising the Gardens board to chase after the money. Another Toronto legal firm, McCarthy Tétrault, endorsed that recommendation a month later.

It was decided that the matter would be dealt with at the next board meeting, scheduled for December 14. The night before, Ballard's three executors, Rocchi, Chapman and McKinnon gathered in Giffin's office to hammer out the agenda. When they left, the big-ticket items were the Mellanby report and to get approval to send a formal letter to Seagram at Molson putting him on notice that the Gardens intended to revisit its 1980 broadcast deal with the intention of looking into the retroactive payments. (Miller Thomson already had the letter drafted.)

But when Rocchi arrived the next day for the meeting, the agenda had been completely rewritten and the broadcast issue had been dropped from the list. In its place, two new items were added: a special dividend and a vote on whether to replace the company's lawyers. Rocchi, who attended as secretary in charge of taking notes of the meeting, was asked to leave the room. McKinnon, who was uneasy about the whole scene, was enlisted to assume her note-taking responsibilities.

Then, a beauty contest ensued, with senior representatives from several major firms parading before the Gardens board. Included were John Tory and former Ontario premier William Davis from Tory Tory DesLauriers & Binnington; Arthur Scace, a senior partner at McCarthy Tétrault; and Darcy Brooks from Borden & Elliot (the firm would later be hired by the Public Trustee in its case against Stavro). Finally, Judson Whiteside was given time to plead his firm's case one last time. Before the meeting, the Rt. Hon. John Turner, former prime minister and now senior partner at Miller Thomson, had made a few last-minute pleas to a handful of board members he knew personally. He called Ted Rogers, who gave Turner an icy (if not rude) reception; McDowell was cryptic and Eaton wouldn't take his call until after Eaton spoke to Rogers.

Crump refused to support Tory Tory because it was Ted Rogers's legal firm and was the same firm giving him headaches at the CFL. However, he did like McCarthy because of its long affiliation with retired Judge Willard Estey. After much discussion around the table, a consensus seemed to emerge. McDowell suggested a resolution that McCarthy Tétrault be selected as new legal counsel for the Gardens, starting January 1, 1991. As well, the firm would be asked to forward the names of two senior partners, one to join the MLGL board as a director and the other as chairman of the board.

Although Miller Thomson was being fired because of its alleged conflicts as a result of its triple function as lawyers to the estate, the Gardens and HEBL, no one seemed too concerned that McCarthy had been legal advisers to Molson and a few of the Gardens directors. Thor Eaton seconded McDowell's motion and the discussion ended. Stavro then advised that a press release be issued immediately.

It all seemed much too tidy for this notoriously unruly bunch— and it was. You can thank Giffin for that. When the chairman and Crump retreated to his second-floor office after the meeting, they found Rocchi and McKinnon already waiting. The lawyer, whose eleven-year association with the Gardens had come to an abrupt end, was visibly upset by their betrayal. Giffin made a lame attempt at consoling her, invoking his pet name, "Rosey Posey," but Rocchi wouldn't let him off the hook. "I felt like Joan of Arc," she says, recalling that night. "I'd bailed them out so many times and I felt I'd done a good job for them."

After sitting around for a while, Crump decided to call it a day. Before leaving Giffin's office, he motioned to his fellow executor to follow him out of the room. "There was no vote taken, you know," and with that, Crump left. By the time he arrived home about forty minutes later, Giffin had been frantically trying to reach him. In the meantime, Giffin had connected with Eaton and Rogers, both of them insisting that a vote had indeed been taken. But McKinnon's notes from the meeting concurred with Crump. So the next day during the Bobby Orr Skate-a-Thon for charity, Crump and Giffin gathered in the Gardens' Directors' Lounge and rewrote the minutes of the meeting from the previous night. "He redid the minutes as having had the vote and appointing McCarthy Tétrault," Crump admits with a devilish grin. "Ultimately, I signed the minutes as secretary." It was the last time Crump and Giffin collaborated on anything.

CHAPTER FIVE

The Salvage Plan

"I believed at that time, and still do, that the estate had found its 'white knight.' The problem was that he also happened to be an executor." — DONALD CRUMP

WHILE MOST OF HIS lot spent New Year's Day 1991 in front of the television watching endless hours of football, Donald Crump had already had his fill for the year. As commissioner of the CFL, he had closed the book on another season, culminating with the Grey Cup game in November. Since then, he'd been busy trying to broker the deal that would see ownership of the CFL's Toronto Argonauts pass from the hands of Harry Ornest to Bruce McNall, Wayne Gretzky and John Candy.

This day, though, Crump was performing a little number crunching of his own. "I sat down at the computer and tried to drag together all of the financial information that I had from the estate, trying to figure out where the heck we were," he says, recalling events that began the year that was to shape the future of the company where he'd worked for the better part of twenty-five years.

Crump was sitting behind his desk in his second-floor office in the northwest corner of the Gardens. It was part of the same three-room enclave (with private shower) that had once served as Conn Smythe's command post and, until recently, had been the storage room for Yolanda's personal possessions. The room, which had been restored by Donald Giffin, was nondescript—dark with an imposing grandfather clock against the back wall separating two narrow windows. A sofa and a couple of side tables offered a rather feeble attempt at making the room feel cosy. A table littered with piles of documents—many of them in preparation for a lengthy court battle—was backed up against another wall, directly beneath a large, framed black and white photograph of opening night in November 1931.

That's the view the bespectacled Crump got every time he looked up from his desk. It's that tradition, Ballard's executor recalled later, he was fighting to preserve and protect during the events that unfolded after Ballard's death.

In late 1990, the bickering among Crump and his co-executors had become so distracting, it had become debilitating. As the discord intensified, it was becoming virtually impossible to separate church and state; estate affairs were seeping into the public company's boardroom and into the Gardens management offices.

"It was clear they had a pathological dislike for one another," Rocchi, who was still the lawyer for Ballard's estate, recalls. So much so that she had felt compelled to provide them with a lengthy letter suggesting they consider selling the estate's assets. Rocchi thought they should strike while the iron was hot; because the Mellanby report had revealed how the company could secure greater value for the broadcast rights in the future, they could likely fetch a higher price for the shares than the $27 range they were trading at the time. "You guys can't execute; you don't get along. You don't trust one another and you're not going to be able to do anything because of that," she recalls telling them.

1990, the first year in the life of administration of Harold Ballard's estate, had been one of stickhandling through one crisis after another. The most pressing issue was paying back Molson. At stake were the thirty-four common shares of HEBL owned by 810756 Ontario Ltd. (indirectly by 810757 Ontario Ltd.) that had been pledged to Molson for the $15.5-million loan and that was payable on December 31, 1990. Since interest on the loan had been accrued (rather than paid monthly) over nineteen months, the total amount owing at maturity was just under $20 million.

The loan was made to one of the two numbered shell companies Ballard had set up in the late eighties when he bought out his daughter. The shares pledged as security to Molson's loan were worth about $12 million (based on a trading price of $28 for MLGL's shares at the time). However, because it was a non-recourse loan, that meant if the loan went into default and Molson seized the shares, the company would recoup only the value of those shares. The brewery couldn't demand that the executors make good on the remaining $8 million by looking elsewhere in the estate to make up the difference.

Not that there would be anything even if Molson tried. The estate didn't have enough liquid cash; it had funds worth about $1.8 million and revenues from dividends of $184,817 a year on its preferred shares. Its overall debt comprised $15.8 million still owed to the TD Bank for Harold Jr.'s buyout; $20 million for Mary Elizabeth's shares; about $3-4 million in unpaid federal taxes, plus probate fees and outstanding lawsuits.

For the executors, the predominant issue was control. If Molson seized its shares—one-third ownership in HEBL—Ballard's estate would own only a one-third interest in the holding company that controlled Maple Leaf Gardens. Bill Ballard still owned his birthright thirty-four common shares. Add the 20 percent MLGL block Molson already owned to the HEBL stock it would get by default. That arithmetic was enough to make Stavro, Crump and Giffin very nervous.

Not surprisingly, the executors' main preoccupation was paying back Molson. The problem was coming up with the money. If they sought conventional financing by borrowing directly from a bank, they'd have to secure a loan, and the bank would want security. On December 13, 1990, Rocchi had written the executors advising them to be careful choosing this route because they could be personally on the hook as executors for loans to the indebted estate. Partly because Giffin and especially Stavro were in a different financial league than Crump and given that relations between them were strained, Rocchi suggested they each seek their own legal opinions to help determine what course they should pursue.

Giffin apparently suggested to Crump that he didn't have to spend the money to hire a lawyer, and that his attorney, Ronald Farano, a tax and estate planner, could take care of them both. But Crump, who was already deeply suspicious of Giffin, was wilting under the weight of the legal material accumulating in his CFL office and had simply stopped reading it. He called David Matheson, a commercial partner at McMillan Binch, for help. After reviewing Crump's files, Matheson joined the crowd that was growing so much; by the end of 1990, there were enough lawyers involved in the estate—all of them on Ballard's nickel—to put a team on the ice.

Two days later on December 15, 1990, Donald Crump and Steve Stavro had lunch at the JJ Muggs restaurant in the Eaton Centre. The eatery is one in the chain of the family-style restaurants owned by Ted Nikolaou, a man Stavro had known for years through the Greek community, and who would join the board of Maple Leaf Gardens as a director ten months later. During the luncheon, Crump said he broached the idea of Stavro lending the money to the estate. "The first time I can recall that the issue of Stavro being an investor in this thing came up and to the best of my recollection it was me that asked him, 'Well, what about you and your bank?'" Crump recalled Stavro was non-committal: "He wasn't pushing his way in to take this position. I think it was sometime after that when I started to put the numbers together."

Three days later, a very upbeat Crump called Rocchi at her Rosedale home from his car phone en route to Agincourt after a steak dinner with Stavro, Bellmore and Matheson. Crump was calling to notify Rocchi that he'd hired Matheson as his personal attorney and to expect a call from him soon. Rocchi remembered that Crump, who'd been depressed of late, was in an unusually good mood—and that made her uncomfortable.

The next day, Matheson did call. He had a lengthy list of requests for Rocchi, including sending over documents that, like Bellmore months before, she thought went beyond those required to represent his client in his personal capacity as an executor. For example, Matheson not only wanted letters and opinions she'd already given regarding Crump's fiduciary responsibilities, he also wanted a copy of the Mellanby report, Miller Thomson's opinion of that study and the briefing materials that had been prepared on a special $30-million dividend MLGL's board of directors had considered—and rejected—in the fall of 1990.

Back then, the new Gardens board had been asked to consider a proposal for a special dividend worked out by the controller Ian Clarke and Peat Marwick's Bill McKinnon. The thinking was that

MLGL would borrow $10 million from the bank to add to the company's $20 million in retained earnings. At the same time, the company's lawyers at Miller Thomson had been urging the Gardens directors to force Molson to remit millions' worth in retroactive payments they argued the company was owed as a result of its broadcast contract—and voilà, instant cash.

The plan would be to declare the dividend before Molson exercised its option and snared the 20-percent stake in MLGL on November 1, 1990. For the estate, the $8.15 a share dividend translated into a $12.5-million windfall. Even Bill Ballard would do nicely, pocketing about $6.25 million.

The hoped-for bottom line would be that Ballard's debt-ridden estate would suddenly be flush with enough cash to pay off the Molson loan. The proposal kit, which was supported by the three executors, was delivered to the board in September 1990.

And it set tongues wagging, especially Ted Rogers's. At a meeting in his office with Crump, Rocchi and McKinnon, an incensed Rogers accused the Gardens lawyer and Ballard's executors of trying to bail out the estate using the public company's assets. Having articulated his point using mostly profanities, Rogers dismissed them and ordered them to leave his office like errant school children.

Surprisingly, Crump agreed with Rogers even though they didn't get along, and not because of any common understanding of business ethics. "A good portion of that dividend would have been taxed, so it wasn't a great big bonanza for the estate," recalls the executor. "We were in a tight spot because we had a fiduciary duty to both the shareholders of this [public] corporation and a fiduciary duty to the estate. And it was difficult on balance to know which was to be the greater priority. I had to agree with him, it wasn't proper for us to pay the dividend."

But his agreement didn't mean he still wasn't sceptical of the cable czar's moves. In Crump's mind, Rogers's adamant opposition to the dividend was another illustration of how he was doing Molson's bidding. By obstructing the dividend, Crump figured, the estate would be left scrambling for funds and Molson could keep holding a gun to the executors' heads.

The day after Crump had called Rocchi on his cell phone, she sent the documents and a cover letter to Matheson's downtown

Toronto office. Over the next two weeks, there were more letters and calls from Matheson and Bellmore asking for more information about the obligations of executors in the event of a takeover bid; what happens when estate assets are sold; and are executors entitled to finders' fees? That line of questioning led Rocchi to mistakenly conclude that the executors were still trying to find a way to broker a deal and earn a fat commission for bringing a successful buyer to the table. What she didn't know was that in the final days of 1990, the lawyers for two of Ballard's executors had begun laying the groundwork for a proposal that would effectively transfer control of the estate's assets to one of their clients.

Ballard's trustees were all motivated by a desire for the same thing: a piece of Maple Leaf Gardens. The consensus among Gardens watchers was that it would be Giffin and Stavro who would slug it out to win control over Ballard's 60.3-percent block of shares, or as Bill Ballard said at the time, "The two of them are fighting to grab a hold of the steering wheel while Crump hid in the trunk." It was said that Molson had Giffin (and, some argued, even a few board members) doing its bidding, and Stavro, despite his protests to the contrary, had cosied up to Bill Ballard and his gang long before Harold died. The only one left out was Crump. "The will provided that an executor could buy it, but they both knew that I wasn't interested," he recalled. Ultimately, the man Ballard had half-heartedly ordered his minions to fire too many times to count would endure long enough to help determine who would succeed him.

The groundwork was set during a meeting on December 29, 1990, in the Directors' Lounge at the Gardens on a Saturday afternoon as four lawyers and three trustees gathered for an executors' meeting. First, they agreed to accept Molson's latest deadline extension to January 31, 1991. Up next was the issue of conflict of interest, namely Giffin's.

The controversial two-page option had first surfaced in Justice Haley's chambers at the time the three executors were committee members in the early months of 1990. Stavro then had been shocked when Giffin unveiled the option, demanding to know why it hadn't been reported before that meeting in the judge's chamber in February 1990. The agreement, dated April 13, 1989, stated "that if Ballard receives an offer from a third party to purchase the shares

[Mary Elizabeth's thirty-four common in HEBL], Ballard may sell to the third party only if he notifies DPG [Giffin] who has thirty days to match the offer." Not only that, the right of first refusal provided that Giffin could purchase the holding company shares (which represented one-third control) at a deeply discounted price. According to the formula, if Ballard decided to sell the shares or get someone else to take over the $15.5-million loan from Molson, he would have to entertain an offer from Giffin first that wouldn't amount to more than half of what was left owing on the Molson loan. The agreement also purported to give Giffin a right of first refusal on all the shares in the event of "death, bankruptcy or permanent disability of HEB."

That Giffin had secured such a benefit without paying any financial compensation especially galled Stavro. "Steve was concerned that this option that had been obtained without any compensation should be challenged," Bellmore later explained. When they sat down to discuss it, Giffin clutched his precious option while Bellmore and Stavro castigated the seventy-six-year-old, and according to some in attendance, they impugned Giffin's integrity by questioning his business ethics because Giffin wanted to keep his option even though it placed him in a conflict of interest. Not only that, Stavro disputed the veracity of the crude-looking document. "To me it didn't look right," Stavro said later. "When I saw the way it was presented, typed, that's when it hit me. I gave him a shot here, I said, 'You know, I don't agree with this,' and I said, 'I don't care, we'll go to court over it. We'll go to the Supreme Court. I don't care if it costs me my life savings.'"

For her part, Rocchi wasn't concerned about whether Giffin had paid for the option because that issue had no bearing on his ability to carry out his fiduciary responsibilities as an executor. What did concern Rocchi was the potential conflict of interest the option posed for Giffin. She reasoned with him (with the support of the other lawyers in the room), explaining that if he insisted on keeping the option, he'd be forced to resign as an executor. He could hardly be involved in discussions to decide on whether to redeem a loan that would have given him an opportunity before all others to buy the shares for himself. As an executor, Giffin was required to do his best to secure a loan to keep the shares in the estate, even though personally he might be tempted to want the opposite.

"That was a decision that had to be made and if the estate decided to redeem the shares, they were redeeming them to benefit Giffin. That would [create] a conflict and as a legal position, she was absolutely right," Bellmore later explained in an uncharacteristic display of support for Rocchi.

At the meeting they all knew the option represented a significant advantage for anyone who wanted to ultimately control Maple Leaf Gardens; whether it was paid for was a moot point. Stavro later admitted he had a hard time believing that Giffin had actually secured an option from Harold—while *he* had not been offered such a boon. "I had a feeling with Harold because I was close with Harold—that close, do you understand? I knew back then that he wanted me to be part of it if I wanted to be. And I just couldn't, maybe, but the way it looked, it didn't look kosher to me." Buying or controlling the shares before anyone else was uppermost in Stavro's mind.

Midway though the meeting, Giffin and his two lawyers Farano and Stanley Freedman (a corporate lawyer in Farano's firm) left the Directors' Lounge and went to sit in the empty arena. Giffin implored his lawyers for help but Farano was worried about calling Stavro's bluff to fight the option because he argued the document was poorly drafted in the first place and he figured it would have been a problem to successfully defend before a judge. Finally, Giffin agreed to relinquish the option, but only because he believed that in doing so, it would bring peace within the estate. At that point, Freedman expressed his concern about the acrimony developing among the executors. "I didn't think that giving in on this issue would achieve the peace Don [Giffin] hoped he was going to get. I expected there'd be more battles down the road," he later recalled telling his client.

When they returned to the group, Stavro was pounding his fist on the table in the Directors' Lounge threatening to challenge his co-executor's conflict of interest all the way to the Supreme Court of Canada. Giffin turned to Crump beseechingly for support in the wake of opposition coming from all corners. "I never thought about the option agreement at that time. I thought, 'Who the hell would want thirty-four shares in a corporation that's got fourteen miles of bad road ahead of it?'" Crump said later. "I never gave it a second thought at the time."

Crump knew that relations between his co-executors were strained; but he played his hand openly for the first time during the rambunctious meeting by joining the chorus of opposition against Giffin. For some reason, Giffin still seemed to trust Crump, asking his co-executor to follow him into an adjacent room (the referees' change room) to talk in private. According to Crump, Giffin told him that despite his reluctance, he'd agree to relinquish his controversial option, saying, "I'm counting on you." Back then, Giffin believed that he and Crump were allies and that the two of them represented the majority vote that Ballard's will said was required to make decisions within the estate.

When the two men returned to the lounge where the others were waiting, Giffin announced he'd do the honourable thing. Everyone seemed relieved. Later, Giffin's wife Patricia would curse those who forced her husband to relinquish something she viewed as his entitlement, a reward for years of loyal service to Ballard. Despite the fact that he had screamed and threatened legal action against Giffin, Stavro later said that he didn't force his co-executor to give up his option: "That was his choice." But Freedman's prescience was right. Giving up the option bought no peace.

By the end of 1990, Crump figured the estate was on a collision course. "There was an agenda I just can't put my finger on," he remembered thinking at the time. "I don't know who it is, but I know that I'm not party to it.... And I'm being wooed by somebody to do something that I don't know." As he sat at his computer on the first day of 1991, Crump figured Ballard's estate would need a saviour to sort out all the colliding interests.

The corporate apparition in early 1991 certainly wasn't the kind of benevolent force that would bring peace and goodwill within Ballard's estate. During the first week in January, Rocchi and Crump had dinner at Giffin's home in Thornhill. Unlike Stavro, Giffin was never coy about his motives. That night, he laid them bare on the table: he openly declared that he wanted the Gardens for his sons. Now, it was Crump's turn to confess. "What do you want out of this?" Crump recalled his co-executor asked. "I don't want anything," came the reply. "I'm not a player." As far as Crump was concerned, Giffin was on the same footing with Stavro now that he had given up his disputed option.

Even so, Crump knew from his lunch at JJ Muggs in mid-December that Stavro was seriously thinking about replacing Molson as creditor and, in doing so, obtaining for himself important rights to buy all of the estate's assets. On January 9, Stavro had lunch with Matthew Barrett, chairman of the Bank of Montreal, his personal and business banker for forty years. "I said, 'We're trying to raise $20 million,'" Stavro recalled of that meeting. "They didn't say no but they said, 'Okay, Steve, we'll take a look at it and everything else [which included a pledge of HEBL's Maple Leaf Gardens shares and a guarantee from Knob Hill Farms].'" A few days later, Stavro got the green light from the bank. Bellmore later recalled that "we said Steve would be prepared to loan the money if they [the estate] couldn't get it anywhere else."

While Stavro was lining up financing from the Bank of Montreal, Crump's personal lawyer David Matheson was taking an active role in creating and writing Stavro's so-called bail-out proposal, which, if nothing else, suggested that Crump was involved too. However, neither Crump nor Stavro, nor their lawyers for that matter, told Giffin at the time.

In the meantime, the small cadre of the BaGa insiders at Molson weren't exactly sitting on the sidelines. Quite the contrary. In fact, the strategy being hatched at corporate head office on the thirty-sixth-floor executive offices of Scotia Plaza was a study in contradictions.

One minute, the company seemed intent on exercising its legal rights by unequivocally making demands for its money at the end of January. The next, Norman Seagram would be freely handing out deadline extensions. "We didn't want to suggest or imply that we were waiving any of our rights under the original loan agreement because we are a public company," Seagram explained. "We wanted to maintain the strength and security of our position and to make sure they understood this. We were mindful of what the public might think and how the league might view it." Molson was desperate to protect its marketing and television contracts with the public company, Maple Leaf Gardens. As a result, Molson had to flush out what was really unfolding inside the estate, even if it meant prejudicing its claim to the thirty-four shares in HEBL that the company had within its grasp.

The problem was that they couldn't get a handle on Stavro. Giffin was an ally; Crump, as one Molson official observed, "seemed to move from one side to the other with enormous dexterity. He was always playing someone else's alter ego; first it was Harold, then Don [Giffin] and now Steve." However, Stavro remained an enigma, a loner. "We never saw Steve as being a player on the other side of the table. He's a pretty private guy and he doesn't leave a trail. He's not the world's greatest personality or conversationalist.... You try to figure out who the other guy is, how he thinks, what he's thinking about, what his motives are. We just came up with blanks."

Seagram remembers a two-hour lunch with Stavro at one of his favourite Greek restaurants in Toronto's east end about a month after Ballard died. "I didn't see that Steve had a role at that time, any more than attempting to fulfil the terms of Mr. Ballard's will."

Another former Molson executive, who lived through most of the BaGa saga, recalls his first encounter with Stavro. "I remember this meeting because when I walked in there [Stavro's home]—and I'm a very, very light drinker—there were not thimbles but glasses of scotch poured and handed to you. We sat and talked for an hour in front of a warm fire and he [Stavro] says he'd like a snack. They bring in whole chickens! We sit for another while and at the end, Steve says it's been a good meeting and let's meet again." What did they talk about? "Anything and everything. It was almost as if we were feeling each other out."

Soon, though, Molson began to understand that Stavro had plans of his own.

A meeting between Molson and Ballard's executors was scheduled for the second week of January 1991 just days after his private meeting with Barrett from the Bank of Montreal. The agenda: to discuss proposals for another possible loan extension. Remarkably, Crump, Stavro and Giffin attended with no lawyers—least of all Rocchi—at the behest of Stavro. "It wasn't like people were coming to us begging for extensions," said a senior official at the brewery. "There was certainly no sense from them that there was real urgency about the loan. That may be the way they portrayed and positioned it at Maple Leaf Gardens and it [later] developed into a leverage point for one of the executors." When they met, Maple Leaf Gardens had given notice to Molson about its broadcast contract. On January 11, Giffin sent Molson a letter in his capacity as president of the Gardens outlining why MLGL planned to review its 1980 broadcast deal with an eye to adjusting and recouping the millions of dollars Mellanby had suggested the company was owed as a result of underpayments during the past few years.

What Seagram and Giffin didn't know at the time was that as the three trustees were sitting down to negotiate with Molson to protect a critical estate asset, Stavro had already arranged his own financing proposal. As well, by the time the group met with Seagram in early January, they had another card to play: the Toronto Dominion Bank had agreed to advance the estate the full $20 million on the condition that the executors agreed to pledge all of the estate's assets, namely the controlling block of MLGL shares, as collateral. There were no other demands, such as an option on the security. However, at the time Stavro was telling everyone—and still maintains today—that the bank wouldn't advance any more funds.

The executors, who had met with Seagram hoping to secure a lengthy extension or even a discount of the loan, left his office empty handed.

Giffin then went off on his annual two-week vacation in the Bahamas. As far as he was concerned when he left, the Toronto Dominion Bank had at the very least offered the money to pay off Molson and the estate was still facing a deadline of January 31. However, on January 14, while he was away, Stavro and Crump met again—without Giffin's knowledge—with TD Bank officials. This time they asked the bank if it would extend enough money only to cover the interest on the $20-million loan for three months. The bank said yes, but it still wanted a pledge of all the estate's assets as security for the loan. Again, the executors (Crump and Stavro) refused to agree to that condition.

The next day, January 15, Crump and Stavro paid another visit to Seagram—again without Giffin's knowledge. The Molson senior executive verbally agreed to consider extending his company's loan for sixty days. Crump later admitted that he and Stavro didn't pursue the Molson offer because in order to do that, they would have had to borrow money from the bank and they didn't want to give up the security TD was requesting. Giffin was not given the chance to voice an opinion.

As a result, Molson remained the estate's bogey man.

At 3 P.M. on January 28, 1991, Stavro made his bold advance. A copy of his proposal to pay out the $20-million Molson debt—known as the term sheet—was faxed to Rosanne Rocchi by Crump's lawyer David Matheson. Rocchi, who, like Giffin, had no idea about the flurry of meetings between Stavro, Crump, Molson and the Toronto Dominion Bank, was thunderstruck. As the last of the four pages snaked through the fax machine, Rocchi thought that Stavro had finally stepped forward to take a run at the company, and he was going to start with an offer to play white knight. More importantly, because Molson's drop-dead date was just three days away, the estate would be forced to give the proposal serious consideration because if Molson was not paid back, the loan would go into default and the brewery would seize one-third of the holding company (HEBL) that controlled Maple Leaf Gardens. Not helping matters was Stavro's tough bargaining stance: his offer was only good until January 31—the same as Molson's.

According to the first draft of the term sheet (there would eventually be four), Stavro's company, Knob Hill Farms, would lend $19,888,198.58 to 810757 Ontario Ltd. to repay Molson. The loan was standard fare: a term of two years with an interest rate of prime plus 5/8ths of a percent, which was well below market rate and wasn't payable until the principal came due on February 27, 1993. In effect, Knob Hill Farms would replace Molson as creditor and Stavro's loan would be secured by the $12-million worth of common shares in HEBL—the same security that the executors had refused to assign to the TD Bank weeks earlier.

As part of its loan agreement with Knob Hill Farms, the estate would agree to a number of standstill agreements prohibiting it from borrowing money or pledging estate shares without prior consent from Stavro, even if the $20-million loan was in good standing. Those covenants are usually what a bank or conventional lender would seek as a way of making sure their money is protected.

However, in exchange for making the loan, Knob Hill Farms would receive an unusually generous—if not, controversial—sweetener. Stavro's company would snare an option in priority to anyone else to purchase, by private sale, the 60.3-percent controlling block of MLGL shares owned by the estate through HEBL and the two numbered companies "at fair market value as determined by two independent appraisals."* The option would be triggered in the event that the estate decided to sell 5 percent or more of HEBL, or was prepared to accept an offer to purchase 5 percent or more of the holding company's shares. And more importantly, "The Estate shall cause such right to purchase to be triggered in any event before January 1, 1996."

In other words, this would not just simply give Stavro the right to match any offer in anticipation that other buyers came to the table by the January 1, 1996, deadline. That sunset clause would go one step further. Ballard's estate would not only grant him the right of first refusal, but would actually bind itself to an irrevocable option that would, in effect, allow Stavro to force the estate into a sale by the end of 1995 based on two independent appraisals.

In return, Stavro would abstain from voting on his own proposal. As well, all three executors would agree to remove themselves from managerial positions at Maple Leaf Gardens, to avoid being in a position to influence the value of the asset that Stavro was seeking to eventually purchase. The only one of the three affected by this provision at the time was Giffin, who was still occupying the president's chair.

Still, Knob Hill Farms would have the right to appoint two directors to the Gardens board and anoint the company's chief executive officer. That wasn't all. Stavro, according to the term sheet, could veto any material decisions made at the corporate level, such as declaring dividends or selling assets such as the hockey team or arena.

---

* Ballard's will said "supported by," and that distinction would become important later.

When all was said and done, Stavro would receive a controlling interest in MLGL for putting up money that would have been available to the estate through conventional financing. In fact, now that Giffin had relinquished his option, the shares had reverted back to the estate unencumbered once Molson was paid off. As a result, the estate could have maintained control of HEBL, and thus the Gardens. However, if the estate accepted Stavro's offer all of the estate's shares would be encumbered and control would be handed over to one of its executors personally. The offer would give Stavro the right to control the shares in HEBL and the right to purchase them. The effect of that would be like giving him a key to the vault.

"The option was there because if you're going to work as hard as he is to build this thing, he [Stavro] should at least have the right to buy it," is how Bellmore explained the debatable benefit his client had requested.

Having received the surprise term sheet, the estate lawyer, Rocchi, promptly called a meeting with her partners, John Chapman and John Sproat, who specialized in commercial law. For the next hour, the three colleagues read through Stavro's offer, arguing its merits, shortfalls and obvious potential conflicts. They called in senior partner John Turner for an objective opinion. The former prime minister is also a seasoned attorney who is considered to take a less rigid approach when offering advice than, say, someone like Rocchi. After perusing the document, Turner tossed it on the conference room table and said, "It stinks."

Rocchi and company had their work cut out for them. With only seventy-two hours to get an opinion out to the executors, they began dividing up the sections among them.

Giffin was the last to learn about the term sheet. He found out hours after Rocchi, while watching the hockey game in his usual seat at the Gardens between the then Minnesota North Stars and the Leafs. Crump stopped by to casually mention that Stavro was thinking about lending money to the estate in return for an option to purchase for himself all of the MLGL common shares in HEBL. Stunned, Giffin went looking for Art Scace, one of the partners at MLGL's new law firm, McCarthy Tétrault, who was in the arena.

It was not lost on Giffin that by the time he learned of the plan, he'd already signed a release giving up his own option on January

12 (and received nothing in return) at the insistent urgings of Crump, Stavro and the bevy of lawyers. Wasn't the irony rich, Giffin later told associates. Stavro wanted to purchase a similar—even better—right by paying off Molson's debt even though the executors had previously turned down Toronto Dominion Bank not once, but twice. Like Rocchi, Giffin still believed they had only three days to come up with the money to pay back Molson. Giffin still did not know that Seagram had verbally offered Crump and Stavro a sixty-day extension while he was away on vacation and that TD offered the money to cover the extension. (When all of this information surfaced weeks later, Giffin declared that caving in to pressure and giving up his option was the biggest mistake he'd ever made.)

Stavro's white knight motives were later described by his lawyer Bellmore. "Steve Stavro has said that if it wasn't for the will and the wishes of his friend Harold Ballard, he would never have lent the money to save the estate. To me, this was about a will and a loan about to go into default. It was a squeeze play with a lawsuit from Bill Ballard on the one hand and Molson on the other side demanding its money. It would have been irresponsible for the executors to play with fire. You can't play chicken in a situation like that."

But others argued that there was no crisis, that the estate was not about to lose control of Maple Leaf Gardens because it didn't have full ownership of the holding company that controlled the Gardens to begin with. Bill Ballard owned one-third of HEBL, Molson had a string on one-third and the estate held the other third. And that ownership structure was vulnerable to change because of Bill Ballard's outstanding lawsuit that asked the court to overturn the deal that had enabled his father to buy out Junior. Bill also wanted the right to buy his brother's thirty-four common shares in the holding company (giving him two-thirds) but the judge still hadn't made a decision. Bellmore used those arguments to explain why no one but his client stepped forward to offer money: they couldn't get clear title for the shares.

Nonetheless, the executors were legitimately concerned about losing a valuable asset because that would undermine the estate's ability to decide its own fate. That's what all the jockeying was about: all three executors spent more time determining "who" bought than they spent figuring out for "how much."

"Harold Ballard made it very clear that he didn't want to leave his estate to his kids," continued Bellmore in Stavro's defense. "All of a sudden [Bill's] become a voracious individual with a plot from the cradle. You're an executor of the man's estate, what do you do? The guy [Bill] was suing the ass off his father's estate, trying to win through the court the control he couldn't get through his relationship with his father. The estate spent hundreds of thousands of dollars to do what the will wanted."

As for Crump, who had to cast a vote as executor, he saw Stavro's offer as a business transaction. "The option agreement was a very modest price to pay for obtaining a $20-million loan on very favourable terms," Crump later declared in a sworn affidavit. This, even though he admitted that the executors had earlier refused to pledge the shares to the bank, with no option or right of first refusal attached. As he headed into negotiations with Stavro on behalf of the estate through his lawyer Matheson (who also drafted Stavro's option), he never attempted to bargain for a deal that didn't include an option. It did not seem to have crossed his mind that the fact that they were negotiating at all raised questions about whether it was a true salvage plan as outlined in Canada's trust laws.

"At the time, I didn't care where the money came from. I had no arrangements, and still have no arrangements with Stavro," he offered. "Remember, this is all being done at a time when Billy was in court with us. So anybody who put money up on these circumstances really had to have their head examined." Or have a good lawyer.

Rocchi would come to a very different conclusion.

Within thirty-six hours of receiving Stavro's offer from Crump's lawyer, she delivered a thirteen-page opinion to Ballard's executors. Basically, Rocchi suggested Stavro's proposal was just too sweet, referring to his option instead as a right of first "opportunity." Among other things, she outlined that even though Ballard's will said that the other two executors didn't need the court's blessing to accept the third executor's proposal, they were still bound to behave in good faith on behalf of the beneficiaries and not for their own personal advantage.

Moreover, trust law in Canada prohibits trustees from profiting as a result of their dealings with trust property. In other words, someone in Stavro's position can't use or deal for his own personal advantage the trust property that he has been entrusted to protect. A trustee's first duty is to find a buyer for the assets, or in this case, Crump, Giffin and Stavro were obligated to find someone to step in and take responsibility for the Molson loan. If that avenue is not available and an executor steps up, trust law in this country states that "if the trustee seeks prior court approval to the purchase, he has to demonstrate that the sale is most necessary, that no other purchaser has been forthcoming or seems likely to come forward in a reasonable time and that his own offer in the circumstances is a favourable one."

"If the executors proceed with the proposed transaction, they would be in breach of trust," Rocchi warned. To avoid this dire situation, she cautioned, the executors must make an application to the court for approval of the transaction.

Rocchi now says she should have seen it coming all along. For weeks, the executors were talking about a so-called white knight among them even before they'd exhausted all other outside avenues. Rocchi was concerned that the executors weren't chasing down potential suitors because they were spending their energy trying to cut a deal with Stavro. On January 24, she had written the three another lengthy letter listing a number of interested parties who had called her directly, enquiring about assisting the estate with its cash problems.

For example, Tim Horton's chairman Ron Joyce had made discreet enquiries; Israel (Izzy) Asper, chairman of Global Communications Ltd., made a bolder overture by writing a letter to Donald Giffin and then following that up with a call to Rocchi. Even Molson maintained an active list of potential partners—including Asper's Global and Tim Horton's—to assist in either stepping in to replace Molson and take custody of the Mary Elizabeth shares or even possibly take over the Gardens. According to Rocchi's letter, Crump had told her that a week earlier, Seagram had called asking him to breakfast. Because their schedules didn't coincide Seagram had allegedly met Crump at Pearson airport on the evening of January 21 before the CFL commissioner boarded a 7 P.M. flight to

Edmonton. During their brief discussion, Rocchi reported that Seagram offered Crump $40 a share for all the estate's MLGL stock. Crump promptly called Rocchi at home after midnight when he arrived in the Alberta capital. Rocchi's first reaction was that Molson's strategy was to divide the three executors and create distrust among them. After all, she thought, Stavro was in town that day and he wasn't invited to breakfast or the airport lounge for coffee.

But Crump now flatly denies all of it. He says the estate did respond to the advances: he personally called Tim Horton's in-house lawyer, and left a message. He called Asper and was told the communications mogul was out of the country. Later, Asper, whose company had the rights to the Leafs' local broadcasts on his Global Television network, said that he'd simply written "an innocent letter" and that reports of his interest were greatly exaggerated. Later, the doughnut company's Ron Joyce claimed he wasn't interested in wading into the legal quagmire.

As for Seagram's offer, Crump says that's bunk. And in a rare display of agreement, even Seagram says Rocchi's version is much exaggerated. It's not that he didn't make the overture, it's just that he wouldn't make a unilateral offer to buy the company.

In the end, Crump dismissed the so-called suitors as those who merely wanted to take the company on the cheap—and he wanted no part of handing anyone the venerable Gardens on a platter.

The lawyers at Miller Thomson believed that if the executors were prepared to contemplate the kind of deal Stavro was offering, they should be shopping that publicly. There'd be a bevy of potential suitors lining up to open their vaults. And why not? By making a fairly standard loan, they could snare a right of first refusal on the controlling block of one of the most coveted sports franchises anywhere. Given that scenario, the lawyers at Miller Thomson believed the estate should be avoiding a conflict of interest with Stavro and negotiating directly with others.

But all of those issues seemed academic now that the executors had to make a decision about Stavro's offer. Around 8 P.M. on the night of Wednesday, January 30, 1991—the day before the expiry of Stavro's offer—the executors and their lawyers paced in anticipation, while Rocchi's opinion came through one of the fax machines at McMillan Binch's offices (which had become the official gathering place for Ballard's executors and their attorneys). In the midst of all this, Giffin had been on the phone to Norm Seagram. It was the first time Molson learned of Stavro's offer to play banker. "Up until then, we were motivated by what would happen if the bank took over, which was all right," said a Molson official. "However, if Steve Stavro stepped in, that would not be so fine."

Giffin returned to the group, announcing that Molson had extended its deadline for another two weeks to February 14. Putting his executor's cap back on, Stavro agreed to accept the extension at midnight. Then he slipped back into his banker's stripes and agreed to extend the deadline for his own financing proposal until February 14.

The pressure was off—at least for now.

Shortly before 9 o'clock that same evening, Don Giffin and his lawyer, Ron Farano, left the offices of McMillan Binch and drove a few blocks north to check in on Rocchi and Chapman. The two lawyers, hyper from their marathon day, were still at their offices. For the next half-hour, Giffin and Farano described the tense scene they had left behind on the thirty-eighth floor of the Royal Bank Plaza.

As they listened to the litany of complaints, Rocchi and Chapman exchanged knowing glances. The estate's embattled attorneys knew they'd come to the end of the line. Weeks of misinformation and new revelations of secret meetings and negotiations between the executors and their camps had all but completely eroded the trust that binds lawyer and client.

At first they thought the "boys" were trying to keep Rocchi out of the loop, preferring to deal directly with Chapman and John Sproat. They had already begun talking about what they could do to help break the logjam that was clearly developing among the executors.

So now, Giffin's wailing about how his co-executors had conspired to snatch control of the Gardens for themselves seemed the height of hypocrisy. "Rosey Posey, why can't you do something?" Giffin whined. Rocchi could barely contain her frustration, explaining for the umpteenth time that her firm couldn't act on its own. If he wanted her to take legal action on behalf of the estate, he was the only one who could give her instructions because Crump and Stavro weren't complaining. And he was the only one with any standing to challenge his co-executors and argue his allegation that they preferred to self-deal rather than consider other proposals.

Still, Ballard's long-time crony backed away from the idea of a confrontation. Remarkably, when everyone else could see the writing on the wall, Giffin's lethal combination of vanity and tenacity wouldn't allow him to see that his future at 60 Carlton Street was dimming. That was because Giffin always hedged his bets; he was keeping an open mind.

The next day, on January 31, Rocchi's partner, John Chapman, met with Matheson. They discussed the merits of calling Molson's bluff—defaulting on the loan and allowing the brewery to realize on its security. It was a tactic Rocchi and her partners had been suggesting to the executors for the past few weeks.

The thinking was that Molson wouldn't foreclose for a number of reasons: one, the company would have to apply to the Ontario Securities Commission for an exemption because the shares represented one-third control of HEBL, and according to Ontario securities laws, by seizing them Molson would indirectly be triggering a takeover. Two, John Ziegler and his kitchen cabinet of powerful American owners were already in a snit over Molson's 20-percent stake. Molson wouldn't want to incur a black eye by staring down the league and taking on even more Gardens stock. And finally, why would Molson foreclose on a deal in which it would lose about $8 million?

Ultimately, Rocchi's message to the executors was not to get hung up on controlling all the shares.

All of this was making Crump very nervous. He had already been suspicious of Rocchi's motives, increasingly viewing her advice as contradictory. "This was an extremely stressful period for Donald Crump," Matheson later explained about his client, who was having a tough inaugural year at the CFL. "They were being inundated with piles of opinions. In the summer of 1990, the advice to the executors was to hold the asset, build it up, and then dispose of it. By 1991, the estate's lawyers had changed their minds completely."

Prior to the meeting, Crump's lawyers hired Burns Fry Ltd. (without telling Giffin) to give a fairness opinion, later to be dubbed the "comfort letter." Later in the meeting, Chapman and Matheson were joined by Robert Bellamy, vice-chairman, and Tye Burt, a director, both from Burns Fry, a large investment firm on Bay Street. During their four-hour meeting, the two brokers told Chapman they believed it was difficult to value the estate's interest in Maple Leaf Gardens and the best way to maximize their worth was by offering the assets for sale on an open market. By holding onto the thirty-four common shares in HEBL that were pledged to Molson, Burns Fry concluded, the estate could control the destiny of the eventual sale, and the control block would fetch a premium at the time of sale.

Even so, the more immediate issue was the option attached to Stavro's loan proposal. Giffin, Crump and Stavro had already agreed that it was reasonable for the estate to pay off the loan and maintain control of the shares. That was a given. The Burns Fry report should have reviewed whether the whole transaction the estate was contemplating with Stavro was fair to the estate from a commercial point of view. Astonishingly, the brokerage house did not do so.

In the end, the brokerage firm's senior people advised against Rocchi's strategy and cast their vote in favour of Stavro's offer, even though it meant all of the estate's shares would be encumbered by a right of first refusal.

Bellmore reiterated to anyone who would listen that Stavro was offering to wipe out a major debt for the estate and in return, asking for future consideration on the shares as compensation. At the time, Bellmore publicly stated that his client wasn't going to buy the shares, so the brokerage firm's line of thinking certainly helped justify its decision.

"It didn't seem unreasonable to me that somebody who was going to put their money up to bail the estate out, that they had some kind of a right to buy them at the end," Crump says. "If what I do is helpful to you, then give me the right to buy them at fair market value. I didn't have a problem with that concept really." He adds: "I believed at that time, and still do, that the estate had found its 'white knight.' The problem was that he also happened to be an executor."

The executors had two more weeks to consider their options—and the tension among their lawyers began to intensify.

Chapman stopped by to see Rocchi when he returned from his meeting with Matheson and the Burns Fry brokers and regaled her with the details of Matheson's involvement. Again, Rocchi was stunned. After her chat with Chapman, she wrote a blistering letter to Matheson (which was later filed in court), accusing him of insinuating himself into the loan negotiations with Molson and the executors to the exclusion of the estate's lawyers. "Notwithstanding our repeated urgings, no effort has been made to our knowledge to discuss a similar proposal or more appropriately structured proposal with an arms'-length lender," she wrote in a two-page missive. By now, Molson had pushed its deadline to the middle of February and Rocchi was still trying to corral the executors into pursuing a number of other avenues that might still be available. By not informing her of their meetings, she wrote, Matheson had relegated her firm to commenting on events after the fact. "Much of the substantial effort undertaken by lawyers has simply been wasted given that one set of lawyers (your firm) has an inadequate historical background and another set (our firm) does not know what is currently occurring."

Four days later, on February 4, she backed that up with a telephone call to her counterpart. Matheson outlined his client's position. Crump thought it was not a good idea to default on the loan. As well, Matheson said his client didn't want the shares to "fall into the wrong hands."

It was during this discussion that Miller Thomson first learned that TD Bank was willing to lend enough money to cover the interest for three months and that Molson had agreed to consider extending the deadline to accommodate that request. Stunned, Rocchi put her thoughts to paper in another internal memorandum, which said, "Since we were not informed of either of these discussions, this led the executors not to pursue a course of action which should have been pursued."

She also suggested that the decision by the executors "not to 'buy' three months' grace by agreeing to pay interest may very well have been a serious error in judgement on their part." If they'd agreed to those terms, Rocchi wrote, the estate would have bought some breathing space to make an informed, rational decision. More importantly, it would have cost very little because the bank would need only about $400,000 worth of assets pledged as security. Putting up half a million dollars for a little peace of mind seemed more than commercially reasonable.

The next day, Matheson and Carmen Theriault, a trust lawyer at McMillan Binch who had previously worked in the Public Trustee's office, visited Miller Thomson's boardroom. Rocchi, Sproat and Robert Fuller, a senior partner of the firm, met with their McMillan Binch counterparts. Matheson said that he disagreed with a number of the legal points in the Miller Thomson opinion although he refused to put them on paper because he didn't wish to "have much time wasted on memoranda flying back and forth." Matheson claimed that the proposal he had drafted for Stavro was not cast in stone and that it could be modified. In fact, Stavro's offer was a last resort and his orders from Crump were to "keep Brian Bellmore warm" in the event that another suitor did not surface with the money to help the estate pay off the Molson debt. According to Rocchi's four-page memo filed in court, Matheson said, "They were therefore careful not to do anything which might alarm Brian Bellmore." Matheson would later explain that he and Crump were concerned that Stavro would say, "Hey look, I've had enough of this. I don't need this."

Sproat and Rocchi told Matheson they believed that Crump favoured the Stavro proposal, and that as a result, he was ignoring other alternatives. Matheson didn't respond; instead, he suggested they all meet to discuss Rocchi's opinion, hinting that changes could be made to the Stavro proposal to make it more acceptable to everyone. However, the Miller Thomson lawyers replied that short of Stavro making a straight loan with no strings attached and no option, they couldn't go along with it.

A few blocks north of the downtown legal hubbub, Giffin's lawyer Ron Farano was fuming. He was complaining to associates about the optics, more specifically, that Crump's lawyer appeared to be orchestrating Stavro's proposal rather than Bellmore. In doing so, it appeared that Crump had been negotiating with Stavro (through Matheson) on behalf of the estate without Giffin.

More galling for Farano and his client was that Stavro continued to sit in on the negotiations with Molson even after he'd declared his interest to take Molson out. Weeks earlier, Giffin had been vilified by Crump and Stavro for a smaller conflict.

When the veteran tax lawyer met with Rocchi and Matheson the afternoon of February 5 he expressed his outrage over what appeared to be a supreme act of hypocrisy at the expense of his client. But this time, the lawyers for the executors and the estate seemed to make progress towards reaching a consensus. According to a seventeen-page letter Rocchi sent to the executors on February 6, she informed the three that "all counsel agreed court approval would be required to permit the executors to accept Stavro's proposal should they honestly believe this was in the best interests of the estate." The letter went further: the estate lawyer cautioned that it was "unlikely that a court would grant such approval unless the executors could present clear and cogent evidence that Stavro's proposal was in fact the only offer available and that he was willing to pay as much as any third party, that the executors were clearly in a salvage situation."

Bellmore was on the phone to Rocchi within minutes of receiving her lengthy letter. He outlined Stavro's position, which was basically to plough ahead with his proposal because Stavro's offer was the only one to come forward, notwithstanding the broad media coverage that the estate was in dire financial straits. Now his client's deadline was only a week away. Bellmore planned to appeal directly to Hugh Paisley, Ontario's Public Guardian and Trustee, who is responsible for the administration of estates and their beneficiaries when they are charitable organizations, as they were in the case of Ballard. Bellmore wanted Paisley to bless Stavro's proposal.

Rocchi papered that conversation too. She wrote another letter to all the various parties on February 7, informing them that the Public Trustee didn't have the authority to give consent on transactions that required court approval. The folks at Miller Thomson had begun feeling like puppets. "We were not going to let that happen while it was on our watch," recalled Rocchi. As the situation festered, representatives from the firm met with Crump and Giffin individually, trying to open the lines of communication. A weekend chat between Crump and the law firm's chairman Judson Whiteside yielded little more than a placid admission from Crump that he felt confused. Sproat and Chapman fared no better with Giffin. The lawyers considered appealing directly to Hugh Paisley. They also considered asking the court to force a lengthy extension out of Molson. But they'd have to get permission from their clients—and that was as remote as the Stanley Cup.

Shortly after reviewing Stavro's proposal, the estate attorneys had even considered the drastic measure of initiating their own court action against Stavro, Crump and Giffin, requesting they be removed as executors for breaching their fiduciary responsibilities. But the law firm had other clients and its own reputation to worry about. That kind of desperate Hail Mary play could backfire. "Much of the disorder in 1990 created chaos that was inevitably harming the business of Maple Leaf Gardens, the affairs of Harold E. Ballard Ltd. and the financial status of the estate," Rocchi said in hindsight. "Because of their inability to agree, we had corporate paralysis and deadlock at every level up the chain. The troika wasn't working."

Finally, in late afternoon on February 7, Rocchi wrote her last letter, a four-paragraph letter of resignation reiterating her belief that they should seek other sources of financing because they were under a legal obligation to do so. She implored them to give notice about Stavro's offer to Bill Ballard for two reasons: first, because the rules of Justice Farley's injunction required the estate to notify Bill of any material changes, and second, because Bill was a shareholder in HEBL and was entitled to know. Her parting shot: "The course of action being pursued by you is fundamentally at odds with what we believe to be prudent, appropriate and in the best interests of the estate."

With that, Rocchi severed all ties with one of her firm's oldest and most high-profile clients by walking away from Ballard's estate, HEBL and Maple Leaf Gardens.

When Giffin later learned of Miller Thomson's resignation, he was devastated. He called Rocchi after speaking to Crump and, according to notes filed in court, he reported that his co-executor had commented that "he's got no respect for anyone who quits their job." No doubt, Crump may have forgotten that he'd committed the same act the previous year.

CHAPTER SIX

Billy Come Lately

*"Selling the Toronto Maple Leafs
would be like offering sex to teenage
boys."* — BAY STREET LAWYER

BRIAN BELLMORE GREW UP in Toronto's West End, loving
hockey and envying the "lucky" Ballard children who lived down
the street. As he studied his way through St. Michael's high school
and later the University of Toronto, the tall and imposing Bellmore
played varsity hockey. As he was being shaped into one of the
toughest courtroom tacticians in the country, he met Hugh Paisley,
who in 1991 was the Public Guardian and Trustee of Ontario. The
two were classmates and friends at Osgoode Hall Law School in the
1960s before Bellmore headed off to Harvard and the jocular Paisley
went off to practise law at a private firm before joining the Attorney
General's office in 1980. So when Bellmore called Paisley in early
February 1991 asking for an impromptu meeting to discuss an
urgent matter, the Public Trustee cleared the decks.

A meeting was scheduled at Paisley's offices at 145 Queen
Street West for the afternoon of February 7. Bellmore, David
Matheson, and one of Giffin's lawyers, Stanley Freedman, were to
explain the state of affairs in Ballard's estate, outlining the debt
problem and the offer by Stavro to play banker. According to Bellmore, Rocchi was expected to attend. The problem to be put
before the Public Trustee was that the executors seemed divided
over the proposal. As a result, each attorney was expected to debate
his or her respective position in the hope that Paisley would be able
to bring some order to the chaos. His responsibility was to protect

the charities, which were the ultimate beneficiaries of Ballard's will. The night before the scheduled meeting, Bellmore had told Rocchi during a telephone call that he was going to seek the Public Trustee's approval for the estate to go forward with his client's offer—and the option it carried. Rocchi had argued that Paisley could only give an opinion and that because of the inherent conflicts of interest and the potential effect on the beneficiaries, a court was the only jurisdiction that could ratify the transaction. However, the court's decision, she conceded, would likely be guided by whatever the Public Trustee decided.

"She was saying that Mr. Stavro couldn't do that [get an option] under the reading of the will and I disagreed," Bellmore recalled. "Lawyers disagree all the time. So we went to the Public Trustee because we felt that he should know about this and know about the proposal and what their position was and [that's why] she was asked to come to that meeting." To that end, Bellmore prepared a briefing binder containing a copy of Ballard's sixteen-page will, the Trust indenture papers and a preliminary draft of Stavro's loan offer.

When Giffin's lawyer Stan Freedman arrived, Bellmore and Crump's lawyer David Matheson were already waiting. That's when Freedman broke the news to the others: Rocchi had just resigned an hour earlier. "What a way to introduce the problem to the Public Trustee," thought Bellmore. But Rocchi later denied that she was ever given notice about the meeting, let alone invited to attend. (Bellmore sent over a copy of Rocchi's lengthy opinion the next day.)

At the meeting, Paisley was seeing Ballard's will for the first time. Although a copy was sitting in Eric Moore's files at the government agency, it hadn't come to Paisley's attention until the dispute between the executors surfaced and Bellmore called asking for the meeting. The group reviewed the will, paying particular attention to clause VII, which outlined Ballard's provisions allowing his trustees to purchase the estate's assets without court approval. Paisley was asked to comment on whether Stavro could proceed with his offer. "They wanted to know if there would be opposition from the representatives of the charities before they went before the court," Hugh Paisley later recalled.

Freedman had been under the impression that they were meeting to sort out all the confusion. Instead, when he arrived, he found them already waiting and was almost immediately thrust into battle with a Public Trustee who appeared to be moving beyond a neutral position. In fact, Paisley took the position that court approval wasn't necessary for Stavro to make his loan because Ballard's will allowed for that. Maybe so, said Freedman, but Ballard's will didn't exclude others from coming to the estate's rescue either. With that, he repeated what had become Donald Giffin's mantra: open up the process. According to Giffin's lawyer, Stavro was the only game in town because the others were refusing to allow outside suitors to come to the negotiating table. At the time, it was well known in business and sports circles that Ballard's estate owed money to Molson but no one really knew the important details of how HEBL was structured and where the loans were at the holding company level. (Matheson and Bellmore had received this information from Rocchi months earlier.)

It was common knowledge within the business community that Maple Leaf Gardens had been underperforming for years. But now Ballard was gone and the insiders knew that the Mellanby report had strongly suggested the company would reap millions more in future television revenues. In fact, they told the Public Trustee during the meeting that the company was considering taking Molson to task to collect millions in retroactive payments. As well, Paisley said Bellmore confided that the Gardens was going to renegotiate its local broadcast contract and that the value of the company's shares would be enhanced and so would the estate. Ergo, the executors could fetch a higher price for the shares and the charities would get more at the end of the day. Add in the usual emotional intangibles, and "selling the Toronto Maple Leafs would be like offering sex to teenage boys," one of the lawyers declared.

Still, Bellmore and Matheson dismissed the allegation that other financiers were being blocked from coming to the aid of the debt-ridden estate. They also said they didn't want to place too much stock in the Mellanby report because it was still speculation and opinion. They preferred to deal with the loan issue separately as it was the urgent matter that had to be resolved. At no time did Paisley consider the merits of the transaction Stavro was proposing. And he said he had no idea that Stavro would receive an option on all of the estate's shares. The meeting ended with only one decision: they would all confer again.

Five days later, on February 12 at Bellmore's request, the Public Trustee met once again with the executors and their lawyers. The group of lawyers and their clients (eleven in all) met in the offices of McMillan Binch at five-thirty in the afternoon. One of the main issues discussed at the meeting was the injunction that had been imposed on the estate the previous November from the Bill Ballard litigation, which effectively froze the estate's assets until the judge ruled.

Bellmore spoke first. He began by outlining for the record that the meeting had been called to discuss his client's offer and to hear what Paisley had to say about it. Bellmore admitted there was substantial disagreement among the lawyers, namely Rocchi versus the rest. Miller Thomson had resigned the previous week so there was no one at the meeting representing the interests of the late Harold Ballard, although the executors seemed well represented by their own hired guns. Bellmore continued, saying that if they agreed to proceed with Stavro, the executors would have to appear before Justice Farley. The reason: to release the executors from their obligation not to make any material changes to the estate's assets until the judge ruled on Bill's lawsuit.

During the meeting, Paisley told the executors that he had "concerns with regard to the orderliness of the administration of the Ballard estate and the functioning of the executors." He confirmed that trustees must act solely for the benefit of the beneficiaries and not for reasons relating to self-interest. According to minutes of that meeting, Paisley commented that "self-involvement by an executor was not necessarily improper or forbidden if full prior disclosure of all the relevant facts was made to the beneficiaries and where the provisions of the will or trust agreement permitted such transactions."

Paisley said one of the conditions for him to consent to Stavro's proposal was that the estate must immediately replace Miller Thomson with attorneys who had "nothing to do with MLGL or the personal affairs of any of the executors." He began by asking about the assets, such as Ballard's cottage in Georgian Bay, his home on

Montgomery Road, bank accounts both in Canada and offshore, cars, a boat and, of course, the HEBL shares. At the time, the executors had still not filed a passing of accounts with the Public Trustee's office for the time during which Ballard had been incapacitated. Crump provided a brief rundown of their status and that of the numerous liabilities claimed against Ballard's estate.

Again, the only consensus among the executors at the meeting was an agreement on the necessity to keep control of the thirty-four HEBL common shares pledged to Molson. After that, the meeting fell apart.

It began when Crump confirmed what many had suspected; he was in favour of Stavro's proposal because it provided benefits to the estate. Giffin was concerned about it because he had opinions from two law firms that said it wouldn't "sail." Since Stavro was offering to abstain from voting on his own proposal, the final decision was left to Crump and Giffin. Given the gap between them, Giffin suggested that it would be foolhardy to expect they could come to an agreement during that meeting.

Paisley suggested that putting it off wasn't the best option given that the Molson deadline was two days away. Had they considered other options besides Stavro?

Farano piped up, complaining the others wouldn't sit down with Molson to discuss a long-term extension. But Crump interrupted Giffin's attorney with a litany of complaints about Molson. He claimed they'd asked about an extension to March 31 and as far away as the end of July but he said Molson had only agreed to February 14. Crump said he had even asked Molson to discount the loan to $15 million and they had refused.

This was all news to Giffin and his lawyer.

Farano couldn't believe it. He'd just talked to Seagram for forty-five minutes that morning; that was when the brewery's senior executive told him he'd let the estate know by noon the following day whether Molson would consider a possible one-year extension on its loan.

Now it was Crump's turn. He mused out loud whether "Mr. Seagram was dealing in good faith with the executors since they were getting such different positions from him."

Paisley, whose role by now had been reduced to acting as the referee between the verbal volleys, enquired about how they intended to deal with the estate's debts. Crump said the estate was collecting about $443,000 each quarter (or about $1.8 million a year) from its MLGL shares and that money was financing the TD loan for Junior's shares. Crump estimated the estate would need about $8 million to meet its debt obligations and that's when he raised the spectre of the special dividend that Rogers had shot down months earlier—and that Crump now says he too resisted.

"The executors have obtained a legal opinion and an accounting opinion that such a dividend would be proper," Crump told the group. "Notwithstanding, the board of directors of MLGL would not go along with it. The next meeting of the board when such a dividend might be approved will be held in August [1991]."

Paisley reminded the executors that they "effectively controlled MLG" and were to act in the best interests of the estate's beneficiaries. Remarkably, the regulator asked them whether "they were prepared to do everything in their power to effect the major dividend for the benefit of the estate," even if it meant changing the directors on the board of MLGL. Giffin, Crump and Stavro already had numerous conflicts heaped on them as a result of Ballard's will, and now they had the Public Trustee brazenly suggesting they raid the public company's coffers to keep the estate onside. No doubt securities regulators and the minority stakeholders might have had something to say about that.

Nonetheless, Crump and Stavro not only agreed with Paisley on pursuing the special dividend, they enthusiastically supported his suggestion of sweeping out the dissident directors, most of them loyal to Giffin. Not surprisingly, their co-executor hung tough, refusing to support the idea of a purge, while lamely suggesting the independent directors might reconsider their position by the next board meeting, in August.

Next up was Paisley's perfunctory lecture to Stavro about dealing in good faith. For the record, he told the assembled that if the grocery magnate's offer was accepted, he would have to act "exclusively in the best interests of the estate and avoid even the appearance that he was not doing so." The Public Trustee then added that he had no reason at this time to expect that Stavro would do otherwise.

The upshot of the meeting was that the executors' choices

came down to either getting a long-term extension from Molson or accepting Stavro's offer. Having said that, Paisley asked what they expected to accomplish by getting another loan extension. Farano suggested the answer was pretty obvious; it would buy the estate some time to look for other financing, something they hadn't done because they'd all been focusing on Stavro's proposal.

Finally, Stavro spoke up. He declared that he was fed up. He'd gone to the bank twice already, practically begging for help, and he wasn't going back again. Then, turning to Giffin, he basically told him to "put up or shut up." He would take his offer and step aside if Giffin wanted to lend the money instead. But Giffin always preferred playing the middleman, the facilitator brokering deals rather than walking away with the prize for himself. Giffin sheepishly admitted he didn't want to put up his personal assets to save the estate. With that, Stavro repeated that his offer was good only until midnight, February 14—two days away.

By the end of the meeting, Paisley seemed to have washed his hands of the conflict. However, according to Paisley, the group was told in no uncertain terms that if the estate was considering a deal with Stavro, the executors must get court approval, especially since the trustees were divided over the proposal. Regardless of what they decided, the Public Trustee wanted to review the estate's accounts within three months.

The gathering finally decided that at the very least, the group was going to appear before Justice Farley (or "Jungle Jim" as he is known in the legal community) to ask that he exempt Stavro's offer from the conditions imposed by his injunction.

The next morning, Giffin's attorney Farano called David Roebuck. A seasoned trial lawyer, Roebuck was hired to represent Giffin's interests before Judge Farley. Immediately upon hearing details of the case during his morning meeting with Farano, the low-key but intense Roebuck was concerned that the executives would be heavily criticized later for cutting a cosy deal with one of their own. As the freshest pair of eyes to view Stavro's proposal, Roebuck asked whether the estate was dealing with a real emergency and began questioning the firmness of Molson's deadline. Later in the day, he wrote to Bellmore saying that if the transaction they were contemplating was reasonable, then it should stand up to court scrutiny. And if that were the case, then the trustees should unanimously be seeking court approval to protect themselves, and more importantly, they should be attesting to the nature of the emergency in writing in a sworn statement.

Ultimately, Roebuck wondered why, if it were a true salvage plan, Stavro was negotiating with the estate. And why would he be securing a personal benefit? Wouldn't he just step into the breach? Bellmore wrote back saying the estate was forging ahead with the transaction with his client because Molson could pull the trigger at midnight February 14 and Stavro was the only one coming forward with money. Roebuck got his first whiff of pending trouble when Bellmore casually said he was appearing before Justice Farley the next morning without the usual motion records and sworn affidavits.

Faced with that kind of fast-tracking, Roebuck became even more apprehensive; now he really wanted everything in writing. Years of experience told him that this deal would likely be challenged at some future time and he was particularly concerned that his client, Giffin, received no benefit but would have been perceived as having prostituted himself. "We weren't opposing the motion to lift the injunction," Roebuck remembered. "We just wanted to make sure that the issue of urgency was being squarely addressed." He called Bellmore that night to argue his point: if this were a true emergency and everyone had followed the letter of the law, then it would be prudent to get a clear record of events. During the telephone conversation, Roebuck said he asked Bellmore and William Sasso (another one of Crump's lawyers) whether the executors were willing to ask Molson for another extension, but both attorneys refused "for good and compelling business reasons," according to Roebuck. Bellmore later explained that Crump and Stavro wanted to stop postponing the inevitable: that is, the estate had to pay back Molson. Roebuck was only twelve hours into the case and he couldn't figure out what they were talking about. "When you refuse to ask for an extension, how can you call what you're doing a true salvage plan?" Roebuck asked. He became even more determined to get the executors to commit under oath that this was a real emergency. He asked his legal counterparts to have their clients swear an affidavit that they had refused to ask Molson for another extension. Bellmore shot down that idea in a letter.

Less than twelve hours after his late-night telephone chat with Bellmore and Sasso, Roebuck was served at 8:52 A.M. the next morning with court papers requesting him to appear in Justice Farley's chambers at Osgoode Hall in exactly thirty-eight minutes. The judge was already expecting the group after having learned a couple of days earlier that Miller Thomson had resigned. When the roll call of lawyers was completed, Bellmore and company hadn't brought the sworn documents Roebuck had requested the night before. It was February 14, the first anniversary after the court had officially declared Harold Ballard mentally and physically incompetent to run his own affairs.

For the next hour, the lawyers argued. Then, the judge ordered a reluctant Bellmore to hand over a copy of Stavro's proposal to Jim Hodgson (Bill Ballard's lawyer) and to produce an affidavit outlining why he should lift the injunction. The motion before Justice Farley was really straightforward but he wanted to make sure that his ruling was handed down for all the right reasons.

Hodgson asked specifically for an affidavit from Stavro outlining why there was such urgency to the issue, but Bellmore harrumphed that he'd be the one to decide who would give the affidavit. It had become obvious to most of the players involved that Stavro had never once signed an affidavit himself. There was no doubt that Crump would be the deponent explaining the reasons on this day and every other that followed. The group was dismissed and asked to reconvene in the judge's chambers at 2 P.M. that afternoon. And that's when the posturing took over.

At 1:17 Roebuck received Crump's affidavit, which contained the claim that the Molson loan was to be paid by midnight that day. What he didn't know was that an hour earlier, Norman Seagram had called Bellmore at his office (where Crump was sworn) to offer the estate a two-week reprieve until February 28. As they gathered for the afternoon session before Justice Farley, Stanley Freedman poked his head through the door, trying to get Roebuck's attention, but Giffin's litigator waved him away. Doug Garbig, Roebuck's law partner, went out to see why Freedman appeared so exercised. Freedman told Garbig about the latest Molson extension.

Moments later the brief proceeding ended. Garbig and Roebuck left the courthouse to head to their office on the thirty-second floor of the Simpson Tower where Don Giffin was waiting for them. As they walked, Garbig explained what Freedman had told him outside the judge's chambers. The two lawyers arrived to find that a power failure had trapped their client in their law offices on the top floor of the building. Giffin was eventually brought down to the lobby by a service elevator and the three men headed north to his office at Maple Leaf Gardens. Once there, Roebuck telephoned Bellmore at his office to ask whether he knew about Molson's latest extension. Bellmore told him he had learned of the extension after Crump's affidavit had already been sent out. More importantly, Bellmore told Roebuck he was prepared to present the letter written by Norman Seagram to Judge Farley when they reconvened later that evening. Seagram had written to "Steve, Don and Don" at around 4 P.M. confirming the new deadline. In his letter, Molson's senior executive vice-president said his company would grant "the third and final" extension, this time until the end of the month. Seagram warned that "if payment of principal and all accrued interest is not forthcoming on 28 of February, 1991, TMCL (The Molson Companies Ltd.) will take all appropriate steps to realize upon its security." Having written the heavy-handed missive, Seagram was fully aware that he might be playing right into Stavro's hands but he was willing to take the risk. "It was always a possibility that he could pull this off," Seagram said. "But it was never a probability."

Roebuck asked Bellmore and Sasso if they would allow their clients to sign a letter drafted by Giffin's lawyers accepting the new Molson extension. They refused. During that conversation, Roebuck recalled, Bellmore told him that Freedman and Farano should stop "hiding behind [Roebuck's] skirts" and continue negotiating with Stavro. As far as Bellmore was concerned, he thought the group was appearing before Justice Farley so that the estate could lift the injunction and negotiate his client's offer. "At the end of the meeting [on February 12] the Public Trustee said he would support the concept of Stavro being able to loan the money to the estate," Bellmore later said. "We all shook hands and left." With that, Bellmore said he thought they were all moving towards finalizing the terms of Stavro's agreement. But two days later in the middle of the motion before Judge Farley, "Giffin did an about face," he said. "He wasn't supporting it but he wasn't opposing it either." That was the gist of Bellmore's complaint during the phone call.

The mild-mannered Roebuck corrected Bellmore, saying that Giffin was not welching on anything because Stavro's proposal was nothing but a bare-bones outline and Giffin had agreed only to keep the lines of communication open. Roebuck resented that his client had been accused of conspiring with Molson. In fact, Giffin was the one begging for extensions to prevent the shares from being seized. It irked Giffin that the lawyers for Crump and Stavro were working in the backrooms churning out financing proposals for their own client while refusing to consider other alternatives.

"It wasn't Don Giffin's fight," Roebuck later recalled. "He was drawn into the thing in the role of protagonist because he was the one executor who wouldn't go along. But Don wasn't duking it out with Steve. His position had always been that if the executors wanted to do the transaction [with Stavro] then they should get court approval. If Stavro becomes the buyer, he should resign because he's in a clear conflict of interest. He has an option to buy the only significant asset in the estate and he wants to stick around to manage it. It wasn't an attack on Steve. It was a sensible legal position." In fact, Giffin's unfailing politeness would not allow him to attack Stavro in public. Even after outlining his position on Stavro's potential conflict in his affidavit, Giffin added, "However, by stating this I am not suggesting that Stavro would act in a manner that would be to the detriment of either MLG Ltd., or HEB Ltd." He never attacked his co-executor in court either, although these were courtesies that Stavro or his lawyers never afforded him.

At 6 P.M. that evening they gathered once again at McMillan Binch's offices to begin the hearing. Justice Farley sat at the head of the long conference room table with Bellmore and Sasso on his right, Hodgson on his left, and Roebuck at the other end of the lengthy table. Ballard's lawyer began the hearing by cross-examining Crump to find out why he'd thrown his unadulterated support behind Stavro's offer to the exclusion of others. It was a lengthy session punctuated by constant protests from Sasso and Bellmore (who objected strenuously to any enquiries that tried to assess the merits of his client's offer) and sarcastic admonishments directed at Crump's lawyer, Sasso, by Justice Farley. A Rhodes scholar who had practised commercial law before being called to the Ontario bench in 1989,

Farley didn't suffer fools gladly.

While this was unfolding in the large conference room, down the hall in another office the very thing Stavro's camp had hoped to avoid had materialized—a bidding war. Bellmore had delivered his client's term sheet to Hodgson during their afternoon session before Justice Farley. After quickly scanning the document, Bill Ballard's lawyer had proof of what had only been rumoured by "outsiders," that Stavro wanted to play the white knight. More importantly, Hodgson, who had been involved in a number of high-profile cases involving shareholders' rights, realized there was an opportunity for his own client to play the same role. Hodgson called Bill Ballard, who immediately rushed down to McMillan Binch's offices. It was a sight to behold—worthy of a Ballard—Bill Ballard conferring with his lawyer about how to put forward a bid in enemy territory, trying to figure out if the prodigal son could snare a piece of the action.

While Hodgson questioned Crump before the judge that evening, Ballard, Michael Cohl (who had been at home watching a movie before getting the call from Ballard) and a group of lawyers were hammering out Bill's proposal. The adrenaline was pumping so much, Cohl recalled, that the barbs shooting between the men transformed the hallowed halls of the law office into a locker room awash in testosterone. "Guys, you have to put your balls on the table now before you lose your chance," shouted one participant, sensing the opportunity at hand. Finally, Bill's handwritten offer to lend $20 million to his late father's estate was scribbled onto one page and delivered to the throng of lawyers. Ballard was upping the ante, tabling his own financing package in writing to the estate. His offer: a loan of $20 million for four years, with interest at 5 percent for the first two years and prime plus half a percent for the remaining years. In all, it amounted to a cost saving of about $3 million for the estate compared to Stavro's loan offer. It too contained an option on the estate shares for Bill. After all, the executors were obviously entertaining the idea of granting an option to Stavro, so Ballard figured he could get one too.

Justice Farley ordered a dinner break at 8 P.M., and copies of Bill's offer were distributed by Roebuck to pass along to the other lawyers. Bellmore and Sasso refused to look at Bill's offer, preferring to continue arguing only the motion before Justice Farley. Sasso wouldn't even physically touch the paper, saying it wasn't evidence and besides, all this would do was prolong the hearing, something he obviously didn't want to happen. Roebuck insisted, and Justice Farley finally stepped in to remind the lawyers that it would be inappropriate for them not to consider the other offer. As a result, they recessed to discuss Bill's salvo.

In one conference room Stan Freedman assessed Bill's offer for Giffin. Meanwhile Bellmore invited Roebuck and Giffin to join Stavro, Crump and his two lawyers, Sasso and Matheson, in another conference room where they had gathered to consider the new proposal. Roebuck recalled that he asked if they'd at least be prepared to request a lengthy extension from Molson, to which Stavro replied, "I'm not going to participate in an auction." Bellmore again rejected that idea, which prompted one lawyer to point out that the rigid stance could leave the executors vulnerable to a lawsuit. "Anyone who's afraid of a frivolous lawsuit shouldn't be an executor of Harold Ballard's estate," came the reply from Bellmore—pure bombast the way only he could deliver it.

Before they began to assess Bill's offer, Roebuck requested that Stavro leave the room since he had a competing offer on the table. Bellmore refused on behalf of his client. Stavro then paced around the room, walking in circles behind Ron Farano's chair. After being jostled a few times from behind, Farano stood up and offered to settle their differences with his fists. Stavro then slammed his index finger down on the table, accusing Giffin of being a traitor. By entertaining Bill's offer, he screamed at his co-executor, Giffin would be "breaking faith with Harold" because their late friend didn't want the breweries or his children to have his beloved Gardens. Stavro knew exactly which buttons to push: Giffin flushed and his eyes welled with tears. Later, Stavro said of that marathon night, "All I know is my relationship with Harold was very close and whether I bought the shares or not was secondary to me, okay? My main concern was to save this place before the breweries took it over. And make sure to guide the place right or you're not going to get the best value. First of all, you try to save it and then increase the value of the corporation. And that's what I tried to do."

David Matheson (who had been working on Stavro's proposal

while his colleague Sasso represented Crump before Justice Farley) suggested that perhaps Crump, Stavro and Giffin should sit down to thrash it out. Having just seen Stavro's display, Roebuck wasn't having any of that. Then, without any further discussion, Bellmore and Sasso declared that Bill's offer was not acceptable. So much for negotiation.

Back they went to sit at the table with Justice Farley. After all the sandwiches had been eaten and the questions mostly dodged, the judge lifted the conditions of his own injunction just enough to allow the executors to resolve the Molson loan deadline without prejudicing Ballard's claim to the HEBL shares. In short, Stavro won this round: his offer could be put to the executors. All that drama and last-minute heroics had achieved what had always been a foregone conclusion. Nothing had changed over the course of the day, except Stavro was one giant step closer to getting his hands on the estate's shares. Bellmore wanted everyone to stick around to discuss Stavro's offer but Giffin's lawyers preferred to get a fresh start in the morning. "After Farley made his decision, we were supposed to negotiate the final terms of [Stavro's] loan agreement," Bellmore recalls. "Giffin's lawyers even said, 'Let's rock 'n' roll, we're ready to negotiate.' But then they came back and said, 'Forget it, we're too tired.'"

The next day began like the rest—lawyers wrangling, exchanging phone messages, faxes and thinly veiled insults. Freedman sent a letter to Matheson outlining his comments on Stavro's proposal. He waited all day for a response, which came from Bellmore shortly before four-thirty in the afternoon via the fax machine. Bellmore claimed that unless his client's term sheet was accepted by the other executors—without any revisions—by five-thirty that day, Stavro would withdraw his offer.

Freedman could hardly believe his eyes. He fired back a missive to Bellmore, accusing him of issuing ultimatums rather than negotiating with the estate. And, Freedman wrote, "Stavro has a penchant for creating unrealistic deadlines."

And so it went. During the next two weeks right up until the end of the month, the relations among the executors and their hired guns deteriorated badly. Nothing seemed certain. Every idea appeared to have a life span of less than twenty-four hours. One day they thought Bill Ballard's proposal might be the only offer on the table, the next they thought Stavro had not really pulled out of the bidding as he had threatened but was just sitting on the sidelines, waiting for the right moment to step back into the fray. If that was the case, should Stavro as an executor participate in the negotiations with Ballard given that he had a competing bid? Roebuck wrote a letter on February 18 telling Stavro to declare himself and stop playing hide-and-seek. It went unanswered.

Meanwhile, Crump said he wouldn't even consider a loan from Bill if it wasn't part of a settlement package that would end his protracted legal battle with the estate. Giffin's lawyers were still clutching at the possibility of another extension from Molson. Bellmore shot down the idea of approaching Molson. In the meantime Giffin's lawyer Farano pushed forward to ask the court to force the executors to seek one anyway. That resulted in yet another letter, this one from Bellmore, who wrote to Roebuck saying that according to Ballard's will, Stavro didn't need court approval because a majority of the executors rule. And if Giffin challenged that, he said, he'd be accountable for the hefty legal fees. Roebuck fired back his own missive, saying thanks for the advice but your client still hasn't declared his intentions on Bill's offer or his own.

Ten days passed before Stavro finally emerged from the sidelines on February 25 with a new and improved offer. It looked remarkably like the offer that Bill Ballard had tabled the night of February 14 and that had been refused by lawyers representing himself and Crump. In fact, Crump's lawyers had been handling both offers: while Sasso was receiving Bill's proposal, his partner, Matheson, had been putting together a competing bid from Stavro. "This was not a true beauty contest," remarked one of Giffin's lawyers in disgust. "There was only ever one contestant."

Stavro offered a four-year loan with interest at 5 percent for the two years and prime plus five-eighths of a percent the following two years. This time, there was one notable change: Stavro was going to break the deadlock by refusing to negotiate any further with his co-executors. He was going to seek approval for his own offer through the court. Apart from everything else that was going on, competitive market forces at least appeared to be working in the estate's favour.

Bellmore sent Stavro's new proposal to Roebuck with an accompanying letter that read, "Mr. Giffin may wish to consider whether to vote on this proposal given his current arrangements with Maple Leaf Gardens." Roebuck was stunned that such a barely camouflaged threat that Giffin could lose his position at the Gardens would be uttered, let alone put on paper.

Nonetheless, Giffin and his lawyers figured they should keep the bargaining going, so they met with Ballard and Hodgson in the hopes of wringing out another offer in the face of Stavro's latest salvo. Crump's lawyers were invited to attend but declined to participate. The reasons became evident a few hours later, when they served Giffin's lawyer Farano with a new round of court papers, ordering him to appear before Justice Richard Trainor the next day at two o'clock. Meanwhile, Farano implored Molson to tender another extension in writing.

"The highest duty of an executor is to give effect to a testator's wishes," explains Bellmore of the chaos. "His will didn't say to give it to Bill. His father fought him every step of the way." Bill Ballard counters, saying he too wanted to see his father's wishes carried out, that is, to maximize the value of the estate for the charities.

It was now February 27, twenty-four hours before Molson had said it would pull the trigger, and guess where the executors and their battery of lawyers were? After a flurry of legal manoeuvrings, claims and counterclaims, applications and cross-applications, the motion before Justice Trainor finally got under way in a public courtroom despite Bellmore's protests that it be heard in camera.

What a scene! At the south end of the room sat a bemused Crump and a confident-looking Stavro, a pillar of the community, a philanthropist trying to get approval for a loan that would make the estate's bogey man go away. On the north side, Giffin, wearing headphones to aid his hearing (he was deaf in one ear), wanted the estate to consider a proposal from Bill Ballard, a man who'd been convicted of assaulting his late father's girlfriend, a Billy-come-lately, Bellmore claimed, who hadn't rushed to save his father's estate until Stavro's offer surfaced. Failing that, Giffin at least wanted a court order forcing the estate to buy more time from Molson. In the middle sat Bill Ballard and his business associate, Michael Cohl, who had undisguised open-mouthed admiration for the courtroom performance of Stavro's hired gun. Turning to his business partner, Cohl said of Bellmore, "Holy Christ, is he good!

Let's hire him if we ever need a gunslinger."

For two days, there were plenty of courtroom theatrics, dramatic moments that only a Ballard story could deliver. When Stan Sokol, the Public Trustee's lawyer (who'd known Bellmore since he was seventeen years old and coached his son's baseball team), threw his unabashed support behind Stavro, Bill delivered his own judgment of Sokol's performance. In a stage whisper he said loud enough for all to hear—"the agony of a C-minus student"—sending the lawyers running for cover to hide their fits of laughter. By the end of the first day, another deadline just got longer. This time Molson's reprieve was extended to March 7. But Stavro was going to play hardball, moving his deadline only until the end of business on March 1—the day Justice Trainor would hand down his decision.

That day, having seriously underestimated Stavro's resolve—and his deep pockets—Molson made an eleventh-hour offer in a letter hand-delivered to the executors. Shortly before 10 A.M., one of Molson's lawyers strutted into the courtroom and declared that Molson would extend the loan for sixty days. Roebuck practically begged the judge to let Molson's lawyer give that testimony under oath. Justice Trainor agreed.

But before the judge had finished giving his approval, the wily Bellmore was on his feet objecting. Ever the cowboy, Bellmore pulled off an audacious performance, lobbing an accusation Giffin's way and claiming that he wanted the executor to take the witness stand so that "he can bring forth evidence that Giffin was on Molson's payroll." Justice Trainor, who was the regional district judge from northern Ontario, said he wouldn't allow the hearing to turn into a "circus." He then did an about-face and refused to allow the Molson representative permission to take the stand. Later, Bellmore said the only reason Molson tried that stunt was because they finally realized the court was going to rule in his client's favour.

He was right. About an hour and a half later, Justice Trainor delivered his decision on the very narrow legal question of whether Stavro needed court approval to vote on his own proposal. Justice Trainor said Ballard's will exempted his executors from seeking court approval; however, he also said that he had great difficulty with the offers put forward by both Ballard and Stavro. "In light of my decision I do not propose to deal with the merits of the dual proposals," Trainor said. Nonetheless, he still went to the trouble of issuing a subtle warning. "My decision should not be interpreted as relieving the trustees from the responsibility to act in the best interest of the estate and, in particular, of the charitable foundations."

Just before noon, as they were leaving the courtroom, Matheson moved quickly to get Stavro's proposal approved. He summoned Giffin like a school boy to attend an executors' meeting at his office in the Royal Bank Plaza in two hours. Having come from a testy court appearance, Giffin was feeling vulnerable. He wanted to know what was on the agenda but Matheson refused to answer. So Giffin was advised by his lawyers not to attend. Instead, Stan Freedman sent a fax to Bill Sasso, asking whether the other executors intended to vote on Stavro's offer. The fax went unanswered.

At around the same time that two of the executors were meeting at McMillan Binch, a lawyer from Blake, Cassels & Graydon faxed them a revised offer from Bill Ballard to the executors. His new proposal really raised the stakes: no interest payable on the loan for the first two years; after that, it would be prime plus half a percent. The offer still contained an option on the holding company's shares—but it would save the estate about another $2 million in interest fees. Not only that, Ballard's offer would have allowed the estate to hold an auction but Bill would have the right of first refusal to match any third-party offers. And Bill even served up what Crump had asked for in writing: Bill was prepared to drop all his lawsuits against the estate. Suddenly, after the executors had spent weeks unsuccessfully trying to find the money to repay Molson, Harold's son had emerged with something tangible—and in writing. Regardless of what the executors and their entourage felt about him, Bill's last-minute heroics were real.

Giffin's lawyer Roebuck attempted to make the point by refaxing his copy of Ballard's new offer to Matheson and the others at 2:37 P.M. Still he got no response.

An hour or so later, Giffin decided he'd had enough and cast his vote via the fax machine. He sent a statement saying he didn't support the Stavro proposal and included a copy of the Miller Thomson fax reminding the executors they couldn't make any material changes to the estate until they resolved Yolanda's demand for $500,000 a year in support from Ballard's estate.

But the day's dramatics had not yet finished. At 4 P.M., after three months, Justice Farley released his long-awaited decision in Bill Ballard's case. The judge essentially ruled in favour of Ballard, giving him a greater say in the way HEBL would be run in the future. It was a major victory for Ballard because it put him on equal footing with Stavro.

In a 160-page ruling, Justice Farley ordered that a neutral board be put in charge of HEBL. Although he didn't give Ballard his younger brother's stock, Bill was given equal opportunity to bid on the shares after a proper appraisal was completed. The judge, who cited passages from Shakespeare's *King Lear*, was particularly critical of Giffin. "It appeared that he would not do anything that conflicted with anything Harold Sr. desired," Farley wrote. "There was the heel-clicking point of view of things."

In a final volley, the judge said, Crump and Giffin were to resign from HEBL's board within a week and were not to stand for re-election "in light of their past disregard for the interest of all shareholders and their apparent complete devotion to the wishes of Harold Sr.," wrote Judge Farley.

Armed with this victory, Ballard acted immediately when he marched straight into another courtroom within hours after that decision was released. Ballard was understandably worried that Stavro's proposal would affect his newly secured position. Using his new-found status, he hauled the middle-aged men in front of another judge—at the court of appeal—and asked if that court would enforce Justice Farley's order. But it was too late. The lawyers representing Stavro and Crump announced that just hours before, at 3:37 that afternoon, the two executors Crump and Stavro had voted in favour of Stavro's proposal. There was nothing any judge could do about it at that time.

In fact, Hershell Ezrin had already dropped by McMillan Binch's offices to pick up the cheque that had been hand-delivered by Howard Wood, Knob Hill Farms' in-house lawyer. There was even a little last-minute drama: the bank draft was short of the amount by thirty-six cents and that forced everyone to dip into their pockets to find loose change that was actually taped to the Bank of Montreal note. "You never saw a sadder face," sniped Bellmore about the Molson vice-president, who picked up the cheque that gave Stavro his hold on the estate shares.

Why did the estate choose Stavro's offer over the one tabled by Bill? "This loan offer from Bill was a late-blooming attempt to prevent the estate from saving itself," Bellmore says. Crump dismissed Ballard's offer. "He's always chasing the best deal, he never really advanced anything."

All of Giffin's protests and letters of defiance couldn't reverse what had happened: he had emerged as the big loser in the war. After a year that began on a sure footing, Giffin was now one step from being banished from the hockey palace he'd coveted for almost three decades. His future at the Gardens as president was tenuous at best, especially in light of the comments made by Bellmore: "It's not a sandbox for a seventy-six-year-old retiree." Crump later said of his co-executor, "He was offered the same chance to put up the money but he wouldn't take it. Steve always gave everyone the opportunity to stand in or match his offer. Now whether he'd walk away or not, history showed that he wouldn't. It was the ultimate brinkmanship." Matheson concluded that Giffin "wasn't interest[ed] in doing that [working with his co-executors] at the time," calling him "extremely naïve to think that someone like Steve wouldn't try to salvage the whole situation." Indeed. That's what it had been for Stavro's team—a salvage operation. Stavro took a risk when no one else would. Defiance against those who would stand in the way of his doing Harold's will (and his own). In return, he received what he thought was a reasonable commercial benefit, the kind of reward, one could argue, that comes to those who display "guts and loyalty," which were the two greatest traits in the eyes of the Gardens founder Conn Smythe.

Still, Giffin wasn't out of the game just yet. He had powerful allies elsewhere.

In the meantime, the three still had one last piece of unfinished business before Crump and Giffin stepped down from the holding company's board. HEBL indirectly controlled the two numbered companies where the thirty-four common shares in question were held. As directors of that company, the three executors had to pass a resolution giving Stavro the right to seize not only the thirty-four, but all of the holding company's shares should the estate default on his loan. Of course, Stavro would abstain from voting on this resolution.

The potential for another impasse had already been anticipated: Crump would be named chairman of the two Ontario numbered companies where the loan and shares were held. That gave Crump two votes in the event of a deadlock between the executors.

An invitation was extended to Giffin and Crump to join Matheson at Stavro's Palm Beach home for a meeting on March 4. Giffin declined but Crump and his lawyer went south. An ice storm in Toronto delayed the conference call, which was really an hour-long formality. Giffin voted no, Crump voted yes and Stavro sat across from Crump in his Palm Beach living room, listening in on the line.

When the call was over, Steve Stavro finally controlled HEBL, the major shareholder in Maple Leaf Gardens. Donald Crump went on a well-deserved two-week vacation in the Florida Keys.

Pomp and pageantry at Maple Leaf Gardens on Opening Night, November 12, 1931.

Harold Ballard and Yolanda at the cottage during his last birthday party, July 1989.

Steve Stavro (left) joins Ballard's birthday festivities with late Gardens' director Ed Lawrence (right).

Jim Devellano invested his life savings in the Gardens.

Harry Ornest began stockpiling shares after Ballard died.

Donald Crump kept Ballard "in control and out of trouble."

Cutting the Maple Leaf cake at the last birthday party.

Donald Giffin finally at the helm of the Gardens in May 1990.

Rosanne Rocchi, Ballard's lawyer for all reasons.

The Winners' Circle after the Maple Leaf Cup at Hollywood Park, Los Angeles, May 1993.

Front Row, left to right: Hollywood Park Goose Girl, Mr. and Mrs. Donald Crump, Mr. and Mrs. Brian Bellmore, Mr. and Mrs. Steve Stavro, jockey Kent Desormeaux, trainer Bobby Frankel, Larry Tanenbaum. Back row: Unknown woman, Jim Proudfoot, Harry Ornest, Ron Pringle, Terry Kelly, Ted Nikolaou.

Brian Bellmore and Chris Dundas leaving the courthouse after Justice
Lederman stopped Stavro's first attempt to take the Gardens private in
August 1994.

Susan Himel, Jay Chalke and Frank Newbould the day after the
settlement was announced on April 4, 1996.

CHAPTER SEVEN

Stavro's Hat Trick

"Pour me another one, and make mine plain vanilla." – BILL BALLARD

I F BILL BALLARD WAS playing out a role in a Shakespearean drama as Justice Farley claimed, he didn't know it. As far as the forty-three-year-old concert promoter could tell, he was merely basking in the glory of his bittersweet victory in court.

Even though he hadn't been able to get a judge to intervene against Stavro, in early March 1991 Bill was still closer to taking control of his father's sports empire than he'd ever dreamed. With 25 percent in the Gardens each—through the holding company—Stavro and Ballard were in a virtual deadlock for control of the famed hockey franchise and arena. Not that his dad had made it easy, or even wanted it that way. If he had, that father whose approval he'd always sought would have made it a lot easier for him when he wrote his will.

But Bill's was no ordinary father; irascible and unpredictable, Harold Ballard had turned his family into a feuding ground. It didn't start off that way. Bill was close to his father in his growing years, increasingly involving himself in the family business, enough to be named a director of HEBL in 1970. A lawyer by training, Bill worked as a vice-president at Maple Leaf Gardens after graduating from law school. Even while Harold Ballard was cooped up in prison serving his sentence for tax evasion, his eldest son toiled at the Gardens; in fact, he had been appointed to the board of directors in 1972 in anticipation of his father's imprisonment. During this time, Bill created Concert Productions International (CPI), a subsidiary of Maple Leaf Gardens that promoted entertainment events, with his friend Michael Cohl. However, when the boss returned from Millhaven, he came back with a vengeance and soon their strong personalities caused them to clash. Bill finally severed CPI's ties to Maple Leaf Gardens in 1974 and resigned from the Gardens board the following year.

Their professional estrangement remained, but never really spilled over into familial relations—that is, until Yolanda came onto the scene in 1984. As the wedge between father and children grew, abetted by Harold's failing health, Bill began openly questioning his father's ability to run the family holding company. The open criticism resulted in his removal from the HEBL board in 1988. According to those who knew Ballard well, he believed his children hadn't done anything to earn the legacy. He'd produced all this wealth for them and received little in return, except for the small consolation of a bedside reconciliation in his final days. Still, Bill had his shares and the pact he'd made with his two siblings to stick together. When that broke down, Bill had to fight for what he thought was his rightful inheritance the hard way—just as his father had planned.

Now only a perpetually tanned, multi-millionaire grocer was standing in Bill Ballard's way.

Emboldened, Ballard tried to break the standstill by appealing to a higher court and another judge to try to prevent Stavro from exercising his option or touching anything in the estate until Ballard could appeal Justice Trainor's decision. On March 5, before Mr. Justice Samuel Grange of the Ontario Court of Appeal, he succeeded. They'd all have to come back for another appearance in the Court of Appeal in early April, the judge decided. Indeed, Bill Ballard was on a roll.

And Harold Ballard's eldest son suddenly had an ally. Although Donald Giffin had the power to contest the actions of his co-executors, the sheet-metal magnate was no longer capable of fighting alone. Instead, Giffin coat-tailed on the legal initiatives launched by Bill Ballard, the same man who'd helped undermine his own power at the Gardens. (As Giffin hid behind the legal skirmishes, there were a number of consolations along the way. For one, Giffin's sixty thousand shares had earned him a tidy paper profit of more than

$382,000 in just three days, courtesy of a 23-percent hike in MLGL's stock price, thanks to all the publicity from the courtroom wrangling.)

But Steve Stavro was also advancing quickly. He wasted no time consolidating his new-found power—and he had plenty of provocation. First, Maple Leaf Gardens announced that Giffin's contract as president had been extended until March 1992. Giffin's friends on the board helped him parlay a temporary position into a two-year proposition that ensured he'd be around even after they hired someone to oversee the company. Stavro and Crump, who had demanded that Giffin step down from his position during a heated argument months earlier, seethed.

Stavro attempted to use a board meeting scheduled for March 25 to unseat Giffin. He wanted to use a provision his term sheet purported to give him—some influence in the selection of the chief operating officer of Maple Leaf Gardens. This, even though Justice Farley had said a month earlier that the clause wouldn't be enforceable because it fettered the discretion of the board.

Before the meeting, held at the arena during a hockey game, Bellmore sent each of the seven directors a letter. In it, he reminded the board that the estate, and thus the three executors, ultimately controlled the board, and that the board should act accordingly (which presumably meant to follow the lead of the executors). Bellmore's epistle did not endear his client to an increasingly hostile bunch.

Ted Rogers, for one, could barely contain himself.

"It would be appreciated if you would take me off your mailing list of people needing legal assistance as to how to behave at board of directors' meetings," Rogers wrote in a scathing retort to Bellmore three days later. "My colleagues and I are undertaking to represent all of the shareholders and to do what is right for this company under the most trying conditions and provocation from the legal activities of various shareholders."

Rogers continued, "Almost from the first day I became a director, we have been hindered in carrying out these activities by the personal activities and altercations between various shareholders and even various executors of Mr. Ballard's estate."

At the board meeting, dubbed the Night of the Knives by some who attended, Stavro was soundly rebuked by the independent directors who rallied around Giffin. Not only was Giffin allowed to stay on as president, they voted to eliminate the executive committee—at the time made up of the three executors—that had been overseeing the company's affairs. From now on, the entire board would participate in managing the Gardens.

Next, the board took steps to entrench Giffin further by supporting a proposal that put him in charge of continuing the search for a chief operating officer. A search committee of Eaton, Rogers and Giffin had been set up in the fall of 1990 and it hired Caldwell Partners to conduct an executive search.

Crump was supposed to write the job description but it never materialized because the CFL commissioner was too preoccupied arranging the sale of the Toronto Argonauts to Bruce McNall (who was represented by Rocchi during the negotiations). The search committee finally settled on hiring someone "with a high hockey profile and equally solid business skills," and the rumour was that their man was Cliff Fletcher. But that choice sparked another row between Stavro and Crump and the rest of the board.

As far as Stavro and Crump were concerned, Fletcher didn't quite fit the corporate profile Giffin was supposed to recruit. The fifty-four-year-old long-time general manager was a hockey man whose number crunching abilities rested mostly with players' salaries and maintaining an opulent lifestyle that included fine wine, European travel and his extensive Canadian art collection. A native of Montreal, Fletcher had worked as a buyer at the Iron Ore Co. before taking on employment as a scout for the Montreal Junior Canadiens. The fact that he'd been associated for more than a decade with Sam Pollock's venerable hockey system would have endeared Fletcher to Giffin. (It didn't hurt that Molson owned the Canadiens, either.) In 1967, Fletcher joined the St. Louis Blues organization as the team's eastern Canadian scout and by 1971, he had worked his way up to the big leagues as assistant general manager (under the auspices of another hockey legend, Scotty Bowman). But that didn't last long. The following year, Fletcher joined the Atlanta Flames as general manager, and he was still there when the team moved to Calgary during the summer of 1980. That team won the only Stanley Cup Fletcher had enjoyed in his twenty-year career in hockey. Giffin was hoping his luck would change.

Crump and Stavro liked neither the size of Fletcher's proposed paycheque nor the wide-sweeping dimensions of his job description. Crump says they were concerned that Giffin and his search committee pals were giving away too much power to Fletcher, whose business acumen was viewed as suspect. Besides, who cared if he came highly recommended by former NHL president John Ziegler and Alan Eagleson, former honcho of the National Hockey League's Players' Association. "Here's a person with no shares and he's given carte blanche to make deals, sign deals, everything," Stavro explains.

Worse, by trying to hire a "top-flight" hockey man like Fletcher, his adversaries believed Giffin was merely trying to solidify his own position as team president.

Stavro and Crump said they needed professional help and they suggested their own man, Lyman MacInnis. Only he and Crump weren't telling anyone they'd already approached MacInnis through Bellmore back in February, around the time they were all scrambling to meet Molson's deadline. And keeping to their secretive style, they had not told Giffin.

MacInnis, a senior executive at Labatt's entertainment division, had worked with Alan Eagleson in the 1960s, negotiating contracts for dozens of players, including Bobby Hull and former Leaf forward Norman Ullman. He'd been on the board of directors of Hockey Canada (one of the discretionary beneficiaries of Ballard's will) and was one of the final candidates to replace Eagleson as chief of the NHL Players' Association. He was also a former partner at Deloitte Touche and perhaps most notably had been singer Anne Murray's accountant, leading her unsuccessful bid for the Gardens in 1982.

Stavro used Bellmore to approach MacInnis because they were neighbours and fellow parishioners. MacInnis said at the time he was flattered to be offered a job as chief executive but he was tentative because he'd been with Labatt for only six months. A few weeks later, he met with Steve Stavro, Bellmore, Crump and Matheson, a fellow Maritimer he'd met in 1966 at a tax course at the University of Toronto. MacInnis had even introduced Canada's songbird to Matheson, who became Murray's lawyer.

After their meeting, MacInnis became very interested and began making plans to hire two general managers: one for the hockey team, and the other for the arena. He wanted John Muckler, from the Edmonton Oilers, for the team, and Brian Connacher, whom Stavro eventually hired, for the building.

But then he heard Fletcher had been quietly offered the job. "I was a little surprised that Cliff would think he could run a public company," says MacInnis. "I know I couldn't run a hockey team but I know how to run a company that owns a hockey team." Nonetheless, he met with Giffin and Thor Eaton for lunch several weeks later but figured they were simply going through the motions when an obviously ill Giffin fell asleep during their meeting.

The battle lines were drawn once again: Giffin forged ahead, putting Fletcher's name before the board while his co-executors countered with MacInnis.

The names of both men were eventually forwarded for consideration during a board meeting on June 4, 1991. Giffin didn't vote, under rumours of a threat that he would be removed as executor, but Stavro and Crump did. Fletcher won easily, becoming chief operating officer, president and general manager. And as Crump and Stavro had suspected, Giffin was appointed chairman of the board and chief executive officer.

And as he had done to show his displeasure a year earlier when Giffin became president of the Gardens, Stavro didn't stick around for the big announcement. "I didn't show up at the press conference," he recalls of Fletcher's hiring. "I got Brian to work on it ... to keep things rolling and keep peace in the family. Brian worked with Fletcher's lawyer." As it turned out, Fletcher produced a winning team and would be Giffin's legacy to Maple Leaf Gardens.

Faced with what looked like defeat, Stavro decided to push to get his man MacInnis appointed as chief operating officer to work with Fletcher, even though the latter had been given a five-year, $4-million contract that carried a whopping $1.5-million buyout clause.

However, it was becoming increasingly clear that Stavro didn't have the kind of support at the board level that he enjoyed with estate matters. In fact, this group of directors didn't appear to like Crump any more than the previous board.

For his part, Crump admits he never got along with Ted Rogers. "I guess I got Mr. Rogers mad a few times," he says. "Ted's got a wandering eye.* You never knew whether he was looking at you or not. I had to keep saying, 'Ted, are you looking at me? Are you talking to me?'"

Having failed in their attempt to appoint MacInnis, Crump and Stavro decided to take another run at the composition of the Gardens board by using their muscle as directors of the holding company to depose MLGL's dissident independents. Crump and Giffin still hadn't resigned from HEBL by the spring of 1991 (even though Justice Farley had ordered that they step down by the first week of March) because they were appealing his decision. And while that case wove its way through the court, the two men continued to wield influence as directors of the company that controlled Maple Leaf Gardens. Faced with that, Bill Ballard went to court in April to complain that Crump was using the reprieve to help Stavro clean house at the Gardens.

As a result, seven weeks after they were first told to leave, another court ordered Crump and Giffin to resign immediately.

That decision created a power vacuum. The estate (which acted as Stavro's faction) was to appoint one new director to HEBL and Bill Ballard could name the other. David Moore, Bellmore's law partner, was nominated by the estate while Ballard named his business associate Michael Cohl. Moore and Cohl in turn were supposed to select a third member but, not surprisingly, they couldn't agree.

So back they went to Justice Farley's chambers. The amused judge asked for two nominees from each camp and he'd decide from the list who would be appointed as the pivotal director. In the old days, Harold Ballard changed the names of HEBL's directors regularly, depending on who was in or out of his doghouse. No one back then would have dreamed that one day the courts would institutionalize those decisions.

Justice Farley was impressed with the offerings. Stavro's group served up George Whyte, a former managing partner at McMillan Binch and vice-chairman of Curragh Resources Inc., the company that owns the Westray mine in Nova Scotia. The

---

* A medical condition called strabismus.

alternate was a banker named Geoffrey Styles.

Bill Ballard countered with David Crombie, a former mayor of Toronto and federal cabinet minister, and a lawyer named Stephen Paddon.

Justice Farley chose the fifty-four-year-old Whyte because of his private-sector corporate experience. A past director of Honda Canada, a board chairman and director of Sun Alliance & London Insurance, and now a senior vice-president with the Bank of Nova Scotia, Whyte had met Stavro in the East York industrial hockey league back in the 1950s when he played on a Macedonian team sponsored by Knob Hill Farms. Whyte later played for the University of Toronto Varsity Blues team before attending law school at Osgoode Hall. David Matheson re-acquainted the grocer with the mining executive almost forty years later. In fact, it was Crump's lawyer who put Whyte forward as a candidate.

Notch up another win for Stavro.

Actually it was icing on an even bigger victory a few weeks earlier. On April 12, a three-judge appellate panel had ruled against Bill Ballard's appeal, upholding Justice Trainor's earlier decision giving Stavro the right to vote on his own loan proposal, which led to acquiring his option. Justice George Finlayson said it was "fully in accord with the letter and the intent of the will," and thus Stavro didn't need court approval to secure his option.

During the argument, Bellmore had claimed the estate would eventually put the Gardens up for sale but stressed that exercising the option was "not the purpose" of Stavro's deal. In fact, he said, "Stavro may not be a buyer."

Ballard's lawyer, Jim Hodgson, who argued the appeal, could only shake his head. Stavro's deal, he said, actually worked against the intent of Harold Ballard's will because it took indirect control of the Gardens out of the estate. Not only that, it breached strict provisions of the Charitable Gifts Act, which as an executor, Stavro was bound to uphold.

But the quick-footed Bellmore shot back: "We're [the executors] accountable if we've breached our trust with an interested party."

Who could blame him? The watchdog charged with protecting the beneficiaries from a possible breach was sitting on the same side of the room as Stavro. In his factum filed with the Court of Appeal in April 1991, Stan Sokol, the Public Trustee's lawyer, said that "after reading the Will as a whole, it does provide in clear terms that the Stavro proposal can be accepted by two of three executors, without court approval, although one of the two is the lender and optionee under the proposal."

The Public Trustee's lawyer also argued that the Charitable Gifts Act didn't apply in this case because the executors hadn't transferred the shares at issue into the Harold E. Ballard Trust. That hadn't yet been done, Sokol argued, so there weren't any beneficiaries to protect as yet.

Without a doubt, having such a powerful ally vigorously supporting his cause helped legitimize Stavro's position before the court. "The message we were getting was full support," Bellmore says. "They supported both the concept of Steve voting on the loan and the loan itself because at the court hearing in front of Justice Trainor, we spent three days comparing the merits of both loans." Still, Bellmore now admits that the judge purposely steered away from actually making a ruling on its merits.

That's the part Bill's lawyer still couldn't figure out. He'd gone to see Hugh Paisley days after Stavro's proposal was accepted to sort out the government agency's position. Hodgson was still stunned from watching what he considered Sokol's overzealous defence of Stavro in court before Justice Trainor. Why wasn't the Public Trustee's office taking a neutral position, Hodgson asked. But Paisley didn't really have an answer.

Paisley said he'd look into the matter and he promised to review Bill's latest offer. Two days later, Hodgson wrote to Paisley restating his argument—that Stavro was negotiating with himself, improving his offer every time Bill put one on the table. And, according to Hodgson, his client's offer was still a better deal for the estate. "A fiduciary has an obligation to come to the table with his best offer and not negotiate with himself," he wrote.

Paisley, however, who knew about the anticipated increases in television revenues, informed Hodgson that he couldn't speak about estate matters because they were confidential.

Having stated his position, Hodgson figured that, at the very least, the Public Trustee's office would take a less proactive role before the Court of Appeal. That assumption would prove to be incorrect.

When the appellate panel of judges made its decision on April 12, it went further than Justice Trainor. Justice Finlayson commented that Stavro's "conflict is very clear," and that "the trustees, however, are in no way relieved of their fiduciary duties to the estate by this court's interpretation of the will." In Canada's legal tradition, judges like to be subtle, often avoiding unnecessary statements. Judge Finlayson seemed to take the extra step of gently reminding Stavro that his fiduciary duties prevailed over all others. If the executors didn't hear the message, their lawyers likely did. Having reiterated that the court "did not accept the task of determining whether the Molson debt could be satisfied in some other way," Judge Finlayson said that if, and when, Stavro decided to exercise his right of first refusal to purchase the estate's shares, "the sole beneficiaries at that stage will be charities who are represented before us by the Public Trustee. The trustees will be answerable at that time for their decision to so encumber the shares." When that happened, the judge said, the transaction would be subject to the provisions of the Charitable Gifts Act. All those words directed at a topic the judge began by saying he was going to avoid. Yet, one of Stavro's lawyers later complained that the court still "could have been a lot clearer."

Bill Ballard would close out the months of legal wrangling with a victory of his own. Yet another Ontario Court of Appeal panel upheld Justice Farley's earlier decision giving the rock promoter a strong say in deciding what went on in the holding company, namely in determining the sale of HEBL shares and assets. Not only that, the court ordered that Ballard be given the holding company's financial statements and other pertinent materials.

By the late spring of 1991, the legal fog had finally cleared with no clear victor. Only now, Giffin was fighting for more than his business life. In April, doctors had removed a large cancerous tumour from the lymph nodes under his arm.

By the summer of 1991 Stavro had asserted his domain over the estate, and the private company HEBL; he finally turned his attention to the public company, Maple Leaf Gardens. It was a time of discontent. Leaf fans had endured another listless hockey season, watching the hometown heroes drop to second-last place overall among the NHL's twenty-four teams.

Not even the arrival of a notable hockey wizard such as Cliff Fletcher on July 1 was enough to quell the angst. That was because even his job seemed tenuous in light of the power play that was mobilizing in the company's boardroom.

Because the terms of Stavro's option agreement allowed him to appoint a chief operating officer and two of the seven Gardens directors, and with the help of Crump, the millionaire grocer had the makings of a majority on the Gardens' board. A few months back when he had tried to impose his power on MLGL, Giffin's loyalists had stopped him. But now, Stavro had David Moore and George Whyte on the board of the holding company whose shares Stavro had secured a right to buy. A purge was in the making. He began taking steps to depose the current directors even though Bill Ballard was once again going to court, this time to the Supreme Court of Canada, to rule on whether Stavro's option was permissible.

Actually, George Whyte says it was his idea to put forward a new board. In fact, it was the first thing he did at his inaugural directors' meeting in June. "My main goal was to keep the dispute between Ballard and Stavro out of Maple Leaf Gardens," explains the court-appointed director of HEBL. "At the time the board was divided into two camps: Giffin and his supporters and Stavro with his group. There was never a cross-over of views."

To bridge the gap, Whyte suggested that his co-directors, Cohl and Moore, each come forward with a new slate of potential candidates. Suddenly the court-appointed swing vote started acting like the decision maker. While he waited for their responses, Whyte says he interviewed some of the existing directors to get their views on the stalemate in the boardroom. But he never did speak with Rogers, who Whyte says was always too busy.

In early July, the two teams handed in their potential rosters. Whyte recalls Moore's wish list included Bellmore (who had played varsity hockey with Whyte); Donald Crump; restaurateur Ted Nikolaou; a criminal lawyer from Oshawa, Ontario, named Terence Kelly (an avid sports fan who'd known Stavro for thirty years); Stavro; Whyte (himself a self-confessed hockey groupie); and a doctor named Shane Cohen from Mount Sinai Hospital.

The obvious omission was Giffin's name.

Whyte recalls telling Moore that it was inconceivable for Stavro to be publicly criticizing Fletcher's business smarts at a time when he expected to get a doctor with no business experience voted onto the board. (Cohen and Stavro knew each other from their philanthropic endeavours.) The doctor was eventually replaced by another Stavro associate named Ronald Pringle, a former chief operating officer of Coca-Cola (Canada) Ltd., who was working as a self-employed consultant after leaving the giant cola company in late 1990. For his part, Whyte knew the former Coke executive well from his McMillan Binch days when the firm acted as the soft drink company's corporate lawyers.

"There were a lot of hockey people, not only businessmen but people who knew hockey. From that point of view, it was not a bad slate," is how Whyte defended his selection.

The team Bill Ballard's side fielded appeared less imaginative by comparison. It included Whyte, Cohl, Moore plus Giffin, Rogers, McDowell and Eaton.

"That's not gonna fly," Whyte warned the former CPI chief. So Bill Ballard's business partner tossed in the name of Sam Pollock (who at the time was general manager of the Montreal Canadiens) to add a little more credibility. But that still wasn't good enough. "He left me no alternative but to go to support the estate's slate," Whyte says, defending his action.

On July 15 the new appointees were officially presented at a board meeting and, as expected, the incumbent directors didn't take too kindly to getting the hook. Another protracted skirmish ensued, this one lasting all through the summer, forcing a postponement of the annual meeting until the third week of October.

Cohl says he wasn't as flippant as Whyte might suggest. "They ramrodded their agenda [slate] through," he says. "It was all very predictable and couched in very proper terms. [But] we knew we were fighting an uphill battle. Everything was done according to a vested interest."

Even so, the practical reality is that most boards do have a strong inclination to support the majority shareholder as much as possible without trampling on the rights of the minority. Bill Ballard, Cohl explains, was being treated like the minority shareholder he was and Whyte felt it was his duty to protect the majority (the estate, which was Stavro and Crump). As a result, Cohl recalls that the HEBL board meetings felt more like shareholder gatherings where decisions had already been made and Bill would get his vote knowing it really didn't count.

Bill Ballard accused Whyte and Moore of "snowballing" Cohl. Ballard, who was not a director, took his shots from outside the boardroom, threatening yet another round of legal action in support of the independents. Yet, he didn't press Justice Farley, who'd appointed Whyte, into investigating his allegations that "Stavro and company were stirring the pot."

By late August, there was slight hope for a truce. The sitting MLGL board members agreed to resign if the board was expanded to nine positions, which would allow Stavro to push forward with his seven nominees but also add two other independents to maintain some semblance of credibility with the company's shareholders.

But Crump and Stavro wouldn't go along with the plan. So the defiant board members nominated themselves for re-election, threatening to face off against Stavro and his buddies in public at the meeting.

Suddenly, Bill Ballard became conspicuously silent.

On August 30, Bill Ballard wrote to Stavro. Not a poison-pen letter, but a terse request to settle a score. He was now ready to sell to Stavro. On the Friday before the Labour Day weekend, it was clear to Bill Ballard he was the last serious threat to Stavro's control—but he was alone and without much hope of winning. A bitter disappointment, really, for the boy who grew up in the dressing room of one of the most prestigious sports franchises anywhere. In Bill's mind, he'd done everything he could to stop Stavro. Just after his father's will was made public a week after his death in April 1990, Bill had asked Rosanne Rocchi if the will prohibited him from buying the Gardens. Rocchi replied that despite what others told him, there was no provision against him specifically taking a run at the company. Since then, having spent over a million dollars of his own money (while his opponents had the right to dip into his late father's estate to pay their lawyers), Bill had lost his appetite for another courtroom battle. Actually, his long-time friends Michael Cohl, Dusty Cohl (co-founder of the Toronto Film Festival and cousin of Michael) and John Perkins had convinced Bill to abandon his quest. "They're very cute and they're very good," one of his friends had told Bill Ballard. "As a minority shareholder [in HEBL] you're vulnerable and this guy looks like he's going to stay and fight in court a long time."

Bill Ballard had other reasons as well. "I saw the way they were jumping all over Giffin's dying bones," he said of his decision. "My wife said to forget it. It's not worth all the tragedy that surrounds this place."

Indeed, Giffin was fading fast. During that past summer he had remained an executor in title only; his authority had been emasculated long before even though he still kept fighting. Giffin was squeezed financially and the vultures began circling.

In July Bellmore had made an extraordinary offer to the dying man: Knob Hill Farms in combination with the estate would pay Giffin's legal bills (these incurred in his capacity as executor) if he agreed to resign from all his positions—his directorship in HEBL, Maple Leaf Gardens Ltd. and the Harold E. Ballard Foundation. He would also have to resign as a trustee of the Ballard trust, chairman of Maple Leaf Gardens and, of course, as an executor. (If he did that, Ballard's will provided that Stavro and Crump name his replacement.) By law Giffin was entitled to have his legal bills paid by the estate. Although Stavro had never forwarded any of his legal bills for the estate to cover, Crump had dipped into the estate's coffers to pay Matheson. Giffin refused to accept those terms.

Bill Ballard had felt sympathy for Giffin but he too had tried to buy his help. In a letter dated July 10, 1991, Ballard had offered the ailing man $250,000 to cover the expenses his co-executors were refusing to pay. In return, Bill wanted Giffin to promise that he'd disclose documents that he believed "constituted proper grounds to commence an action to have the two removed as trustees." Ballard wanted Giffin to call a press conference to launch a lawsuit, which would be fought by a lawyer of Bill's choosing.

Ron Farano, one of the lawyers whose bills Giffin was trying to pay, showed up in the offices of Molson after receiving the offers from both Bellmore and Ballard and asked for financial help because Giffin didn't have enough liquid cash. On July 12, Norman Seagram approved a cheque for $300,000 to Giffin to retire his legal debts; it was a demand loan at an interest rate of 12 percent a year. The loan, backed by a promissory note from a very grateful Giffin, had no strings attached.

"We did it out of friendship and long-standing recognition," Seagram says. "We very much disliked the way Don Giffin was being treated in his capacity as an executor. I don't think he had an enemy in his life. He may have had a lot of people who thought he was a bit of a bumbling fellow, but here's a man who started with nothing in life and had become a very successful businessman." Giffin's family repaid the loan after his death.

Giffin never did take his co-executors to task for putting the financial squeeze on him; nor did he ever go public with his allegations as Bill Ballard had hoped. Rather, he was still clinging to some far-fetched notion that the Public Trustee's office would ride in to the rescue. After all, it was really the government agency's fight. Giffin had already done what he could as an executor. To that end, his lawyer kept up the campaign, writing letters entreating Hugh Paisley to probe the conduct of Crump and Stavro before his client was unable to testify. The urgency was real: Giffin's health was declining rapidly and the trip to Los Angeles for a special chemotherapy treatment was not adding to his life expectancy.

Still, the man Bill had trusted more than his own father wasn't the only disappointment. The mighty blue-chip directors could have at least tried to sue Stavro as he was taking control of the board because of his obvious conflict of interest. But they had nothing at stake other than personal pride and principle, and Bill had become demoralized watching them surrender. On Labour Day weekend, he made his own deal with Stavro.

When Bill Ballard sent his advisers to negotiate on his behalf, he had his own little secret. Bill had an ally; he had been Molson's fall-back position all along. Stavro was leading the race then, but he could always stumble. Because Molson's priority was protecting the brewery's exclusive sponsorship rights with Maple Leaf Gardens, the "BaGa" file was always stocked with any number of plans waiting to be deployed. Molson was also a major sponsor of Bill's concert production company. Hundreds of millions of dollars were at stake.

Bill's circle of business associates had been meeting with Edmund Clark, who was the chief operating officer of Morgan

Financial Corp., as well as a director of a number of trust companies, including Canada Trust. Every Wednesday morning for weeks after Stavro asserted his control over Harold's estate, a group (which sometimes included John Bitove Jr.) would gather in Clark's office in the Canada Trust Tower. Clark, who was also an adviser to Molson and a close friend of Mickey Cohen, was considered a top-notch strategist. His assignment: devise ways to work around Stavro's option.

A bunch of power plays were floated around, including trying to dissolve the holding company and converting the shares into common shares of Maple Leaf Gardens, which would protect Bill. The brewery and the prodigal son made a deal: they would protect each other against Stavro's advance on the Gardens. And, more importantly, Molson would throw its support behind Bill and together they would make their own "Play" (as they called it). Ultimately they promised not to abandon each other.

Thus as he headed into the meeting, Bill Ballard felt obliged to honour his commitment. The strategy heading into the meetings with Bellmore and McKellar in the offices of Weir & Foulds on the sixteenth floor of the Exchange Tower was to first get a handshake on a deal for Bill and then play the Molson card.

Cohl and Perkins negotiated a deal that would see Bill Ballard collect about the same amount of money as his brother Harold Jr. had when he cashed out two years earlier—only Bill was out about $4 million in interest. As well, both sides agreed to drop the myriad remaining lawsuits in the Supreme Court of Ontario and the Ontario Court of Justice.

According to Stavro's lawyer, after they hammered out their agreement in principle during the Labour Day weekend, Michael Cohl excused himself from the room to call his partner, who was at his cottage. Bellmore says Cohl returned "looking very sheepish" and declared that he and Bill had a "moral obligation to our friends at Molson and we feel we don't want to leave them high and dry with a 20-percent block of shares."

Bellmore says he was stunned because he'd always figured Bill was in bed with Labatt, which owned a 25-percent stake in CPI. Instead, Cohl claimed that Bill and Molson were a package deal and that unless the estate made Molson an offer for the block of shares held in trust, Ballard wouldn't settle.

"Molson wanted to sell right then and there at market price," Bellmore says emphatically. "They knew they had no allies on the board any more. That board was not going to have Mr. Giffin on it."

Bellmore, who would get a seat on the new board, says Cohl's remarks simply confirmed his suspicions that Molson had always been trying to squeeze the estate through Ballard's lawsuits.

The estate wasn't interested, he said, and didn't want to add to its debt load. At the time, the market value of Molson's block was about $23 million.

Stavro didn't need the shares either, Bellmore says, because he already had a right to buy an indirect control block of Maple Leaf Gardens through the estate. But control wasn't the issue then. Molson's shares were important for Stavro's long-term plans. In any event, his client hadn't decided whether he was going to exercise his option. "Stavro didn't want the Molson stock because the place was in a mess. The company at the time was in disarray. Steve had an option to buy a mess."

Still, the millionaire businessman dealt with the devil. "Since Bill wouldn't settle without Molson," Bellmore explains, "we decided that when Steve was going to exercise his option, then he'd buy their shares. So we ended up splitting the difference and that's how the put/call agreement came to be."

For Stavro, securing a deal with Molson was the last piece of important business—if you will, closing the loop. He already had control of Ballard's estate as a result of his position as executor and his option on HEBL's shares. Through the estate and HEBL, he could control the public company once he secured his domain over the Gardens board of directors. Once he had control, he didn't really need the other stock unless one day he wanted Maple Leaf Gardens to be a private company—free of securities regulators and pesky minority shareholders and the duties that come attached to them.

The Molson block was critical for the final step in Stavro's plan to take the company private. After all, it was the way the self-made millionaire preferred to conduct business: no pressure and added costs from minority shareholders and the watchful eye of the securities watchdog. With just over 60 percent in the estate and another 10 percent from Molson, Stavro now had a whopping 70 percent of MLGL stock within his grasp. Ultimately Molson gave Stavro the kind of positioning he needed to make a takeover offer on a different level.

There was another reason to deal with Molson. The brewery still held a right of first refusal on Gardens shares in HEBL courtesy of the 1980 loan that had bailed out Harold with TD Bank. And that posed a problem for Stavro: if he attempted to exercise his own option, he would inadvertently trigger Molson's right. Given the litigious nature of this bunch, they'd probably have been battling that one out in court for years.

Worse, from Stavro's perspective, there was always the threat that Molson would keep its string on the Gardens by simply transferring its right to a friendly third party. It was no secret that Molson was determined to participate in the arena, if not the hockey team.

Thus by obliging Molson, Stavro removed the last and potentially the most formidable obstacle in his path to securing total control of the venerable sports institution. Now, after months of demurring, Bellmore was making bolder claims in a Toronto newspaper. "I think he's obviously seriously interested in buying the estate's shares. If things go very positively, and he thinks they will, it would be the natural thing for him to do." The singer had changed his tune.

For Molson, it became a strategic divestiture. The company, which now owned a small part, had, as one manager said, "wasted a lot of time on it." The company's quandary was apparent: how to protect its exclusive sponsorship and broadcast rights while extricating itself from a battle it appeared to have lost.

"We didn't have something truly marketable until Steve had declared his ultimate interest," explained a Molson executive. And he did that when he offered to buy the brewery's shares. The estate didn't even consider making an offer because, as Crump explains, "our role was to wrap it up as quickly as possible. We didn't think it was appropriate for us to acquire all the shares. That's for some entrepreneur to do, not an estate." The estate became a party to the put/call deal that required Stavro to buy Molson's shares by April 15, 1994. In fact, the estate gave up the rights it had to acquire any part of the Molson block (which, you'll recall, came out of Ballard's estate in the first place) and handed them to one of its executors. When Crump signed the

September 21 agreement (Giffin didn't sign it), he hadn't asked the estate's bankers to even consider lending the money to Ballard's estate to buy back Molson's interest. Obviously, Stavro, in his capacity as executor, hadn't pushed the matter either.

That the company chose not to sell its shares on the public market was a bit surprising, given that Maple Leaf Gardens stock is so thinly traded. Investors are often willing to pay a premium for such stocks: that's why they're not often pre-sold by a lock-up agreement. Unless, of course, there's some kind of favour in return. In fact, Molson could have thrown a wrench into Stavro's plans by simply holding onto the shares for as long as the NHL would have allowed. Instead, at least on paper, it looks as if Molson seemed content to give up much more than it received in return.

"We just did not feel it was prudent to go out and actively shop those shares," explained a senior Molson executive. "To be quite honest, why own 10 percent of something when there is some other guy, that you will never invite home to meet Mom, who owns the other 90 percent?" However, there may have been other pressures forcing Molson to sell.

Mickey Cohen made the call for Molson. The cigar-smoking CEO took one look down the road to 1995 when Molson would renegotiate its broadcast contract with Maple Leaf Gardens, and that was enough to make his decision final. "We were scared. Mickey did it because he knew the brewery would have to sit down with the Gardens people. He didn't want to create problems that would sour Stavro," explained a Molson official.

Stavro had his hat trick.

Having secured the reins of control on the shares, Stavro had to arrange the financing to pay for it all. He accomplished that in surprisingly quick fashion. In the fall of 1991, Harold Ballard's indebted estate had been able to raise $21 million on very short notice, a remarkable feat given that it hadn't been able to scrounge together roughly the same amount to pay off Molson at the beginning of the year. And it wasn't because its weak financial position had improved since March. There was still about $15 million worth of debt to be paid and the $1.8 million in dividends flowing from the Gardens to the holding company still wasn't enough to cover its financial obligations.

The TD Bank would lend the estate $21 million, which had to be paid back in full on December 1, 1995. Given that it had no cash flow, the estate's inability to cover the hefty monthly interest payments, the bank also agreed to provide a separate interest facility of $4.5 million. In other words, TD provided the principal money to repurchase Bill's shares and, at the same time, advanced the funds to cover two years' worth of interest on that same loan. So every month when the interest was due, the bank would simply roll the amount into a separate account. The bottom line: the estate didn't have to pay a cent for a $25.5-million loan to buy out Ballard's son until four years in the future.

In return, Bill's thirty-four common shares in the holding company were pledged to the bank as collateral for the principal loan. (The other shares in HEBL had been previously pledged by Harold.) At the same time, Knob Hill Farms guaranteed the $4.5-million interest facility, which had a due date of November 23, 1993. Given the estate's precarious financial state, Stavro wasn't taking any chances on losing his stranglehold on the Gardens shares he'd fought so hard to secure.

Bellmore argues that his client was protecting the estate's financial position. Maybe so. But it was also glaringly obvious that Stavro was desperate to hold onto the shares that were optioned to him in March 1991. An astute businessman such as Stavro would understand that the value of his option would increase appreciably if the estate could finance a buyout from Bill. In order to do so, Stavro was prepared to give his consent, allowing the shares in the estate to be pledged to the Toronto Dominion Bank. And that's how the heavily indebted Ballard estate was able to raise the $21 million to pay off Bill. But because banks don't like to be exposed to risk over the long term—and given there was virtually no cash flow in the estate—Stavro also guaranteed the $4.5-million interest facility on the loan for two years even though the life of the principal loan was five years.

Ultimately, there was really no advantage for Stavro in this deal. In fact, he might have actually been worse off because he'd agreed to release his grip by pledging the shares to the bank as collateral for the loan. Still, it was highly unlikely that any bank would go after a guarantor like Stavro if the bank could get full repayment of its loan simply by realizing its security. The bank would call in its interest facility if it thought its security was in danger.

In return for guaranteeing the interest facility, Stavro secured an agreement from the Toronto Dominion Bank that entitled him to step in and take over the bank's position as lender if the bank decided to call in the loan. If that were to happen, the shares would be assigned to Stavro. That arrangement gave him a security interest in Maple Leaf Gardens. In other words, if there was a default, he could take possession of the 60.3-percent block in the estate and either sell the shares or try to keep them for himself, by foreclosure.

All of the financing obligations were interrelated because Stavro wasn't taking any chances. He made sure that nothing could happen to the estate's shares without his involvement. Stavro now had another means to take the estate's controlling block of Maple Leaf Gardens shares without actually making an offer to buy them.

And that's the package deal Stavro and company put on the table when they all convened at Weir & Foulds on September 19 for the actual signing of their agreements. Two days later, Molson and Stavro publicly announced their deal. Under the terms of a put/call agreement (dated September 21, 1991), Knob Hill Farms had until April 15, 1994, to acquire half of Molson's 20-percent stake in MLGL. Steve would have to queue up to get consideration on the remaining half.

Ultimately, Stavro had until the middle of April 1994 to "call" on Molson's shares and purchase them according to a complicated pricing formula, which worked out to the average trading price of MLGL stock twenty days before purchase. If by that time he hadn't made his move, then Molson could "put" the shares to Stavro, forcing him to buy them.

Bill Ballard had started the dealmaking because, he later explained, he was trying to stop from being ambushed himself when he recalled the conflicting accounts of Molson's role. He says that when he and his lawyer, Hodgson, showed up at McKellar's office to pick up the cheque, the estate lawyer walked into the room with Molson attorney George Vesely, a senior partner at Osler, Hoskin & Harcourt, to declare they had a deal. "They'd been meeting all along with Molson, who always played both sides against the middle," Bill Ballard says. "If they hadn't already arranged it, how did Stavro put together a deal in about three minutes? It's not his style. I'm telling you, he already cut a deal with Molson and was putting a gun to my head, trying to force me to go along."

Still, if they deny that's what happened, Bill Ballard laughed, when he recalled the manoeuverings, then "pour me another one, and make mine plain vanilla."

As two hundred people jammed into the Hot Stove Lounge for the annual shareholders' meeting on October 22, 1991, Steve Stavro finally emerged from the shadows. By now he was in firm control of Ballard's estate, the holding company and, now, Maple Leaf Gardens. When you ask Brian Bellmore what he remembers most about that meeting, he recalls that "Steve Stavro spoke." Actually, he didn't. Donald Crump spoke for him, reading a mission statement as Stavro—the new boss—sat impassively in the front row. "What I want is teamwork and harmony on and off the ice," Crump quoted Stavro as writing. "Let's roll up our sleeves and get to work. There's a big job to be done."

It was a watershed meeting, one that changed the course of the sports institution for good. In her typically melodramatic manner, Yolanda carried two bouquets of flowers—one for the "new queen" of the Gardens, Sally Stavro, and the other for the former queen, Patty Giffin, whose husband Don was chairing what would be his last meeting.

Ted Rogers delivered an eloquent speech about the integrity of independent directors. "Perception is reality," he said, waving a share certificate. The cable baron argued that unbiased independents should be named to the board to protect the minority shareholders. Having made his point, Rogers officially pulled the incumbent slate. Crump would later dismiss Rogers's valedictory address as pure rhetoric.

With the slate put forward by Stavro supported by the estate, the vote became merely a formality. After the meeting, the new board retreated to the Directors' Lounge for a private meeting to appoint the company's officers. As they were milling about in the corridor, Crump whispered a request to Stavro, whose first order of business was to distribute two season's tickets to each new director.

Before heading into the room, Stavro pulled aside Blair Cowper-Smith (the other lawyer who had replaced Rocchi) and asked him not to join the meeting. In fact, the Gardens new honcho informed the lawyer that his firm was now officially fired as the Gardens corporate lawyers.

In the meantime, Crump sought out his own attorney, David Matheson, and invited him to attend the meeting as the company's new solicitor. "It was his reward for a year's hard work," Crump explains. "There's nothing wrong with that."

Inside, the niceties continued. The new board agreed to accept the contract its predecessors had signed with Fletcher. It seems that a series of private meetings between Fletcher and Stavro in early October had resolved their differences. Fletcher even secured a $300,000 interest-free loan to relocate to Toronto from Calgary.

Actually, Stavro had little choice.

Lyman MacInnis, the man the new boss always wanted instead of Fletcher, had walked away from a revised offer tabled over lunch by Bellmore in late August. The proposal offered MacInnis equal footing with Fletcher, making him a vice-president in charge of business operations while the former Calgary Flames GM took care of hockey. MacInnis balked; he just wanted to be CEO.

At the same time, the board resurrected the executive committee now made up of Stavro, Bellmore and Crump, to keep an eye on Fletcher. The new chief operating officer would report directly to this group, which included the same man who held the rights to buy the company.

Crump was allowed to maintain the executive title of secretary-treasurer he had never relinquished after resigning from the company in 1990.

And finally, Stavro was appointed chairman and chief executive officer. This, even though the term sheet he had put before the courts clearly stated that all three executors agreed to remove themselves from managerial positions in the company.

Crump defends the decision because Stavro was a natural for the top positions, despite the apparent conflicts. "It would have been a worse conflict if you had let the place be run by an outsider and it had gone bankrupt." Stavro explained it this way: "I was responsible more or less for the estate and the funds that I'd advanced. I wasn't there to stifle Cliff or anything but to watch more or less the operation; not to get involved with his day-to-day at the club or anything. It was just a matter of, you know, just to be there."

Then, as if Stavro had waved a magic stick, the fighting in the Directors' Lounge stopped. "From the time Harold was declared incompetent in February 1990 through to October 22, 1991, it had been a constant struggle," recalls Crump. "It was a terrible time."

Later that night, the board members (past and present) attempted to bury the hatchet. In what was intended to be a show of solidarity, they all gathered together at the Albany Club for a testimonial dinner honouring the outgoing directors, including Donald Giffin.

On this night they would carve up the roast beef instead of each other. There was even talk of naming Giffin an honorary chairman for his years of service at the company, but not surprisingly, nothing would ever come of that idea. Still, Stavro's peace would be short-lived. He may have successfully ousted Giffin from the operations of the hockey arena, but the dying man's family would carry on the fight their patriarch could no longer wage.

CHAPTER EIGHT

Hunting Leafs

"We're in for a brutal fight."

— J. PERRY BORDEN

NICHOLSON ISLAND CLUB IS a place where big city boys converge to hunt game birds. It's an exclusive millionaires' club on Nicholson's Island, four hundred acres of fields located just southwest of Prince Edward County, one mile out from the north shore of Lake Ontario, off Huckeye's Point. On most fall days, packs of five or six small-game hunters—all there by invitation—chase pheasant in fields of colourful hedgerose and mature forests of oak and maple.

During the first week of October 1991, a group of amateur hunters gathered in the club's dining room for the traditional pre-shoot meal. Among those at the table were a mining executive, a cement dealer, a lawyer from a blue-chip Bay Street firm, the son of the Maple Leaf Gardens chairman of the board, and a family member of Canada's largest department store owners who was also a director of the Gardens.

The group of mostly middle-aged men, who spent their summers prancing around islands in Georgian Bay, were sharing a joke about what one called "the imminent demise of the independent directors." In a few weeks, Ballard's estate—that being Crump and Stavro—would vote to appoint its own slate of directors at the annual shareholders' meeting, removing all the current independents, including Thor Eaton, who was the subject of much of the dinner table banter. Thor himself had had a number of heated exchanges with Stavro and knew his head was on the block.

The conversation may have been light-hearted but the air of

resignation about Stavro's ultimate victory was palpable. At that point, a voice interjected, calling the talk of Stavro's inevitable conquest as "a lot of crap." It was the lawyer speaking. He argued that, like everyone else, including the media, his friends at the dinner table were acting as if the court's decision upholding Stavro's right to get his option had been wrong.

Instead, the lawyer, John Perry Borden, gave them another perspective: just accept that maybe the Court of Appeal's ruling was right in saying that Stavro had the right to vote on his own proposal and then, he said, look at whether Stavro had obeyed the letter of the law subsequent to that decision. That was the ticket.

"It was very wrong for him to be moving in that manner," Borden said of Stavro, "removing the independent directors, asserting his own dominion and control over the Gardens and, at the same time, continuing as an executor of the estate."

The fifty-three-year-old son of one of the founding partners of Borden & Elliot recalled that he told his dinner mates that "nobody was looking at the question of whether the beneficiaries, through the Public Trustee, or independently of the Public Trustee, ... could attack that type of aggressive act on the part of Stavro."

Borden was referring specifically to Stavro's rather bold intention to purge the board and then to sit in the chairman's seat himself. A clear overstepping of his position, the group agreed, the very breach of fiduciary duty the Court of Appeal had cautioned him about earlier in the year. "The court said it was a permissible conflict but went to great lengths to caution Stavro to make sure it didn't become an intolerable one," Borden said. "He crossed the line when he assumed influence and control over the asset that was optioned to him at fair market value."

Better yet, the trust expert told the assembled men, something could be done about this "outrageous" conduct. Emboldened, they decided to knock out a course of action.

The next morning while they were out in the field, the group stopped for a coffee break. With their guns parked by the side of a bench, Borden used a cell phone to call his office, asking his assistant to dust off the opinion he'd put together with colleague James Stratton for Thor Eaton during the summer.

Back then, Eaton had requested a legal interpretation of the Court of Appeal's decision giving Stavro the green light to vote on his own option. Eaton had read the opinion at his Georgian Bay cottage. In fact, he had an extra copy made for Donald Giffin, who was convalescing at his son's island near Parry Sound.

The men at the shoot ate lunch and drove back to Toronto.

Having shed their hunting garb, they retreated to their offices and began plotting a strategy. First, they would establish a credible legal argument to challenge Stavro. "The only way you can do anything about it is to know there is a legal wrongdoing and his game plan could be unwound," said one of the lawyers involved.

Second, they'd commission an appraisal of the Gardens to be performed by a credible investment house. And finally, they would discreetly shop around the legal and commercial evaluations to potential investors. Their plan hinged on big money—the kind required for a hostile takeover. The group, with its strong ties to Toronto's establishment, didn't just want to stop Stavro, they wanted to unseat him and take control for themselves. But by the time their campaign kicked into high gear, Stavro would already be sitting in the CEO's office.

Philip Giffin, Donald's intense and cool second son by his first marriage, became the benevolent face on the increasingly unfriendly play being assembled.

Because Philip was a minority shareholder through his family's two-percent stake in the Gardens, the plan was soon known as "Philip and his buddies' play." By this time, his father was preoccupied with his rapidly deteriorating health and knew little, if anything, about his son's plans.

For the next six months, unbeknownst to Stavro, a group of trust and estate lawyers at Borden & Elliot began probing for his soft spots, isolating alleged breaches of trust. But even they soon became divided over the controversial issue of whether you could breach a duty by actually crossing the regulatory lines or whether you just have to be in the position to be able to do it.

"The instinctive reaction of a number of people was that there was something wrong, but they couldn't put their hand on just what it was," explains one of the lawyers. Some argued you needed evidence of wrongdoing, while others argued that all you needed was the so-called "doctrine of temptation."

Borden was one of the latter. He wasn't looking so much for the evidence of what, if any, damage had resulted from Stavro's position of effective control over the value of the estate's assets, because that was almost impossible to assess. He argued that all you had to do was call the Public Trustee's attention to Stavro's managerial positions and the temptations they carried and the Public Trustee would have to intervene to protect the beneficiaries. Up until then the interests of the charities had been lost in all the power plays. They had yet to receive a penny from Ballard's will.

It was easier said than done. Blowing the whistle on Stavro was only the first step in a complicated, self-interested plan, shrouded in secrecy.

In the plan's infancy stage, a group of three lawyers (Lorne Saltman, Larry Wright and Borden) were working on a retainer from Philip Giffin and Thor Eaton. Code-named "Nokin," based on a billboard advertisement outside a New York financier's office, the plan began to expand. Borden was responsible for sussing out a cogent legal argument to carry the plan forward and Philip looked for the deep pockets. In fact, from the outset it was decided that Philip would get a piece of the action, some sweat equity, and all he had to do was find four or five partners to broker a deal. Like father, like son.

There was a deadline focusing their minds: Stavro had to make his move by April 15, 1994, because of his put/call deal with Molson that allowed him to take half of Molson's 20-percent stake.

The legal strategy focused on the conditions under which Stavro had slyly moved into the chairman's seat.

Stavro would have had no conflict if his option had set a fixed price because whatever decisions he made as CEO, he would not influence the value of the asset he was trying to buy. However, because his option does not state a price—it would be determined by two appraisals—Stavro's position in the chairman's seat afforded him the opportunity to materially change the price he would eventually pay for the Gardens' shares. That was a conflict of interest, the thinking went: his role as executor should have been to get a higher price, but as the buyer, he would want to pay as low a price as possible. "It was a breach of his fiduciary duties every time he woke up in the morning and decided whether to drive to the Gardens or Knob Hill Farms," Borden explained.

By Christmas 1991, a legal argument had been crafted. However, the members of the group still hadn't contacted the Public Trustee even though they had isolated six alleged breaches of Stavro's fiduciary duties. Instead, Wright, who was head of the corporate department at Borden & Elliot, put together a takeover plan while Borden took the legal brief to investors. Morgan Guaranty Trust Co. (J.P. Morgan), an investment house based in New York, was hired on February 3, 1992, as its financial adviser. For a one-month retainer of $25,000, J.P. Morgan was instructed to produce an evaluation of Maple Leaf Gardens, a takeover strategy (to be known as the Nokin Opportunity) and a dog-and-pony show initially to be presented to Ronald Joyce, chairman of Tim Horton's.

J.P. Morgan's draft proposal contemplated an outright takeover of the Gardens through a fully financed public tender offer: about $75 million in equity would be raised from a group of four or five investors and an additional $45 million would be debt financed. They anticipated a total tab of between $115 million and $125 million—or between $26.50 a share and $34 a share.

With the report in hand, the younger Giffin, Peter Hunt, a vice-president of the New York-based investment banker, and the trio of lawyers paid a visit to Tim Horton's corporate head offices in Burlington, Ontario.

Back then, Joyce didn't have much of an appetite for the legal entanglements that intertwined the public company with the private holding company. He knew the problems only too well because he was embroiled in a similar family dispute. Tim Horton's widow, Delores, was suing her late husband's company for the 50-percent stake she had sold to Joyce back in 1975. Her husband had founded the coffee and doughnut chain in 1965 and taken on Joyce (who was the first franchisee) as an equal partner the following year. The all-star defenceman died in a fiery automobile crash in 1974, and the following year his wife sold her half of the company to Joyce for $1 million and a tan-coloured Cadillac Eldorado. Seventeen years later, in 1992, Delores Horton claimed that at the time of the sale she had been mentally incompetent, the result of her addiction to alcohol and drugs.* "It would have been wonderful to bring Tim Horton back to the Gardens," Joyce says, "but all I could see was a whole lot of legal infighting."

Joyce was still sincerely interested but needed foolproof assurances. The doughnut company's lawyer was particularly concerned about whether a strategy that relied so heavily on a government agency could ever work, especially a Public Trustee that, until now, had not stepped in to confront Stavro about his moves, let alone banish him from the estate.

The talks never went any further. In fact, the topic of money was never broached, even though Joyce always maintained that he'd have to be part of a team of buyers because he couldn't afford to take the Gardens on his own. "I perceived a lot of problems with it," Joyce recalls. "We didn't want to get involved because of the legal quagmire." They never met again. Three years later, Tim Horton's became a 15-percent owner of the Calgary Flames and Ron Joyce one of the team's alternate governors.

Obviously, shopping around a legal strategy whose success depended almost entirely on a civil servant wasn't going to be nearly enough to attract investors. The only way to hook them was to bring to the table a tangible incentive, namely the 10-percent block of MLGL shares Molson still owned but had not yet committed. It would be the financial security that could provide investors with the flexibility to take a run at the Gardens and recoup any losses in the event of a failed bid.

Philip, Borden and Norman Seagram met on March 20, the same day Donald Giffin succumbed to his illness. Borden, who was in Florida vacationing with his family during the March break, flew back to Toronto for the day. Shortly before their 9:30 A.M. meeting, Borden called Philip's office to let him know he'd arrived, but his secretary informed Borden that the elder Giffin had passed away during the night. Nonetheless, Philip planned to go straight to Borden & Elliot's offices from the undertaker's at the appointed time. The subsequent meeting lasted for the better part of the business day.

Borden hoped to discourage Molson from handing over the

---

* In February 1993, Madam Justice Patricia German ruled that Mrs. Horton had not been mentally incompetent at the time and received fair value for her shares.

second block of its shares to Stavro. He appealed directly to Seagram, who was an old school friend of Borden's from the 1950s when they attended Trinity College School, an all-boys' school in Port Hope, Ontario. Borden had admired Seagram's athletic prowess as an all-star football player. But on this day, Borden would carry the ball to the Molson senior executive, outlining his argument that Stavro was ultimately out to defeat Molson's right of first refusal to acquire all the shares of MLGL. In effect, explained Borden, Stavro was end-running the brewery because Molson's right of first refusal could be exercised only if there was actually a sale of Maple Leaf Gardens shares. Because Molson and Stavro both had a right to purchase the same shares, Borden argued Molson's right to the estate's MLGL shares took precedence over Stavro's. In fact, Borden figured that Stavro merely wanted to buy Molson's shares as a way of taking away the company's right of first refusal. As protection, Borden continued, Stavro also arranged the financing of the estate's affairs in such a way that if there were a default, he could step in and take over the shares without actually having to make a direct offer, which would trigger Molson's right of first refusal.

Norman Seagram agreed to bring Borden's argument to the attention of Molson's corporate lawyers at Osler Hoskin & Harcourt. When the day-long meeting ended, Philip went to the funeral home and Borden flew back to his wife and four sons in Florida.

Meanwhile, the group was also canvassing to enlist the support of the eight charities and foundations named in Ballard's will. Ultimately, the plan called for one of these designated beneficiaries to take the legal case to the Public Trustee, who would be responsible for their interests. But the charities were not keen on the idea. They don't like battles, at least not the public kind. There's nothing worse than a beggar looking choosy. It's better to turn the other cheek. "They just didn't want to initiate through the Public Trustee a contentious legal battle with Stavro. They were worried as to what he could do to their longer-term interests if they were to complain about him," said a strategist. After all, the charities were only discretionary beneficiaries. Stavro could simply cut them out.

Instead, they compromised. In August 1992 the chairmen of the Princess Margaret and Wellesley hospitals wrote a joint private letter to Stavro—not the Public Trustee—enquiring about the status of their positions under Ballard's will. At least that was more than the senior Giffin, Bill Ballard and Thor Eaton had been able to get the beneficiaries to do the previous year. The charities were supposed to be receiving an annual income from the estate's MLGL shares, which should have been transferred to the Harold E. Ballard Trust shortly after his death. However, the letter received no reply and that stony silence only increased the charities' paranoia.

Still, the Nokin team was pressing the hospitals to get their own legal opinions about whether or not Ballard's executors had breached their duties. At the very least, given that they were getting no response from Stavro, the charities had justifiable concerns.

In the fall of 1992, a year after they first hatched their plan, Philip and the boys weren't any closer to unseating Stavro and real-izing their dream of owning the Gardens. Their frustration contin-ued to mount in the early months of 1993.

It was around this time that the three lawyers from Borden & Elliot started hearing complaints about their deadbeat case. By then, the three lawyers were spending an inordinate amount of time on their little conspiracy that some said had questionable legal merit and, worse, wasn't bringing any money into the firm. Lawyers are generally obsessed with billable hours. In fact, their standing within the firm depends inexorably on their ability to gen-erate profligate paper and bring in cash.

Indeed, hell hath no fury like a law firm without receivables. And since the trio wasn't generating much of those, their reputations within the firm were beginning to suffer. With their commitment increasingly viewed as a boondoggle, it wasn't long before Nokin became known as project "No-Can-Do." And soon their relations with each other and their colleagues inside Borden & Elliot began to deteriorate badly.

But the project received its death blow from outside the legal firm's halls. At an early February 1993 meeting a few floors down in the Molson offices, Larry Wright, Philip Giffin and Eaton were told that Molson wouldn't commit its remaining 10-percent hold-ings to the group. Mickey Cohen and Barry Joslin (a senior vice-president at Molson who'd replaced Ezrin as Cohen's new right-hand man after Ezrin left the company in the summer of 1992) explained that they had an informal obligation to Stavro. Cohen claimed that handing over the shares to a competing interest would be destructive to his company's relationship with the new boss at the Gardens.

It was a stunning blow to Philip, whose father for years had been a close friend of Cohen's and a staunch ally of Molson.

"It was so sensitive then. Stavro put some pressure on. Stavro was aware that Molson was interested in disposing of their discretionary block but there was someone interested in acquiring it. So there was pressure from Stavro," one of those who attended the meeting said. "Mickey Cohen wouldn't tell what it [the reason] was, just that he couldn't do it."

Cohen also went on to explain that he wasn't confident himself that he would be backing a winner if he did assign Nokin the block. Essentially, Cohen wasn't convinced that Stavro's option would be set aside by the courts. He saw the reluctance of the beneficiaries to prod the Public Trustee into action, and even if they succeeded, he wasn't convinced the public guardian would prevail.

Not surprisingly, Cohen was hedging his bets, like everyone else. "He didn't have the confidence that anybody could dislodge Stavro and it would not be in Molson's interest to be backing a loser in a contest against Stavro," says someone who attended the meeting.

A senior executive at Molson sums it up this way: "We were coming from the position that we wanted to stay neutral. We were very meticulous in making sure we didn't take sides. Our motivation was strictly defensive. We wanted to make sure we protected our hockey network."

(At the time, Cohen didn't tell his visitors about a brief conversation he'd had with Stavro a few months earlier at the Royal Winter Fair. Stavro had reiterated his interest in Molson's remaining 10 percent, and Cohen admitted that he had people who were interested in acquiring that 10-percent block. Stavro merely reminded Cohen that they were partners.)

Cohen's decision was the death knell for the eighteen-month Nokin project, just as the group had made some headway with Lyman MacInnis, who had agreed to use his vast network to drum up potential investors for the plan. That Molson block represented the protection potential investors needed against any risk by giving them a way to recoup their money in the event of a successful competing bid. Now the one crucial building block the group needed was not available.

"Anybody that was looking at it saw an enormous battle with Stavro—a real tough street fighter—and a lot of legal costs. This man is holding an option and he is the CEO. We're in for a brutal fight," said Borden. "It was too big a battle to entice people to put up capital unless that could be covered and the risk of those costs eliminated. And the only way to offset that cost liability was by holding that discretionary block. Otherwise they were not prepared to assume the risk."

Still, Philip Giffin and Borden continued beating the bushes through the spring and summer of 1993, even though it was clear that bringing together a pool of players without Molson was highly unlikely. Even the timing seemed inopportune. With the Leafs in the Stanley Cup semi-finals—a feat they hadn't accomplished in more than twenty years—the public, more specifically hockey fans, would view a hostile takeover in a much worse light, given the continuing progress Stavro and his management team appeared to be making in rebuilding the company, particularly the hockey team. Although these measures actually did very little to enhance share value, Stavro was winning big in the court of public opinion.

So how could the Public Trustee quibble when the executors were saying they wanted to rebuild the company and add more value for the beneficiaries before selling it?

Thus, the Nokin group concluded that without any recourse or way to recoup their losses in the event of a blood bath, and an unco-operative Public Trustee, they had no other option but to walk away. And with no investors, there was no client for Borden & Elliot to represent.

Deeply disappointed, the firm pulled the plug. And although Borden & Elliot packed away in storage the files on the controversial deal, the lawyers who worked on the case continued to harbour a burning interest not to let all that time and effort go to waste. For now, though, they would sit on the shelf.

By the end of August 1993, Larry Wright had left the firm to take a position as a senior executive at a Markham, Ontario–based high-tech company; his departure was followed shortly after by

Lorne Saltman who crossed the street to Cassels, Brock & Blackwell.

In September, Borden wrote a letter to Philip Giffin making it official: it was the end of the road for Nokin and for Borden, who was leaving the law firm his uncle Henry Borden co-founded in 1936.

While the Nokin conspiracy lost its momentum, Ballard's executors received an unsolicited offer from another, less hostile suitor. In March 1993, Glen Day, a vice-president in corporate finance with brokerage firm Midland Walwyn Inc., called McKellar enquiring about the estate's block of MLGL shares. Day had read about the Court of Appeal's decision ordering an end to the long, twisting Michael Gobuty saga by forcing the estate to pay National Bank. The broker figured that with debts mounting, the executors might be receptive to the idea of selling. Maybe, he thought, his firm could get a piece of the action. He told McKellar that he could get a group together, including offshore investors, who might be interested in buying the estate's holdings. However, McKellar was instructed to inform Day that "the executors [were] not now interested in selling."

By this time, Tony Van Alphen, a business reporter at the *Toronto Star*, had written two letters asking pointed—if not leading—questions about the administration of the Ballard estate. In his letters, the reporter specifically asked acting Public Trustee Susan Himel and Attorney General Marion Boyd to investigate Stavro's conduct since obtaining his option on the estate's property. (Hugh Paisley had been reassigned to the Ontario Native Affairs Secretariat.)

In her response to the letters, Himel reiterated what the Court of Appeal had decided in 1991: "the executors will be answerable for encumbering shares at such time as the right of first refusal is, if ever, exercised." She continued, "The management of the estate's finances by the executors will be reviewed by the court on a passing of the estate's accounts." In other words, Himel was assuming two things: that Stavro would in fact go before a judge, and that once all the paperwork had been processed, her office would look more closely at assessing any damages.

That policy was reiterated by the Attorney General in her response to the reporter's entreaty. "Since this estate will come before the court again, I am not able to comment on the matter specifically." Boyd and Himel explained that they'd take no action until the administration of the Ballard estate was complete and the necessary paperwork was filed with the court (known as a passing of accounts). And after that, if there was conduct on the part of the executors that was damaging to the interests of the beneficiaries, then those executors would be personally accountable for whatever that loss was. This, even though the executors hadn't processed the accounts of the Ballard committee for the Public Trustee's Office and the Surrogate court to approve, which is required by law.

All the while, the government agencies assumed that it was either Bill Ballard who initiated the letters or one of the NBA franchise applicants who wanted to use the Public Trustee to damage the community image of Stavro in the eyes of David Stern, the commissioner of the National Basketball Association. In the fall of 1993, there were a number of consortiums that had assembled bids to win the NBA's expansion franchise in Toronto. Among those was the Palestra Group, headed by Stavro's good friend Lawrence Tanenbaum, president and controller of a private holding company called Kilmer Van Nostrand Co. Ltd., which controlled the Warren Paving and Materials Group (a steel and construction company) and a stake in CUC Broadcasting Ltd. Stavro, who knew Tanenbaum's father, Max, the founder of Warren Paving, was linked to Tanenbaum's application, which included a proposal to build a new joint hockey and basketball arena. The Bitove family, which had businesses in food services, also had tabled a bid, as had Bill Ballard and Michael Cohl.

Perry Borden couldn't believe Boyd's and Himel's replies to Van Alphen. Waiting until after the event was, in law, "an absolutely stunning position." By then, he argued, the horse would be out of the barn and the ensuing lengthy and costly court battle would be tantamount to closing the barn door. How could you prove what losses had actually been incurred? "It's not what he does, it's the fact that he's in a position to do it." That was when the so-called doctrine of temptation kicked in.

How much more evidence did the Public Trustee need? he

asked. Look at the put/call deal with Molson. It was in Stavro's interest to ensure the value of the shares stayed low for the time that they were put to him by Molson or he decided to buy them on his own volition.

What about his role as chairman of Maple Leaf Gardens? By virtue of that position, he would cast the deciding vote in the event of a tie at the board level, but also got to set the agenda of board meetings. (In fact, the company's by-laws had been amended in 1992, folding the CEO's functions into the office of the chairman.)

Stavro was expressly ignoring the terms of his own option agreement, which stated all three executors would withdraw from management of the company. Instead, he was now sitting as chairman and chief executive in full control of the value of the asset optioned to him at market value. It was a position that appeared to violate the terms in the option agreement that were intended to protect the estate and its hapless beneficiaries.

The Nokin file may have been officially closed but it did not break the trio's resolve to resuscitate the proposal at a later date. By now, Borden had his own practice while Saltman was the new kid on the block at Cassels, Brock. The next prong in their strategy was to find the kind of investor who had the resolve—and the resources—to take on what looked like a nasty fight.

During a dinner at the Toronto Club on December 1, 1993, hosted by Cassels, Brock for U.S. ambassador James Blanchard, Lorne Saltman pulled up a chair next to John Bitove Sr. The wily sixty-eight-year-old was the driving force behind the private family food-services company that caters to Pearson airport, SkyDome and hospitals in Toronto and that had just been awarded the NBA franchise for $125 million (U.S.). The son of Macedonian immigrants, Bitove Sr. parlayed the small coffee shop he opened in Toronto in 1949 (called the Java Shoppe) into a multi-million-dollar operation that today owns all of the Hard Rock Café franchises in Canada and Wayne Gretzky's eatery in Toronto. While his five children (four sons and a daughter) operate the day-to-day activities of the company, Bitove Sr. is politically active. He's what they call a backroom guy, a bagman who boasts friendships with former prime minister Brian Mulroney, Tory senator Trevor Eyton (chairman of Brascan Ltd.) and former Liberal Ontario premier David

Peterson. Two other things distinguish Bitove Sr.: he wears an Order of Canada pin (bestowed on him in 1989), and he grew up with a rivalry with his first cousin, Steve Stavro.

During the dinner, Saltman and the client talked generally about project Nokin. The elder businessman expressed concern that Stavro was a "very unique person" and "very determined." For years, there'd been whispers of bad Macedonian blood between the two families but nothing that anyone could ever prove. Still, Bitove Sr. assured the young lawyer that he had a good rapport with Mickey Cohen, adding, "We think we know enough to be able to do the deal; that we can convince Molson."

A few days later, Saltman stopped by David Peterson's office. The former Ontario premier was now chairman of the board of the Toronto Raptors Basketball club, and a colleague of Saltman at the law firm. Saltman told Peterson about his brief chat with Bitove Sr., at which point Peterson weighed in with the fact that he too had a cordial relationship with Cohen, the result of shared directorships on various boards. Not only that, Peterson was still being paid as one of the three trustees who were supposed to be babysitting the brewery's Maple Leaf Gardens shares.

The two lawyers agreed to arrange an exploratory meeting early in the new year.

In the meantime, Peterson had a scheduled appointment at Maple Leaf Gardens with Fletcher, Stavro, Crump, Bellmore and Allan Slaight, the Raptors vice-chairman and CEO of Standard Broadcasting Corp. Ltd. The purpose of the meeting was to discuss architectural drawings and financial analyses sent over by Murray Beynon, an architect from Stadium Consultants International. Since the Palestra Group had lost the bid, the Raptors organization thought Stavro might consider them as a partner to build a joint-use facility. Although the Raptors' winning bid included building a 22,500-seat basketball-only arena next to the Eaton Centre, they approached Fletcher that fall soon after they sealed the franchise. They'd heard rumours that Stavro might be looking for a partner to help finance a bid to take over Maple Leaf Gardens. Although Stavro prefers not to take on partners, the word on the street was that he had approached Labatt twice already. Fletcher suggested a meeting to open up the lines of communication with Stavro.

The folks at Labatt told Ballard they suspected that Stavro's overtures were linked to a falling-out between him and Molson, mostly aggravated by Stavro's connection to the Palestra Group bid, which included backing from the Canadian Imperial Bank of Commerce and arch-enemy Labatt.

Ever the opportunist, Bill Ballard used this information to his own advantage. Bill and his partner, Cohl, had already received approval to build a concert theatre/arena at Exhibition Place, which had been the cornerstone of their bid to the NBA. Indeed, Bill was thinking that maybe he and Steve could do a little business. He arranged to make a presentation to the Gardens board on November 16. His proposal would see the Leafs play at a combined concert hall/hockey arena at Exhibition Place.

The plan looked like it had legs: Bill had $80 million already secured (courtesy of the funds he'd scrounged for his failed bid), plus the green light from Toronto City Council to develop the CNE lands. But Bill never heard back from Stavro.

And Stavro later cancelled the meeting with Peterson and Slaight.

Meanwhile, Philip Giffin and Borden were still plugging away, sensing that new economic forces had been unleashed as a result of the Palestra Group's failed bid. If Bill Ballard was looking viable— and he was, given that he was flush with cash—then he'd be the perfect partner; the deep pockets Philip Giffin had been looking for all along.

Talk about history repeating itself. Philip was still scrambling to get a piece of the action. Not by putting up his own money, but by brokering a deal and delivering those elusive Molson shares, just as his father had done with Bill's dad.

Back he went to Molson's head office, making an impassioned plea to Barry Joslin that he was Molson's "saviour" and the brewery "owed something to his father."

By the end of 1993, it looked as if Giffin's son would team up with Ballard's eldest son to take a run at the Gardens. But Bill Ballard didn't know it at the time. He was led to believe by Borden and Thor Eaton that he was teaming up with super heavyweights Galen Weston, of grocery fame, or former newspaper mogul Kenneth Thomson.

Peterson kept his promise to Saltman and by late January 1994, he delivered John Bitove Sr. and his son John Jr. for a meeting at Cassels, Brock. During the meeting on the twenty-first floor of Scotia Plaza, Peterson introduced the senior Bitove to Saltman and Borden as "my adopted father."

They talked mostly about the underlying legal strategy and how that could be the foundation on which to build their competitive bid. Perry Borden whipped into his well-worn speech about how the law, if argued properly, would force a public auction, and the Bitoves could enter the fray, taking advantage of the Public Trustee's desire to create a bidding war to benefit the charities. But Borden didn't tell them whom he was representing. In fact, the Raptors group were left with the impression that Borden was trying to solicit their business.

Meanwhile, Bill Ballard was pressing Borden about the identity of the investor he was representing. But he'd been left cooling his heels on the sidelines for too long and finally bowed out of the race on January 31. Remarkably, Giffin's hopes were now tied to Stavro's cousins.

A few days later, Peterson took a ride up the elevator in Scotia Plaza to pay another visit to Mickey Cohen. Without ever mentioning price, the two men talked for roughly an hour about what Cohen intended to do with the remaining shares. Like everyone else before him, Peterson came away empty-handed.

"I guess the view was they were tied up somehow or other," Peterson explains of Cohen's position. "There were commercial arrangements between Molson's and Maple Leaf Gardens, as I understand it, and I guess he valued that relationship."

"Molson's concern was to make sure that it didn't fall into unfriendly hands," explained a senior executive. "If you're going to back someone, you'd better be damn sure they're going to win. From our perspective, if we do this deal with Stavro, we can be sure that it doesn't fall into unfriendly hands."

Undeterred, the Raptors' board of directors met a month later with Perry Borden. The roll call included Borden Osmak, the senior vice-president from the Bank of Nova Scotia responsible for the bank's $12-million equity investment in the Raptors (he made it well known even before the meeting started that he was reluctant to get involved in this kind of play); father and son Bitove; David

Kassie from CIBC Wood Gundy, who would act as the financial advisers (and underwriters); Phil Granovsky, co-founder of Atlantic Packaging Products Ltd. (by telephone); Allan Slaight, who had an equity position of $44 million in the Raptors (making him an equal shareholder with the Bitoves).

The meeting lasted a little over an hour. For the umpteenth time, Borden and Saltman reiterated their plan—outlining the legal arguments, the alleged breaches of trust and the commercial requirements to take it forward. When they were done, they retreated to Saltman's office where they waited forty-five minutes before David Peterson returned to give the proposal the thumbs down.

The risk was too high and they didn't think it could be done without a long, drawn-out fight, and worse, they were not convinced the Public Trustee would get on side. There simply was no assurance of success. Besides, "We hadn't done it to date," Peterson explained, "and there was no evidence that it would occur in the future." Hugely disappointed, Borden and Giffin called it quits on their plan for good. The Giffin family sold their 60,000 shares, invoking closure on their dream of one day owning the Gardens. By the fall of 1993, Stavro saw nothing but open field as he planned his final assault on the Leafs and the Carlton Street cash box.

CHAPTER NINE

The Carlton Street Cash Box

"Everybody is dreaming." – STEVE STAVRO

JIM DEVELLANO WAS ONE of Harold Ballard's happy "little guys" for almost twenty years. He was a certificate-carrying member of the paying public that really mattered most to Harold, the company's shareholders. Season's tickets had been in Devellano's family for more than thirty years. These poor fans had endured over a quarter-century of some of the worst teams in the National Hockey League and watched ticket prices increase disproportionately to the team's on-ice performance.

In Ballard's day, dividends to shareholders (of which he was the biggest) were far more consistent than victories ever were for the fans. Say what you will, Ballard knew how to run a business where the bottom line was the only score that counted.

There were no underachievers in Ballard's personal playground. The crafty king of Carlton Street pinched pennies by severely underpaying the building staff and hockey talent. But he did cash in on the team's long tradition and the convenience of operating in the country's largest and most lucrative market; advertisers couldn't stay away from the most fabled arena in Canada.

As the revenues kept pouring into the yellow brick box, dividends flowed out, the one constant during his reign at the Gardens—a few cents every business quarter, of which he enjoyed the greater spoils.

That was what Devellano bought into in 1976. At the time, he was earning the princely salary of $9,000 a year as a scout for the New York Islanders. Devellano, a Toronto native, required little incentive to buy a piece of the shrine. He purchased his first twenty-five shares in Maple Leaf Gardens for $4 each.

"I could see in the annual report that it was a debt-free building, that revenues constantly went up." So much so that by 1994, a major portion of his life savings were invested in the company. He owned 32,375 shares in all—most of it thanks to the five-for-one split of the common shares in late 1986, when Devellano already owned five thousand. That split transformed Devellano into a potential heavyweight with a sizeable twenty-five thousand shares. (That same split helped Steve Stavro parlay his hundred shares into the five hundred he later flipped to his wife, Sally, at the time he took over the company.)

Devellano continued buying stock as long as the dividends kept flowing his way. By the time Stavro made his offer to all the outstanding shareholders in 1994, Jimmy D. was sitting there with the second-most share certificates—after his friend Harry Ornest.

And it hadn't been easy amassing this stockpile. Devellano had endured temptation and pressure along the way. NHL president John Ziegler had written to him in the late 1980s about his holdings, asking Devellano to stop buying Maple Leaf Gardens shares because he was affiliated with another NHL team. By this time, Devellano had become a senior management executive with the Detroit Red Wings and Molson had just fessed up to its secret slice of Maple Leaf Gardens. The league was frowning on both accounts, and Ziegler, ever conscious of what the other American governors were saying, didn't want another problem festering in Joe Louis Arena.

Still, like so many NHL executives, Devellano took no notice of Ziegler's complaint because in his mind, there wasn't any cause for concern. Jimmy D. had always been a passive investor; in fact, he'd only attended two annual shareholders' meetings. In any event, his boss, Mike Ilitch, was fully aware of his stake in the Leafs—and if it was all right with the guy who signed his paycheque, then the rest could live with it too.

Around the same time as Ziegler's half-hearted complaints, Devellano received a surprising offer from Harold Ballard. It was during the governors' annual meeting in Palm Beach in December 1988 when the ailing owner of the Maple Leafs offered him $42 a share for his holdings. Ballard was becoming increasingly paranoid about Molson and Labatt, who he was convinced were duelling each other to snatch the company from under his nose. At the time, Ballard had negotiated a loan with Molson to buy out Mary Elizabeth's HEBL shares. Devellano's stock would help cement Ballard's control of the company.

Devellano refused the offer. He wanted $50 apiece but the stingy Ballard, no matter how desperate, wouldn't budge. That price was the same number the perennial bachelor went looking to get from Stavro or anyone else who wanted to buy his shares.

"Fifty dollars is the magic number. I always thought that was what it was worth," Devellano quips, admitting sheepishly that he'd been looking to sell ever since Ballard's overture at the Breakers' Hotel during dinner with Yolanda.

But he hung on in anticipation of breaking the $50 barrier. With Ballard soon out of the picture, the musings coming out of the Gardens were that Stavro and company were going to put the place on a sound business footing. "We, as a board, are committed to give our Leaf fans the best possible on-ice product, and committed to our Gardens' shareholders to operate in their best long-term interest," Stavro said in the 1993–94 Leaf media guide. "And I find those goals dovetail perfectly because the better the team does, the better it is for the shareholders."

Sounded good, at least on paper.

Under the new regime, dividends increased. In early 1991, the company doubled quarterly dividends to twenty cents, up from the ten cents it had been paying since 1987. And the post-Ballard Gardens even paid out a special dividend of $2.75 a share four months after his death.

The problem was that the stock price headed south. When Ballard died, the pent-up anticipation of a sell-off shot the trading value on the Toronto Stock Exchange up to $44.25. But three years later, it had dropped 42 percent to the mid-$20 range—and worse, it stayed there.

Devellano blames Stavro for the stock's lethargic state, accusing him of deliberately depressing the value of the shares. In 1995,

Maple Leaf Gardens posted a net loss of just over a million dollars for the first time in its history, due largely to a 104-day player lockout that started in the fall of 1994 and cut the hockey season in half. Naturally, dividends were also cut—another first for the company.

This, he complains, even though the company had $17.4 million in retained earnings. But what about the era of inflating players' salaries; wouldn't it be prudent to stash some money in reserve in the hopes of building a better team with quality players?

"If a company is a public company, you also have to be concerned with the people that own that company," explained the Red Wings' vice-president. "And the people that own that company, small shareholders, have a right to some profit, to some income. It was not a privately held company."

And therein lies the paradox that has always been the Carlton Street cash box.

Maple Leaf Gardens is Ballard's multi-million-dollar legacy; an entertainment business that employs about 150 people full time. It derives all of its operating revenue—about $67 million a year—from the arena and the ownership of the hockey club. Revenues are generated from admission fees; the sale of broadcast, promotional and advertising rights; food and beverage concessions; and souvenirs. Players' salaries, which total about $34 million, account for more than half of the company's total operating expenses.

Broadcast rights for television and radio are the two items that have always lined the company's coffers, even though, in hindsight, those rights were grossly undervalued for years.

Molson Breweries, which, as we've seen, has juggled many positions in the life of the Gardens as banker, shareholder and corporate supplier, owns the national network rights to "Hockey Night in Canada" as a result of its deal with the league, which controls the rights to broadcast two games nationally a week in Canada. The brewery paid about $55 million (U.S.) in 1994 for a four-year deal to broadcast the Saturday night game, featuring at least one Canadian team, preferably the Leafs, in the roster. (Despite what NHL commissioner Gary Bettman says, the large audiences are still in Canada.) The money is then split equally among all twenty-six teams, which means the Leafs get only a fraction even though they are the dominant draw. Maple Leaf Gardens also collected $950,000 in 1995, thanks to the television deal NHL head office in New York inked with the Fox cable network to broadcast games in the United States.

In Canada, the Toronto Maple Leafs and the Montreal Canadiens command the highest premiums because, as perennial fan favourites, they can deliver more male beer-drinking viewers than any other teams. In the case of the Leafs, the local broadcast rights were the source of much angst in the months following Ballard's death. There were plenty of hints coming out of the Gardens that strongly suggested they would be worth much more. In fact, the company had previously issued a press release saying as much. All the while the insiders knew that the Mellanby report had predicted a huge windfall in broadcast revenues. Word on the street was the new post-Ballard management team would capitalize to its fullest on the potential of the national treasure.

"Anybody with hockey experience could have done a better job than Harold Ballard," figured Harry Ornest. He bet his own money on that happening. So he began buying Gardens shares for the first time seven weeks after Ballard's death. On May 31, 1990, Harry purchased one thousand shares at $31 apiece. By the time he stopped in February 1994, he was the single largest public shareholder in the company with 130,640 shares, worth $4.45 million at market value. Ornest was ready for the auction—and the bidding war that he was sure would follow.

Ornest wasn't one of those who thought Stavro's option would depress share value. In fact, he bought all but 24,300 of his own shares after Stavro secured his option on all the MLGL shares held directly and indirectly by Ballard's estate. If Stavro was going to take a shot at the Gardens, Harry figured he couldn't afford to take it alone. There would be room for a few players on Stavro's team.

Ornest first broached the idea when he was in Toronto for a few days for the Rothmans horse race at Woodbine Race Track in October 1992. Stavro had invited Ornest, along with Ted Kennedy, a former Leaf captain, to watch the team play the Chicago Blackhawks. During the first intermission, the group retreated to the Directors' Lounge, where Sally Stavro and Ruth Ornest chatted while the men talked business.

"I want to buy some shares, Steve," Ornest recalls saying. "When are you going to sell me some shares? How do I buy some shares, Steve?"

A man of few words who plays his cards close to the vest, Stavro's reply was curt: "Leave it with me. I'll keep you posted, Harry. Don't worry about it."

In hindsight, Harry says, "It was a stock answer and I accepted it." He tried again the following year at the Breeders' Cup in Santa Anita, California, again to no avail.

Harold Ballard had always intended that his company was to be sold and the proceeds from the sale were to be doled out to charities. That was a given. The big question for the executors was deciding when to effect that sale. For two years following Ballard's death, the official reason for not putting the estate's controlling shares on the auction block was that the trustees wanted to build up the value of the company before actually turning it over. This, even though there was never any doubt that the estate's shares were destined to go to Stavro because of his option.

But that line of thinking changed by the middle of 1992. Donald Crump began advocating the opposite.

Crump left the CFL with a year remaining on his three-year contract to return to his full-time position as Gardens secretary-treasurer—at an annual salary of $250,000 a year plus benefits—in July 1992. The estate's deficit position was suddenly worsening and that raised two problems: first, Crump and his co-executors could be liable for any shortfall, and second, Ballard's beneficiaries would get nothing.

First, he assembled a financial analysis, listing the estate's current liabilities: $3.5 million to the National Bank of Canada to cover the Michael Gobuty fiasco, courtesy of a court order; Yolanda's claim for $500,000 a year or $10-million lump sum; about $4 million in taxes owed to Revenue Canada; and up to $43 million in loans to the Toronto Dominion Bank. The estate's shares at the time were worth roughly $12 million.

"Crump was telling us, 'Look guys, you have to have a sale sometime soon,'" recalls estate lawyer John McKellar of an executors' meeting in his office in November 1992. "You can't afford to do anything else."

During that meeting, the group decided to commission two independent evaluators to "attack the situation," because if they eventually did sell—and they had not yet made that decision, he says—they were required by law to satisfy Ballard's will.

At the time, McKellar says he didn't know if Stavro, who attended the meeting, was interested in buying the shares through his option. Even so, the executors and their lawyer knew two things: that the estate had signed a deal to sell the Gardens to Stavro by 1996 and that Stavro had a put/call arrangement with Molson that expired on April 15, 1994.

True to his character, Stavro wasn't betraying much verbally, although he did agree to personally pay for half the costs of the appraisals—which totalled about $500,000. He really didn't have to say anything; the paper trail of deals did the talking for him.

Despite repeated equivocations from Brian Bellmore, Stavro was ready to make his move. And Crump would be the first to know.

On Friday, January 4, 1993, Crump received a call at his Gardens office from Stavro, asking him to drop by Teddington Park the next day. Ever dutiful, Crump was at Stavro's place by 7 A.M. on Saturday morning and the two men took a drive out to Stavro's 100-acre farm south of Peterborough.

"We talked about the weather, horses and all kinds of things," Crump says of the two-hour drive. "We didn't talk about the interest in the Gardens probably until we were out there. He said, 'I was giving it some thought that I would be interested in [exercising] the option.'" Stavro says he told his co-executor that he was interested in buying provided "I see what the shares are worth." After all, he says, "I couldn't very well decide to buy the company and then see what the shares are worth."

On February 12, Crump, Stavro, Terence Kelly, the sports buff and Oshawa criminal lawyer who had replaced the late Donald Giffin as executor in March 1992, and McKellar met to consider what was listed on the agenda as a "special matter." Kelly was a tireless fundraiser whose relationship with Harold Ballard dated back to the 1960s, when the Leaf owner helped raise money for charity by bringing the team to practise in Oshawa, Ontario (Kelly's hometown), once a year. Kelly, who spent as much as $20,000 a year travelling around the world to sporting events, testified as a character witness on Harold's behalf during his trial for tax evasion in 1971. A classic Irish charmer, Kelly describes himself as "the only person who has left Don Cherry at a loss for words." (Kelly joined the board of Maple Leaf Gardens in 1991 when Stavro cleaned house but the Public Trustee, Hugh Paisley, didn't support his nomination as Giffin's replacement to the estate. Paisley wanted Harold's daughter, Mary Elizabeth; but Stavro prevailed, arguing that Kelly, the ultimate shmoozer, would be good for the fans.)

At the meeting, the three executors and their lawyer discussed formally evaluating the estate's shares "so that proper future decisions could be made." They agreed to retain Burns Fry Ltd. and RBC Dominion Securities Inc., two of the country's largest and most venerable brokerage houses, to evaluate the estate's holdings.

Both firms made a pitch before all three executors in March 1993. Robert Bellamy, then vice-chairman and a director at Burns Fry, came in for a presentation while his counterpart at RBC DS, George Dembroski, sent a letter. Bellamy was already familiar with the Gardens, having written the so-called comfort letter that helped persuade Crump and Matheson to accept Stavro's offer to pay off Molson and keep the shares within the estate in early 1991.

Back then, Bellamy had said that it was difficult to evaluate the estate's holdings and that the only real way to enhance the value of MLGL shares was to put them out for public tender. Even Crump a few months earlier had said under oath that "there [was] no clear-cut way to value" the company "at any given time really." Two years later, Crump would become directly involved with efforts to value Maple Leaf Gardens.

With that meeting, the wheels were set in motion.

The Gardens board of directors was told about the pending evaluations on March 30, but they were not informed about Glen Day's enquiry. A code of silence descended on the place; Crump and Gardens lawyer Matheson became the designated point men, providing information to the evaluators, who were officially retained by the third week of April. In the spirit of silence, the firms began adopting code names for their respective reviews.

Ultimately, Burns Fry would call theirs "Project Slapshot," while RBC would use the rather cerebral, if not ironic, moniker, "Project Trust."

Neither firm ever had access to senior management officials at the Gardens, most notably company president Cliff Fletcher. Instead, Crump played messenger, providing the brokerage firms—who were unaware of each other's work—with detailed five-year financial projections based on pro forma cash flow statements he'd assembled.

"I think we said to them, 'What we want you to have is free rein,'" explains McKellar. "Are you happy with the arrangements through Don? 'Yes.' Are you satisfied that is the one way you are going to get the full information? 'Yes.' I can't remember what they said at the time, but it was something like, 'we might have to qualify our report by saying we only talked to Don.' And we said, that's fine, you have to say what you have to say."

RBC DS would not only put that on the public record, the brokerage firm would go further in its final report, indicating that requests were made to speak to other company officials apart from Crump but were repeatedly denied. (However, later a securities regulator said the brokerage houses were "willfully blind" for accepting those unusually restrictive conditions to produce evaluations that would be used to make an offer to public shareholders.)

"We didn't want all kinds of rumours going around that there's going to be a sale," explains David Matheson. His concern, as lawyer for the Gardens, was securities regulations that would require the company to publicly disclose the fact that it was being put in play.

Although Stavro bowed out of the estate's formal dealings with the investment firms, he did attend meetings in May 1993 when the brokers gave updates on their progress. So did his lawyer, Brian Bellmore. In fact, Bellmore was actively involved in helping the estate's lawyer John McKellar determine the terms under which the brokerage houses would produce their appraisals.

By the end of June, Burns Fry and RBC DS had completed preliminary reviews, pegging the value of Maple Leaf Gardens at between $100 million and $125 million. The estate's control block was valued at between $60.3 million and $75.3 million, given a price range of $27 to $34 a share, which also included a premium for the estate's control block.

As well, both brokerage firms unequivocally concluded that the share price would increase if the company either built a new arena on its own or joined forces with the future NBA basketball franchise to build one, or if a strategic buyer, say someone such as Stavro, decided to buy the shares.

However, the appraisers were never allowed to delve into those possibilities because the estate gave them strict instructions to limit their reviews based on the existing, debt-free building. This, even though at the time Stavro had allied himself to Larry Tanenbaum's Palestra Group bid for Toronto's NBA basketball franchise, which included building a new joint arena.

Perhaps more significant was that the cash flow formulas used by the appraisers factored in only modest growth in advertising and broadcast revenues of about 2 to 6 percent even after the anticipated signing of a new television contract with Molson for the 1995 season. The Mellanby report, at the very least, could have told them that MLGL's broadcast revenues should triple once a new deal was signed. But Burns Fry and RBC didn't receive the Mellanby report because, astonishingly, it wasn't included in the materials Crump passed along.

When asked about all this later by the Public Trustee's lawyer, Frank Newbould, Stavro begged off. "Mr. McKellar and the group looked after it. I didn't get involved with any of the details of it," he said, later adding, "That was a very good price, the estimate to the estate.... Everybody is dreaming."

With the evaluations in hand, Stavro was now ready to shop around for his equity partners.

On September 13, 1993, Stavro and Bellmore visited senior officials at Nesbitt Thomson Inc., in the Sun Life Tower in downtown Toronto. Nesbitt was the brokerage house owned by the Bank of Montreal, which is Knob Hill Farms' banker. (Nesbitt merged with Burns Fry the following year.) The men talked about Stavro's interest in buying not only the MLGL shares in the estate, but all of the outstanding shares in the company.

The objective of this preliminary meeting was to give the brokerage house information to devise a financing strategy for Stavro's takeover. Nesbitt code-named its plan "Project Stanley."

According to notes from the meeting, Nesbitt officials were told about the appraisals being assembled by their colleagues on Bay Street and that their preliminary estimate of the total acquisition cost was a maximum of $125 million. In his notes, a broker wrote that Steve thought the shares were worth $25 to $26 apiece and that he "would want to do" at that price. However, the price tag of $125 million Bellmore and Stavro were shopping around was the equivalent of $34 a share.

According to the notes, Stavro informed Nesbitt that the Gardens' television revenues could increase as much as 300 percent in 1995. The brokerage firm was also tipped to the fact that other outstanding matters—read Yolanda—might be resolved soon.

Stavro and Bellmore met again with Nesbitt ten days later, this time at the Bank of Montreal's corporate head offices in First Canadian Place. In the mezzanine-level conference room, they were joined by representatives from the bank.

During the meeting, "Silverbirch" (the code name for Stavro) and his lawyer were walked through a twenty-page presentation. Ultimately, Nesbitt didn't advise that Stavro go the public route. Instead, the brokerage firm suggested a financing strategy that would see Stavro put up $40 million; another $50 million would be raised through debt financing, either as a private placement (which is the sale of securities privately to a limited number of sophisticated investors) or other sources, such as an equity partner. Nesbitt even provided a list of the kinds of players who would be chomping at the bit to get in on this play.

Stavro's camp targeted the deep pockets of the largest institutional investor in Canada. And he dispatched one of his most trusted advisers to extend the invitation.

Christopher Dundas had been pitching possible financing scenarios with Bellmore and Stavro since the spring. An MBA from the University of California (Berkeley), Dundas specialized in corporate and real estate financings. Dundas, a partner at Murray & Co., a Toronto-based investment banking firm, was given the nod in September to make the call to his contact at the giant Ontario Teachers' Pension Plan Board just after Nesbitt tabled its blueprint.

Dundas floated a trial balloon to Michael Lay, a portfolio

manager in the pension fund's hyperactive—and highly success-ful—merchant banking division. Released from rigid investment limits set by the province, the $40-billion fund (which manages pensions for 200,000 Ontario teachers) is the largest single invested pension fund in Canada. It had been moving aggressively into acquisition financing, with a hefty $677 million worth of invest-ments in Canadian companies.

"Conceptually, would you look at a participation with Steve Stavro in potentially putting together a bid on the Leafs?" Dundas asked. He was cautious even though Ontario Teachers, a formida-ble player in the Canadian financial markets, had a good reputation for confidentiality. And Dundas knew the pension fund had shown a penchant for certain kinds of entertainment companies. But Lay was hard to figure out; he never got too close to business associates. Lay, whose father, David, is a senior partner at accounting firm Price Waterhouse, had already taken a pass on another Dundas offering a few months earlier.

The two men agreed to meet. But Dundas still didn't put all the cards on the table, because, as he says, "I still wasn't in control of the train at this stage." However, he did pique Lay's interest enough to take the idea back to his immediate boss, George Eng-man. The architect of the pension fund's merchant banking arm, Engman was a graduate from the University of London and an MBA from York University in Toronto. More importantly, the English-man Engman brought little of the emotional baggage to the invest-ment that others seemed to tag along on this one.

After a few more enquiries, Ontario Teachers was interested enough to sign a standard confidentiality agreement. That's when Dundas embarked on a very delicate balancing act as the middle-man trying to satisfy the incessant demands for information from Lay while at the same time not rankling Stavro, who was trying to stay on the right side of his own potential conflicts. As usual, Bell-more became the conduit for information.

It was the middle of October 1993 and Dundas was frantically playing both sides of the fence selling the deal. The big-ticket sell-ing items were merchandise souvenir sales, something Stavro had long complained weren't being exploited enough, and future broad-cast revenues. Dundas informed Lay that Maple Leaf Gardens would be negotiating a new long-term contract with Molson and that annual revenues should increase substantially as a result.

Lay wanted more information, so Dundas pressed Bellmore. "Has there been any study done or anything you can show us to give an indication as to what it's worth?" he asked. "Because it's a pretty difficult set of contractual rights to try and evaluate."

No problem. Bellmore sent over a copy of the Mellanby report. Dundas, who recognized Ralph Mellanby's name from the latter's days as executive producer at "Hockey Night in Canada," passed the study along to his counterpart at the pension fund. One of Stavro's potential business partners had the controversial Mellanby report while the two evaluators and Bill Ballard did not.

Bellmore also told Dundas that MLGL was planning to hire a specialist, Barry Frank from International Management Group (IMG), to renegotiate the next local television contract with Molson and those talks should formally begin in September 1994.

Cliff Fletcher and Frank had met for preliminary discussions during the All-Star game break in February 1993. Back then, the consulting company was in the last stages of renegotiating the NHL's new four-year deal with Molson. About six months after the initial meeting with Fletcher, Frank flew into Toronto and met with Stavro before being officially retained on October 22, 1993.

The numbers for the broadcast revenues the consultant was tossing around in the fall of 1993 were about $10 to $12 million a year higher than what the Leafs were getting annually from the old contract. Mellanby had predicted as much a couple of years earlier, which Frank knew, because he'd been given a copy of the Mellanby report by Fletcher. However, when Frank delivered his final recommendation in August 1994, that number had jumped to over $20 million, but the total also included radio and marketing rights, such as the rink boards.

Predictably, Lay had some questions about the controversial Mellanby report. If this study suggested the Gardens was receiving well below the market value, he asked, what was the history behind the deal signed back in 1980? Bellmore recounted the story of how the company's management had sought independent advice about whether it could reopen the broadcast contract for renegotiation. "The conclusion was that they could not and so we were stuck with this contract and it would be open for negotiation one year hence [1995]," Dundas recalls Bellmore explaining.

In the meantime, the pension fund's president and CEO started poking his head into the file even before it was sent up several floors to his desk. It was an unusual move for Claude Lamoureux to stray into the bowels of the organization, but as gatekeeper of what got sent to the board for approval, he was less concerned about the return on this investment than he was about the politics of the proposed deal.

"I asked if this was something we want to be associated with," he says in his easygoing manner. "You know you read so much in the newspaper and I knew there was a bit of a problem. In the end, I trust our people that we could get a decent return and they had done a fair amount of work on Steve, and I knew we had a good partner."

Part of that work included obtaining a legal opinion on Stavro's controversial 1991 option from Wolfe Goodman, a tax expert at Goodman & Carr. "I read this and I think that Stavro has a good case," explained Lamoureux. "Every investment has a risk and this one is more in the papers. Yeah, we think it makes sense...you know we might take some flak but we can live with that."

That's not to say Lamoureux and his group didn't anticipate potential trouble down the road. To cover that risk, Ontario Teachers would later negotiate an escape hatch in its contract with Stavro that would allow the pension fund to walk away from the deal if Stavro ran into regulatory problems.

Lamoureux gave his blessing and, as he did with most of the fund's high-profile deals, got a preview of the presentation to the investment committee at a dress rehearsal with his senior people, George Engman and Robert Bertram, a senior vice-president. Lamoureux made suggestions, with an eye to selling the plan in thirty minutes or less. Ultimately, he was making sure that whatever deals he personally approved got the board's blessing too.

A week later, Engman presented "Project Blue" to the Ontario Teachers' Pension Plan's eleven-member investment committee at an 8:30 A.M. meeting in early November 1993. After a few cursory jokes about hockey jocks, the high-profile directors, who included Gerald Bouey, former governor of the Bank of Canada, Edward Medland, former CEO of Wood Gundy Inc. (and neighbour of Stavro's) and Gail Cook-Bennett, a former economics professor at the University of Toronto, heard about how the fund intended to invest $44.43 million for a 49-percent equity partnership in a company with Stavro that planned to take control of Maple Leaf Gardens and, ultimately, privatize the fabled entertainment company.

During the course of the slide presentation outlining the proposed structure of the new company, the directors were told that Ontario Teachers intended to pay less per share than Stavro—around $31 on a pro-rated basis at the time—to achieve their target returns.

Although the board normally reviewed only deals worth more than a $50-million discretionary limit, Lamoureux still thought that, all else considered, this one should get their approval anyway. In just under half an hour, Michael Lay's last deal before leaving to join a burgeoning high-tech investment firm got the green light.

But Lay's legacy was only half complete. Next was the critical shareholders' agreement, which defined the structure of the partnership between Stavro and Ontario Teachers. They hired two corporate lawyers specializing in finance at Goodman & Carr, to work with Lay and the pension fund's in-house attorney, Michael Metcalfe, in hammering out a deal.

For the next five months, the three drove a hard bargain with Michael Melanson, their counterpart at Fasken Campbell Godfrey (who'd worked as a policy adviser to the TSE and as a legal adviser to the OSC), now negotiating on behalf of Stavro. But Ontario Teachers hammered out a bullet-proof deal with all kinds of protection for the pension fund and a host of wide-ranging powers in the newly created takeover team.

According to the Shareholders' Agreement, which was signed on March 30, 1994, not only would Ontario Teachers pay a lower price per share, the pension fund had the right to approve all capital expenditures. Two positions on the Gardens board of directors were to be created for George Engman and Robert Bertram (pushing the total to nine) and Engman would become a member of the audit committee.

As well, there were all kinds of clawbacks in the event that certain targets weren't met. Most important, Ontario Teachers had the right to put its shares to Stavro, forcing him to buy them back at 110 percent of the fair market value determined by the average of two estimates. Sound familiar?

There were five events that could trigger this happening, including Stavro's death, a change in control of MLG Ventures or an offer by a third party for the shares that Ontario Teachers wanted to accept but Stavro rejected. As well, the pension fund had a window of opportunity to unload its shares to Stavro every five years; that's important for a fund whose investment horizon in cases like this is usually about three to seven years.

By this time, the two independent appraisers had sent in their final reports: on October 1, RBC Dominion Securities concluded that the fair market value for the estate's interest in Maple Leaf Gardens was in the range of $27 to $34 a share. Two weeks later, on October 15, Burns Fry said those same shares were worth between $25.83 and $29.91 each.

Based on the average of those two ranges, Bellmore began negotiating with McKellar at $29.19 a share. Bellmore says he was not aware that the anticipated increases in television revenues, the same ones that his client's future business partners and IMG knew all about, had not been factored into the brokers' values.

However, instead of the Mellanby report, a few weeks later Crump did see fit to send along to the two evaluator's copies of a feasibility study that had been cobbled together by the Gardens controller and Cliff Fletcher, who presented it to the board in November 1993. The study, which has been described as "rough and dirty" and "a sort of back-of-the-paper analysis" by MLGL officials, was handed over to RBC DS and Burns the following week.

Stavro, Crump and McKellar asked the two brokerage firms to review this study, which included current management projections on how broadcast revenues would be affected by the construction of a new building, to determine if it affected their appraisals. Still, the Bay St. firms were not given the opportunity to review the controversial Mellanby report.

Both firms said the Fletcher report wouldn't materially change their earlier conclusions. And Stavro had in his back pocket a couple of valuations bearing the corporate imprints of two of the most credible dealers in the land. Next, he went looking for his second partner and the blessing of the Public Trustee.

On November 26, 1993, Eric Moore was buzzed by the front-desk receptionist in the Public Trustee's office. Tanned and relaxed from a week of waterskiing in Mexico, the lawyer walked out to greet his guest, John McKellar. Moore hadn't dealt with McKellar before; his boss, Hugh Paisley, had taken care of the attorney personally. But Paisley's successor Susan Himel had passed McKellar along to Moore when he called asking for a meeting a few weeks earlier. Moore was surprised to find Donald Crump and Brian Bellmore waiting there too.

The director and legal counsel for the Public Trustee's office had been with the government agency since 1988. Prior to that, the University of Victoria graduate had had a private practice specializing in corporate and commercial law. A high-ranking civil servant, Moore collected an annual salary of $103,171.

Once they made their way through the myriad cubicles to Moore's windowed office, McKellar informed the head of the charitable properties division that Ballard's executors were considering whether to sell the estate's shares. They had prepared and brought with them appraisals, which McKellar marked Confidential and highlighted the mean price of $29.

Crump offered that at the $29-a-share price, the estate would net $67 million and $10 million would be used to pay for corporate liabilities, such as the claims of Yolanda and the National Bank, unpaid federal taxes, executors' compensation and, of course, the ever-growing legal bills. However, that price would leave almost nothing for the charities.

"I think [Moore] was told at the meeting that he was given the evaluations for the purposes of sale, and he said, 'Is Stavro going to buy?'" McKellar recalls of the thirty-minute discussion. "And we said, 'We don't know yet. But if he does, these are going to be used in that regard. If Stavro isn't buying, they will be utilized for the usual purpose of evaluation, so you know whether you have got a good deal, if you get one."

Moore then asked what the executors were planning to do— sell the 50.75 percent held in HEBL and hold onto the 9.53 percent directly held by the estate or sell them both together. He was told that they hadn't decided but that they were "likely to make a decision within the next one or two weeks."

There was no discussion about the process of how the evaluations were put together, nor did they review their terms of reference.

Moore, who can be curt and dismissive, asked them why the estate had not advertised the fact that its shares might come up for sale. Crump tackled that one first. He said the estate's holdings in MLGL were a matter of public record and the marketplace has known for years that these shares were presumably available. There was no reason for the executors to change their passive stance.

McKellar was perplexed by Moore's question. He thought the answer was obvious: Stavro had bought and paid for the right to buy the shares in a private sale and the estate agreed to it. So why was this guy asking about an auction? But McKellar said nothing.

Bellmore barged in, arguing an auction wasn't necessary. Moore assumed Stavro's lawyer was referring to clause VII in Ballard's will, which clearly said the sale price would be set at fair market value supported by two independent appraisals. There was nothing about a public auction or an expensive advertising campaign in that document. Besides, as Dundas would later say, "Why would you waste half a million dollars on appraisals if you're supposed to have an auction?"

And because the bureaucrat didn't object, Bellmore said he assumed Moore accepted this position. After all, the attorney's strategy from the start was getting the Public Trustee on side.

Bellmore informed Moore that his client might exercise his option if the executors decided to sell. And, he continued to Moore, "The whole purpose of the meeting was for the information only of the Public Trustee; the transactions were really none of the Public Trustee's business." Moore later said that he expected Stavro had intended to seek the court's approval.

But Bellmore later claimed that Moore merely asked if his client was going to get court approval if he went ahead with his option. The answer was an unequivocal no; they never contemplated asking a judge to bless such a move.

Later, during eleven gruelling days of pre-trial questioning in August 1995, Moore repeatedly denied that part of the conversation ever happened. In fact, the whole time he was expecting Stavro to seek the court's permission—even though no specific offer was discussed during the meeting—because that was what he was told back in 1991 when Stavro's option was reviewed by the court. At the time, the merits of the option agreement weren't debated before the court; it was the narrow legal issue of whether Ballard's executors could vote on the term sheet and whether Stavro could vote on his own proposal. Stan Sokol, the Public Trustee's lawyer, and Paisley strenuously supported Stavro's position.

"I don't recall him asking very much," recalled Crump. "We had the intention of keeping the Public Trustee informed because after all, they had supported the issue of course before, and we had no reason to believe otherwise."

In retrospect, the government agency should have had a pretty good hunch that Stavro was about to pull the trigger. The sudden appearance of two valuations that satisfied the requirements of Ballard's will should have been enough to at least turn the bulb on inside the trustee's office.

But Moore merely put the appraisals on a stack of files on his already-crowded desk and eventually got around to telling his boss, Susan Himel, about the meeting a few days later. He then filed the appraisals in a locked drawer, even though McKellar had told him that the Public Trustee was entitled to review them and make objections.

Moore was a lawyer, not an appraiser. He didn't do any math to determine whether there'd be anything left over for the charities, which he was supposed to be representing, at the $29-a-share price. In fact, he didn't actually read the valuations until after Christmas. Even having done that, he still didn't form an opinion either way.

"I didn't see that we had any obligation to review and comment at any time," Moore said dismissively later. "We had no obligation to the executors or any of those parties involved in the transaction." What about your obligation to the beneficiaries of the estate, did you have that obligation to them? "It is the executors who are obligated to the beneficiaries of the estate," Moore shot back. Lederer, one of the executors' lawyers, would later say he was stunned by what he called the "arrogance of power" displayed by the civil servant.

What was remarkable was that the estate of Harold Ballard was unlike any of the others cluttering Moore's office. He had a box of documents to prove that point, including two letters from Miller Thomson raising the red flag over Stavro's proposed option in

1991, and the minutes of a meeting between Stavro, Crump and Giffin with Hugh Paisley (which Moore also attended) during which the executors were bickering over Stavro's deal.

More recently, he was also aware of the two letters sent by the *Toronto Star* business reporter to Himel and the Attorney General.

And he also knew that the estate had not passed its accounts for Ballard's affairs, even though the province's Charitable Gifts Accounting Act requires executors to produce a mini audit and financial statement for the Public Trustee's office, before taking it before a judge for rubber-stamping.

In fact, Ballard's executors still hadn't passed the accounts for the time during which he was incapacitated, even though the documents had been prepared by Miller Thomson and handed over to McKellar after the firm resigned back in early 1991. Moore says they weren't passed at the estate's request because the executors didn't want to "tip their hand" in settlement negotiations concerning Yolanda and National Bank.

In a letter dated March 13, 1993, Moore had written requesting they pass their accounts because three years had passed since Ballard's death. Instead, McKellar provided draft accounts of the estate up to the time of Donald Giffin's death in 1992 and asked that they be kept confidential.

McKellar offers a slightly different version. "The Public Trustee's office was in a state of chaos," he says, at the time he showed up with his papers asking Moore for his advice and thoughts. "Give us a month or so to look at these," the estate lawyer says came the reply. "I called back in June and said, 'How's it going?' and they said, 'Well, the truth of the matter is that we haven't looked at them. Our office is in the course of moving, we're swamped here, we'll be cutting back staff. But we will get to them.'"

By the fall, around the time the valuations were coming due, McKellar called again and they still hadn't reviewed the accounts. "It looked to me that they were never going to look at them," he says.

The assets of Ballard's estate, namely his shares in Maple Leaf Gardens, were to be transferred to the Harold E. Ballard Trust in no more than twenty-one years. Because the seven charities and the Gardens employees' scholarship fund were named as discretionary beneficiaries of the trust, they were entitled to receive first consideration for annual income from the dividends earned from the estate's MLGL shares.

Once the trust was liquidated, the proceeds were to be used to pay off the estate's debts. Anything left over would be passed into another entity, called the Harold E. Ballard Foundation, where it would be open season for every non-profit organization to curry favour with the executors. Moore had the heft of two acts to press the estate into co-operating. Because Ballard's estate was destined for charities and held more than a 50-percent controlling interest in a business, the law required the Public Trustee to meet with the executors every year to discuss dividend distribution and other matters affecting the beneficiaries.

Accordingly, the Public Trustee should have set up a tickler sys-tem to ensure that happened as well as ensuring that the estate received its share of the undistributed profits of the business it. transferred to the trust, ergo, the charities had never received a penny.

McKellar said the executors didn't transfer the estate's shares into the income trust because of all the debts still owed. Once the assets were moved, the executors would have become personally liable for the debt. Others, however, dismissed that as a lame excuse, and charged that Stavro was trying to use provisions in the will to keep him from putting the shares into the Ballard trust—and putting money into the hands of the beneficiaries.

Still, the Public Trustee's office wasn't exactly enforcing the let-ter of the law either.

In any event, other than a voice-mail message left by McKellar for Moore in early December 1993—which went unanswered— there was no contact between the government agency and the estate.

With the appraisals safely tucked away in Eric Moore's filing cabinet, two things were standing in Stavro's way: a $3.5-million judgement that had to be paid out by the estate to National Bank, and, of course, Yolanda.

Harold Ballard's former flame was looking for some hefty pay-back for her years of companionship and nursing heroics. The fact that her dearly departed had seen fit to leave her only $50,000 a year was inconsequential. Yolanda had a way of getting what she wanted; in this case, she was hoping it'd be $300,000 a year or a $10-million lump sum to walk, and not in the calico dress Ballard had suggested she put on when she asked him for more money a few months before he died.

When Ballard's will was read in 1990, she promptly sued his estate as a dependant. As a result of her lawsuit, the court placed an injunction on Ballard's executors, prohibiting them from making any material changes to the estate's assets—for example, forbidding the sale of shares. The ban could always be lifted if there was a court resolution or if Yolanda could be persuaded. At the time, the court awarded her $70,000 a year until her case was adjudicated.

The executors began trying to get Yolanda's permission in early 1993 by initiating negotiations for an out-of-court settlement. This, even though the estate had a draft report from a private forensic accounting firm (hired by Weir & Foulds) stating there was insufficient evidence that Yolanda had actually lived with Harold. And even if she had, it wasn't long enough for her to qualify as a common-law spouse.

The report also said there was evidence indicating that the signature on the marriage licence signed in the Cayman Islands back in early 1990 wasn't Ballard's.

Nonetheless, the executors opted for expediency. "Our lawyers told us we had less than a 50-percent chance of winning," Crump explained. Not only was their case shaky, but the executors could not afford another lengthy court battle. Instead, Stavro visited the Toronto Dominion Bank in early December 1993 and requested an "urgent credit" to permit the estate to settle with Yolanda. Christmas would come a few weeks early for Mrs. MacMillan, née Babic, when she received a certified cheque for $4 million from the estate of the late Harold Ballard, courtesy of a loan from the TD Bank. In fact, she would receive money even before the debt-ridden estate's creditors—including the TD Bank and Revenue Canada—and its beneficiaries.

With Yolanda out of the picture, it was time for Stavro to secure money and one more partner for his takeover. He picked the TD, which could not have known that his request—and Stavro's involvement—would become so controversial. Stavro called Richard Thomson, chairman of the TD Bank, to request an audience. The following day, on December 23, Stavro and his lawyer met with William Brock, an executive vice-chairman at the bank, and Robin Korthals, who at the time was TD's president (and would later join the board of Ontario Teachers). "He just came in and said, 'I have a proposal to buy the Gardens,'" Brock remembers. "My first reaction is 'What price?'"

Stavro told the bankers that he intended to proceed with an offer to take over Maple Leaf Gardens and he'd like to extend them the first opportunity to hand over a $33-million loan to help finance the launch, preferably in the week between Christmas and New Year. Of course, that was in a matter of days. It was a typical pattern of negotiating for Stavro: he would meticulously line up his own pucks, no matter how long it took, and then give others as little time as possible to respond to his shots.

Stavro knew that the bank didn't want to lose out to a competitor, like Bank of Montreal, Knob Hill Farms' banker. At the meeting, he also volunteered that he was seeking an equity partner. Would TD Bank like to consider it? That one fell into the lap of Korthals, who fired up an internal review.

The next day, Stavro returned with Bellmore and Dundas for another visit with Brock in the hope of nailing down the credit. The career banker had been with TD Bank since 1963, beginning as supervisor of the institution's agricultural loan department. These days, the no-nonsense Brock was in charge of the bank's credit department and promptly greeted Stavro with a term sheet for the loan Ballard's executor had asked for the previous day.

The trio outlined the plan in greater detail, explaining how Stavro planned to roll the $43 million in loans already piled up in Ballard's estate over into his takeover company, as yet unnamed, and then have them amortized over twelve years. Once that happened, cash flow from the merged company would service the debt owed to TD.

It was obvious that despite what Crump, Kelly and McKellar might be saying about not having made a decision to sell, Stavro and his team were lining up the financing as if it were already a done deal.

Brock put on his banker's cap and asked whether the MLGL shares had enough value to actually allow Stavro and his partners to pay out his bank's loans. Or more precisely, he needed to know whether TD's $43-million exposure was covered.

"What concerned me is how are we going to get repaid," he recalled of the December 1993 meeting. "Even on a preliminary basis, you know it's going to be a stretch and furthermore, you know that if player salaries continue to escalate, is the value of this franchise going to go down because it's financially underperforming?" Enter the two appraisals, which at the time, Brock remembered, seemed like "an extremely highly credible process." But after flipping through the evaluations, he noticed the cash flow projections weren't exactly awe-inspiring—or comforting—from his perspective. Given that Stavro said he had no plans to move the Leafs out of the existing arena, Brock wanted to know how Stavro was going to improve cash flow, even to pull off the $1.5 million in capital expenditures he'd earmarked.

"That's when he expresses a view to me that the contracts will be up for renewal and I forget exactly what he told me about when they'd be up for renewal but they will definitely be negotiated at a higher level." Brock continued: "In fact, this is what he said, 'that I am of the view that $15 million is the floor,' which is in my note." According to his notes later filed in the court, Brock wrote that "the key in this deal is that the broadcast contracts are up for renewal in 94/95 and Stavro confidentially advises that these will rise from $5 million now to [an] absolute floor of $15 million." Brock also wrote that Stavro had already hired a media consultant (Barry Frank) to negotiate the new local broadcast deal.

Not only that, but according to Brock's copious notes, Stavro said "that fact was not taken into account in the two evaluations conducted by Burns Fry and RBC Dominion Securities and explains why the Teachers' Pension Fund and Stavro think $34/share is a very attractive price."

Indeed. Enough to clear away debts, like the TD's $43-million loan and Stavro's $20-million loan, and other expenses, say about $6 million by now in unpaid federal taxes. And if all went according to well-laid plans, Ballard's beneficiaries might even get to divvy up a million bucks between them. Stavro said that "only $1 or $2 million" would be left in the estate after debts and expenses were paid.

The part Stavro didn't tell Brock was that his negotiations with Ontario Teachers had hit a snag. "Teachers was having serious difficulty in recognizing the value of the $34 a share in terms of the going bid," Dundas recalled. "It's extremely relevant in terms of what's happened historically in that here is truly one of the most sophisticated institutional investors in the country and they just don't think that they could go forward at a price that was five dollars above what the appraisers had indicated. It took a bit of creativity before we were able to resolve that impediment."

And shrewd businessman that he is, Stavro would be proven right: the TD would not be able to resist his overture. The bank performed its own due diligence, credit searches of Knob Hill Farms stores, including the mortgages on old and new buildings. In fact, TD would have felt a lot more comfortable if Stavro had given a personal commitment backing up the $4-million guarantee he was offering to put up in support of the loan he was requesting. But Brock didn't push too hard, fearing that would be a deal breaker. Brock admits in his memo that "this is a tough deal and not easy to support"; however, "clearly in my judgment, we tightened the deal as far as we could without losing the whole deal to B of M," Brock wrote to his boss, Dick Thomson.

Having given the loan a green light, the bank's minions handed over the information Stavro had given Brock to the investment arm, where they began assessing a proposed 10-percent equity interest in MLGL, through an investment of $9.75 million in Stavro's still unnamed holding company. TD Capital also extended a loan—this one worth $32 million—personally to Stavro, making the brokerage arm's total exposure worth about $42 million. The return, based on a 20-percent ownership in the takeover company, would be about $600,000 a year. And there were intangible benefits too.

"The bank's market research group has recognized that the professional hockey sports fan represents the same demographic segment the bank is targeting," wrote Jim Coccimiglio, manager of commercial services. Sounds like a page out of Molson's marketing book.

Worse, "if we do not capitalize on the opportunity, we are certain that another bank will and the end result will likely include losing the entire MLG connection," warned the memo. They saw about $400,000 in annual profits from interest paid by Ballard's estate to the TD's main branch walking out the door. However, if the bank jumped into the equity pool with Stavro, the branch would see its profits jump to $650,000 in the first year and $450,000 after that.

A week later, the file was perused by Bruce Leboff, a director of corporate investments. The math wonks performed serious financial gymnastics with Stavro's numbers. The result: valuations that ranged from $27.19 to $32.62 a share on the low end to between $38.07 and $48.94 on the higher scale. The latter values were worth substantially more because they factored in Stavro's assurances that the Molson broadcast deal would be negotiated to include a more than threefold increase over current levels and Brock's confirmation that Stavro had hired a media consultant "and was reasonably confident of achieving these increases."

Keep in mind that the folks at TD knew the two evaluations they were given by Stavro didn't include that important fact in their appraisals. "The potential impact of this increase in revenue is material (i.e. a 40-50% increase in value) and may have impacted the determination of value," Leboff wrote in an internal memo to Charles Baillie, a vice-president of TD Bank. "Given that these valuations will be referred to in any disclosure to public shareholders in the context of a going private transaction, legal counsel should review this issue in detail." And the prescient bank executive noted, "Notwithstanding TD's intent to become involved only once MLG is private, TD's role as lender, followed by purchasing an equity interest may be perceived negatively in the market, if it ever became public."

Further up the chain, another senior vice-president cautioned in February 1994 that "we may be perceived to have inside information vis-à-vis potential for television contract and concluded would be preferable to hold off on investment negotiations until deal had been announced."

By the third week of January, the pinstripes had given the investment a tentative yellow light, preferring to wait until Stavro actually made his bid before jumping into the fray. Meanwhile, the estate's lawyer McKellar was already sending out draft copies of lock-up agreements.

In the meantime, the suspender-clad hawks over in the TD's brokerage arm were getting ready to join Stavro's takeover team. In fact, they were fretting because the Ontario Teachers' pension fund had already snared many favourable terms in its Shareholders' Agreement, including a better price than Stavro and possibly TD Capital.

They complained among themselves that "Stavro's advisers seem to be outmatched by Teachers," and that "it would be difficult to convince Stavro at this stage that he has been badly served by his adviser, and counterproductive to try." That was why, the brokers said, TD should get in on those talks as soon as possible.

Even the bank's group of legal gunslingers at Tory Tory DesLauriers and Binnington, weren't thrilled about joining what looked like an entry draft after all the top prospects had been chosen.

But banks are fastidious creatures; Stavro's option became the next obsession. "Any conflict of interest for Stavro in his role as executor of the estate seems to be covered off. Nevertheless, it might be preferable to have a formal court approval of the proposed purchase from the estate," wrote Warner Lambert, manager of investments at TD Capital.

He argued that as the negotiations continued, more players were being added, widening the circle and increasing the potential for leaks. Lambert suggested the broker jump into the deal as soon as "we are completely satisfied with the propriety of the whole transaction now."

Presumably, that satisfaction would come from the Public Trustee, because at least from the bank's perspective, the government agency was the other stakeholder. TD was clearly under the impression that the Public Trustee was in fact aware of what was going on every step of the way. "Additionally, our solicitors have advised that a majority of all parties other than the publicly traded company (MLGL) must provide consent. While written consent from the Public Trustee [on behalf of the estate] will not be provided, John McKellar, secretary of HEBL and solicitor for the estate, meets regularly with the Public Trustee, and this transaction would also be made the subject of a meeting. If opposition was encountered the deal would be reconsidered or restructured."

However, no such meeting took place. But TD Capital didn't know that when it signed a deal with Stavro on March 31, 1994, becoming an equity partner in the new ownership of Maple Leaf Gardens. At the same time, the TD Bank obtained exclusive rights to call itself the bank of the Toronto Maple Leafs, complete with automated teller machines in the building's front lobby. Bill Brock would get something too: a seat on MLGL's board of directors.

Only one obstacle remained: Harold Ballard's executors had to finally declare that his estate was up for sale.

Crump and Kelly made that decision on March 30 when they agreed to sell the shares held in the estate of Harold Ballard to Steve Stavro. "We reviewed what he had done, where we were and if there's anything else we could do," Crump explains.

Apparently not much. Three days later, they signed a lock-up agreement with Stavro, allowing him to buy the MLGL shares held directly and indirectly by Ballard's estate for $34 a share.

The man who Terry Kelly said he'd seen scribble generous donations on the back of serviettes and who'd been paraded as the estate's white knight would be allowed to buy the assets knowing there wouldn't be much left over for the charities.

When asked if he thought that one or two million dollars was the amount his old friend Ballard had intended, Crump replied, "It was better than going into bankruptcy."

The same day, Stavro also bought Molson's 735,575 common shares, or 19.9-percent stake, in MLGL at $29 (which was the average of the previous twenty-days' trading value).

On April 4, Stavro unveiled his takeover team, which included the giant Ontario Teachers' Pension Plan and TD Capital. Together, they made an offer to purchase all the outstanding shares in the company for $34. Stavro also topped up Molson's offer from $29 to $34, as required in their deal. The players were in their places and the power play was just about to begin.

CHAPTER TEN

Charities at the Gate

"If it was going to go to court to be discussed, someone else had to take it."

– DAVID PETERSON

"**S**IR STEVEN OF THE** Gardens" was now in his rightful place. So proclaimed the newspaper headlines that had championed his takeover offer. "Stavro in the driver's seat;" "Stavro enjoys rink to himself...offers $125 million for parent company he already controls."

The predictable happened too. Even before the offering circulars were sent out four days later, Crump was fielding dozens of telephone calls from shareholders.

"We had fathers and grandfathers who worked on the place and had taken shares in the building and it was an emotional issue. I got back to Stavro and told him that you should at least say people can keep their share certificates. For the most part, though, I didn't hear any complaints." The pieces began to fall nicely into place.

Gardens director George Whyte had received a phone call from Brian Bellmore about a special board meeting on April 2, the day the lock-up agreement was signed with the estate.

"It's the first inkling we had, those of us who weren't executors," he recalls. "It was kept very quiet." At the Saturday morning meeting, he was told by Bellmore that the executors had decided to sell based on the two evaluations and that not only had Stavro secured Molson's block, he also wanted to take over the public company.

Whyte, a former securities lawyer and general counsel of the

Bank of Nova Scotia, was appointed to head up a special committee of independent directors to review Stavro's offer. The other members included Ted Nikolaou, of JJ Muggs, and Ron Pringle, the former chief operating officer of Coca-Cola Canada.

The first thing they did was to issue a press release on April 14, the same day Stavro's offer was made public. They didn't actually receive details of the offer until April 8, so Whyte and Pringle, who were both on the company's audit committee, began assessing MLGL's financial statement.

In all, they received the two Bay Street appraisals, Fletcher's new arena feasibility report and Crump's five-year forecasts—but once again not the Mellanby report. In fact, Whyte claims he'd never heard of it. Even so, "it wouldn't have affected me because it was a staledated report," he says.

One of the first issues they grappled with was whether to obtain another evaluation. "We came to the conclusion that it was not necessary to get another one. Quite frankly, if there'd been one evaluation only," Whyte says, "my view would have been different. But since there were two, why not get three, four, five, six. Where does it go?"

In the end, he says, it was the pedigree of the two brokerage houses that made the decision final. "These were two prominent brokerage houses and they were good enough for us." Still, Whyte says he didn't know that Burns Fry had written an opinion for Crump and Matheson a couple of years earlier in which it stated, among other things, that it would be difficult to value the shares of Maple Leaf Gardens. That was better left to an auction.

Part of the committee's assessment included interviews with a shell-shocked Cliff Fletcher, who had just learned of the takeover bid from Bellmore. In fact, Fletcher claims he was out of the loop completely, learning about the appraisals only when Whyte and his group asked for a meeting to discuss rising players' salaries.

The committee also met with RBC Dominion Securities and Burns Fry. It was during one of these meetings that RBC's George Dembroski told Whyte to "take the money and run" when he was asked if Stavro's offer was fair value for the company's minority shareholders. "I thought that $34 was a pretty damn good figure," Whyte concluded.

"The committee felt very strongly," says David Matheson, who was providing legal advice to the Gardens directors, "based upon all the information they exchanged from evaluators and people they talked to, that they were very clear that this was a fair price."

And that's the opinion they took to the entire board. They decided not to commission their own evaluation and there was no discussion ever at the board level about soliciting other offers.

"Don't forget, Mr. Stavro has a lock-up on over 60 percent of the shares," Whyte explains. "Beating the bushes would have been futile. There was nobody out there prepared to put an offer on the table," he continues, later saying that he was not aware of the overtures made by Glen Day the previous year or of any others previously made to the estate.

Whyte had a point. With Stavro's right of first refusal, anyone else straying in to make an offer would be setting up—at their own expense—for Stavro to swoop in and grab the company anyway, albeit at a higher price. And even if another bidder tried, Stavro could have tried to prevent anyone else from taking the company private because he owned Molson's 20-percent block. That was an enormous disincentive.

So MLGL's board agreed to the offer, all the while assuming $34 included a premium for the controlling block of shares. A Directors' Circular was sent out on April 15, advising Maple Leaf Gardens' disparate bunch of shareholders to accept Stavro's offer.

"They did things properly in terms of appearances," says a lawyer involved in the case. "Stavro said, 'I am an executor, but I'm backing out of this.' They had an independent committee look at the deal, but the reality is clearly, these fellows wanted to say, 'Sure Steve, let's do this deal. Steve Stavro has been good for Maple Leaf Gardens.'"

With that done, Crump allowed himself to actually think about the prospect of not having to prepare for another annual shareholders' meeting—ever again. That would be premature. Jim Devellano and Harry Ornest would see to that.

For a while, Stavro's march to his elevated post in the hierarchy of Canadian sport looked easy. Except, unbeknownst to him, his offer finally flushed out all the other predators who had been circling his prize. Bill Ballard, the Bitoves, even the charities, all began looking to the Public Trustee. Increasingly they viewed Susan Himel as their weapon—their so-called white knight. The pressure began to mount. The backrooms started getting crowded with securities lawyers.

Now that Stavro had publicly declared his intentions, the Bitoves hired Goodman & Goodman to look into devising a strategy to take a serious run at beating his offer.

Securities laws in Ontario require offers to remain open for twenty-one days, giving shareholders some time to consider their options. It's also a window of opportunity for competing bids to emerge from the sidelines.

The Bitoves knew that Stavro's offer for the estate shares was $75.37 million—and the overall price tag once the outstanding shareholders were bought out would jump to $125 million.

At the outset, financing wasn't the problem for the Raptors. It was Stavro's option: Maple leaf Gardens' equivalent of a poison pill.

The law allowed other interested parties to bring their bids forward, even though Stavro had signed an "irrevocable lock-up agreement" with the estate. Because the executors owed a duty to the beneficiaries to maximize the return on the shares, Crump and Terence Kelly (the man who replaced the late Donald Giffin as Ballard's executor) would be forced to consider all offers—not just Stavro's.

But here was the rub: by wading into the fray, the Bitoves would trigger Stavro's right of first refusal, allowing him to simply match the highest offer.

Although it should have kept potential bidders honest by forcing them to come to the table with their best offers, Stavro's option nonetheless took away the board's ability to create a bidding war (which should benefit the shareholders). Why would any company or individual spend all the money on investment bankers and lawyers to make an offer that essentially only forced Stavro to pay more? It was tantamount to a disappointment fee—and it scared suitors away.

Besides, how much appetite would there be to shop around the company and risk increasing the bid price if the only offer on the table had come from the chairman of the board? After all, Ballard's will established a floor price as "fair market value supported by two appraisals." Stavro had offered that much, but if another, higher bid came in, the will went out the window and a new floor price would be set.

Worse, if he couldn't tough it out in a bidding war, Stavro could decide to do what everyone else was trying: broker a deal by flipping the shares to another player who could afford to pay a steeper price.

Finally the Bitoves, knowing all this, decided not to test the market—or Stavro—let alone call the estate's lawyer, John McKellar, to enquire about a possible arrangement.

(In his cross-examination for discovery, Peterson later said that approaching McKellar or even the Gardens lawyers at Aird & Berlis "would be fruitless. It was not an open tender. And there was no interest in selling to outsiders.")

Another Bitove strategist is more blunt. "Who are you going to make an offer to? The board of directors of Maple Leaf Gardens. And who's that? Steve Stavro's cronies."

Instead, the Bitoves engaged in private war, complete with corporate intimidation designed to divide and conquer the executors and Stavro's financial backers. That plan could only work with the help of the Public Trustee.

It began with a telephone call to Susan Himel's office a few days after Stavro's offer was publicly tabled. After a number of exchanged voice-mail messages, Patricia Robinson, a lawyer at Goodman & Goodman, told Dana DeSante, a lawyer in the Public Trustee's charitable properties division, that she had a client who was interested in buying the estate's shares in the Gardens.

Robinson didn't tell DeSante on whose behalf she was calling, except to say that she had some information that would be of interest to the government agency. At the time, DeSante was involved in the process of hiring an outside lawyer to assist the Public Trustee in assessing the recent events. However, DeSante told Robinson that he "would be happy to receive any information she wished to provide."

Himel herself took the information from Robinson. She listened carefully as Robinson told her about an unidentified interest in buying the Ballard estate's shares for a higher price than $34 a share. Of course, Bitove's lawyer was hoping Himel would step in and force a public auction. Failing that, Robinson hoped the Public

Trustee would use her authority to remove Stavro from his position as an executor and then force the estate to entertain outside bidders. Robinson wanted to know if the acting Public Trustee, who had assumed the mantle after Paisley left, was investigating Stavro's offer and his conduct leading up to his bid. Was she prepared to intervene and temporarily stop the sale? Himel replied that she was considering it, but didn't have any definitive plans to step in just yet. Himel, however, didn't call the estate's lawyer, John McKellar, even though she'd just been placed in the position of auctioneer.

It was a whole new ball game for Himel. A lawyer by training, and a former law school classmate of Rosanne Rocchi, she'd spent most of her sixteen-year practice in family law, specializing in mental health and child protection. She joined the Public Trustee's office in 1986 as a lawyer in the Child Representation Program and became Deputy Official Guardian in 1987. Seven years later, she was being called in to protect a bunch of unnamed charities.

Meanwhile, the Raptors group discussed their strategy, which included requesting a private meeting with all three of Ballard's executors. As well, they would invite representatives from Stavro's business partners, Ontario Teachers and the TD Bank, putting them on notice of their planned bid.

The thinking was that by putting their private offer directly to the independent executors—Donald Crump and Terence Kelly—they would be forced to seriously consider the offer. If they turned it down, they could become personally liable for any loss to the estate as a result of accepting a lower offer from Stavro or anyone else.

By tabling it privately, the two executors would be given the "opportunity to avoid a bidding war." However, if that didn't work, the Bitoves would launch a very public hostile takeover. And if that happened, they threatened, the Public Trustee would get involved, as would the directors of Maple Leaf Gardens, who would be required to review the new offer and make a public statement.

As well, Ontario Teachers and the TD would be given notice about the pending legal assault that they hoped would be launched by a number of the charities (gently prodded by the Bitoves' strategists), including a class-action suit and complaints to the OSC and the TSE for lack of material disclosure.

For added effect, they'd also make Stavro's partners aware of the serious allegations they intended to level against him for breach of trust. That strategy, they hoped, would be particularly effective in crippling Stavro's ability to maintain the support of his partners in the event of a bidding war.

On April 25—the last day that Stavro's offer remained open— the Raptors board assembled on the thirty-eighth floor of First Canadian Place in the offices of Rothschild Canada Ltd. to meet with Garfield Emerson. He's reputedly one of the shrewdest corporate strategists around and that's what the Bitoves would need to pull their plan off. The usual cast was present: Peterson, Bitove Sr. and Jr., Scotiabank's Borden Osmak, Phil Granovsky, Allan Slaight and Cassels, Brock legal hound Lorne Saltman.

At Emerson's request, the meeting began with a preliminary discussion about the Court of Appeal's decision in the spring of 1991 that gave Stavro the right to vote on his own proposal but stipulated that he seek court approval when he finally exercised his rights. After that, updates were given by Peterson, who told the group about his telephone discussions with Stavro regarding a joint facility. His view was that Stavro was stalling, refusing even to schedule meetings. John Bitove Jr. lent support by reminding everyone that Stavro cancelled the meeting with the architect a few months back.

Allan Slaight told the assembled group that Cliff Fletcher and his aide, Bill Waters, had been telling him to keep pursuing the idea of a joint facility because except for Stavro most of the Gardens directors liked the idea.

Emerson, a lawyer formerly with Davies, Ward & Beck, warned the group that they needed credible plaintiffs to launch the bevy of lawsuits necessary to pull off the complex scheme. And more important, the court papers had to be framed in such a way as to break up Stavro's lock-up agreement with the estate.

They discussed the draft copy of a twenty-page letter written and signed by Patricia Robinson at Goodman & Goodman. The letter, addressed to Susan Himel, outlined in detail legal reasons to halt the Stavro sale. It did not, however, contain any information about a proposed offer.

By this time, the group was plugging in numbers and formulas crunched by the brokers at CIBC Wood Gundy. The most likely proposal they were giving consideration to would have Canadian Imperial Bank of Commerce and its investment arm Wood Gundy, along with Bitove and Slaight, make an offer of $37 a share for all of the 3.68 million MLGL shares. The total tab: $136.16 million to be capitalized with $113 million worth of debt financing from the bank and $30 million from the Raptors and Standard Broadcasting. The additional $6.9 million was earmarked for the brokers, the strategists and, of course, the lawyers.

The offer would also include a promise to sell the venerable Gardens building for its net book value of $11 million and build a new arena for approximately $150 million.

After painstakingly devising their grand strategy, Bitove Sr. backed off from actually firing off his assault. Instead, on the last day that he could enter a counter-bid to shareholders, Stavro's cousin agreed only to have Robinson's draft letter sent to the Public Trustee.

Robinson called Himel again, informing her that her client had after all decided not to make a competing offer. But she told the Public Trustee that she'd done extensive legal research for her client and that they had no objection if the results of that work were forwarded to the government agency. Himel gladly accepted the offer.

The Raptors seemed content to wait it out, hoping that the Public Trustee would force a public auction, at which point they'd be ready.

"We looked at it very carefully and came to the conclusion that we were not the appropriate plaintiff in this situation," recalls Peterson. "We weren't a shareholder. If it was going to go to court to be discussed, someone else had to take it."

The Bitoves soon found someone to front their fight. A few blocks south of Maple Leaf Gardens, a large brown envelope appeared on the desk of Bill Gillett, the vice-president of Teamsters Local 847, which represents 450 full- and part-time employees at the Gardens. The anonymous package contained numerous documents, including a copy of Ballard's last will and testament and papers setting up the trust fund and the Harold E. Ballard Foundation.

Until those papers arrived, no one at the brotherhood knew that a trust was supposed to have been set up by the executors after

Ballard's death—and more importantly, that the Teamsters' children were to receive scholarship money from that fund through the yet-to-be-created Maple Leaf Gardens Scholarship Fund.

Strangely, there were also newspaper clippings and other documents reciting the history of Maple Leaf Gardens since Ballard's death—all of them focusing on Stavro. Gillett was vaguely aware of press reports about Stavro trying to buy control of the Gardens. Part of the information in the package indicated that the only people who could halt him were the beneficiaries—people such as the Teamsters.

"They seemed to be suggesting that the charities were going to get screwed, and they didn't have, excuse my language, the balls to stand up to them," he remembers. "And if anybody was going to do it, it would have to be the Teamsters."

Gillett called the union's lawyer Linda Huebescher, who requested that he send the information to her office in Mississauga, Ontario. One thing was clear, thought the union representative: there seemed to be lurking in the background a group of people who didn't want to see Stavro taking over the Gardens.

After assessing the information, Huebescher wrote a long letter to the Public Trustee, based on the information that had been provided clandestinely. Gillett hand-delivered the eleven-page missive, which he signed, on April 29. The Teamsters urged Himel to step in and stop the sale to Stavro. They wanted her to force the estate to put the shares onto the open market so as to fetch a higher price.

Oddly enough, the Teamsters' letter bore a striking resemblance to the one sent by Goodman & Goodman on behalf of the Raptors. That was no coincidence. Some of the research materials stashed into the envelope had been put together by Robinson. The package itself was sent to the Teamsters by one of Bitove's lawyers.

On the same day, another government agency was receiving complaining letters about Stavro's offer. Perry Borden emerged again. He fired off a four-page letter complaining to Leslie Milrod, director of the Ontario Securities Commission's general counsel office.

Then on April 29—the same day that Stavro and company were meeting with NHL commissioner Gary Bettman in New York to get the league's blessing for the sale of the team—Borden burned up the fax lines between league offices in Manhattan, Detroit and

Toronto. David Zimmerman, the NHL's associate legal counsel, was faxed three times over a five-hour period. Borden sent copies of his own letter to the OSC and the Teamsters' letter to the Public Trustee to Jim Devellano's office at Joe Louis Arena in Detroit (Devellano was the senior Red Wings manager and one of the two dissident MLGL shareholders publicly opposing Stavro's offer). Last on the list were Thor Eaton and Philip Giffin, who were sent copies at their respective offices in Toronto.

The NHL's Zimmerman was told by Borden that Ontario's Public Trustee had just sent a six-page letter (written by Eric Moore on April 28) to Ballard's executors, taking the position that they were not complying with the Charitable Gifts Act, which required them to get court approval for Stavro's takeover offer. Zimmerman's secretary called back, confirming receipt of the fax and requesting that they send her boss (who was in the conference-call meeting in Bettman's office) a copy of Eric Moore's letter, which was later sent.

On May 4, copies of the letters were also sent to Claude Lamoureux, chief executive officer of the Ontario Teachers' Pension Plan, and Robin Korthals, who at the time was president of TD Bank. The same day, John MacNeil, senior legal counsel from the OSC, called Perry Borden's office to respond to his letter to the securities commission. He informed him that the watchdog was "not proposing to intervene" at this time.

Then, as the Teamsters' Gillett would say, "the shit hit the fan, and people started coming out of the woodwork." The charities stopped being coy. By the time Stavro made his move, most of the non-profit organizations already knew they had been singled out in Ballard's will. They'd even had copies of that document sitting in their donor files for years. In fact, back in 1991 when the battle between Giffin and Stavro first erupted, Giffin, Thor Eaton and Bill Ballard implored some of the organizations to protect themselves against the power play unfolding within the estate. Bill Ballard went directly to Wellesley Hospital, which had always been dear to the Ballard family, but the hospital chairman wasn't about to step in front of the Stavro juggernaut on Bill's behalf. The hospital was uneasy about taking such a huge risk based on Bill Ballard's word. Besides, the Public Trustee wasn't complaining. Instead, they took a pass, fearful of compromising their own positions on D-Day

(Division Day) when the spoils of Ballard's estate would finally be divided among them. This time, however, they heeded the call.

The campaign to mobilize the beneficiaries continued, with letters to Dr. Ian MacDonald of Hockey Canada (one of the beneficiaries which promotes the development of hockey). Wayne Shaw from Stikeman, Elliott responded to the letter with a call to the Public Trustee's office on behalf of the hockey organization, trying to set up a meeting. In the meantime, Peter Rideout, a lawyer from McMillan Binch, wanted to talk to Himel on behalf of his client, the Wellesley Hospital. Himel referred him to Frank Newbould, who had now been officially retained on her behalf.

"Why did the Public Trustee say it was okay back in 1991?" mused a lawyer for one of the charities. "Was it better for Stavro to get it than Bill Ballard? Was that it, they didn't want this son-of-a-bitch's son to get control of it?"

Harry Ornest kept up the letter-writing campaign he began shortly after his early-morning call from Stavro on the day of his offer. He wrote directly to Edward Waitzer, chairman of the OSC, in an unpolished letter mocking the regulator's very public stand as champion of minority shareholders' rights. Ornest quoted Waitzer freely from recent newspaper articles in an attempt to drive home his message that this was the bandwagon on which the regulator should hitch a ride. In the meantime, he also kept up his verbal assault against Stavro and the Public Trustee in the Toronto news media. Meanwhile, Bill Ballard stood watching quietly in the sidelines.

During the summer of 1994, Frank Newbould began to corral the support he needed to freeze Stavro in his footsteps. In July, Richard Wise, the Montreal-based business evaluator hired by the Public Trustee to assess the two appraisals used in Stavro's takeover bid, produced his own critique. Wise said the two brokerages emphasized MLGL's costs, such as players' salaries, while not properly considering the growth in broadcast revenue, which is a key value driver in any sports franchise. They appeared to ignore the obvious, he said, even though it was common knowledge that Molson's fifteen-year broadcast contract expired in 1995. "The valuations look to the future increase in player salaries but not the expected increase in different sources of revenues," Wise wrote in his evaluation. As a result, their assumptions, particularly with respect to revenues, placed a value on the Gardens shares that was substantially below their fair market value. (Fourteen months later, Wise valued MLGL shares at between $50 and $53.)

Finally, the Public Trustee intervened. Newbould filed court papers on August 4 which sought an injunction to temporarily prevent Stavro and his business partners from taking the Gardens private. According to the Statement of Claim filed by her lawyer, Susan Himel wanted the court to force Ballard's executors to seek another court's approval for the sale of the estate's shares to Stavro.

The Public Trustee claimed that guidelines set out in the Charitable Gifts Act clearly stated that a buyer or seller of any estate assets destined for charity was required to get approval from the courts before closing the deal. Because Ballard's executors hadn't done that, Susan Himel sought to have them removed as executors and the controlling block of MLGL shares purchased by Stavro to be returned for a public auction.

As well, the Public Trustee lobbed a serious accusation at Crump, Stavro and Kelly when she accused them of breaching their fiduciary duties to the estate. Himel wanted a declaration under the Business Corporations Act stating that the "affairs of MLGL have been carried on in a manner that is oppressive, unfairly prejudicial to and unfairly disregards the interests of the security holders, including the estate and beneficiaries under the estate." To that end, she sought the court to declare Stavro's purchase of Ballard's shares "null and void" and wanted the controlling block of MLG shares returned to the estate unencumbered.

This time, the charities sent a couple of lawyers to the injunction hearing at the courthouse to protect their interests. "We wanted to be able to say to the judge, 'Okay, maybe the Public Trustee in 1991 supported this. But we knew nothing about it and we didn't support it then and we certainly don't support it now,'" explained one of the lawyers involved. "So to the extent that you're going to hold that against the Public Trustee, don't hold it against us.'"

Darrell Gregersen, executive director of the Hugh MacMillan Children's Foundation, sent her lawyer because "we wanted the judgment simply to leave the option open for the charities to make their pleas for the money to come from the will. We took our cue from the Public Trustee."

The timing of this imbroglio couldn't have been more inauspicious. Late summer is the high season of annual fundraising campaigns, and coincidentally for some, those plans included Steve Stavro and Maple Leaf Gardens. For example, the Charlie Conacher Throat Cancer Fund (which is affiliated with the Toronto Hospital Foundation) had a sixteen-team round robin hockey tournament scheduled at Maple Leaf Gardens for the final weekend of September. Even so, the charity decided to send a representative to the courthouse.

Others demurred. Princess Margaret and Wellesley hospitals had been on the receiving end of Stavro's generosity and wouldn't even consider the notion of locking horns with him publicly over a business deal. The Teamsters, who were always ready to roll with the punches, didn't get an invite.

By the time they all gathered in the court on the morning of August 9, hundreds of shareholders had already surrendered their shares. A sixty-three-year-old homemaker in Etobicoke named Gwen Maxwell, who owned four thousand shares, was one of them. No less than three different brokers had told her to sell; one even said she was better off tendering because Stavro was going to squeeze everybody out and her shares would be worthless.

A week later, Justice Sidney Lederman handed down his decision: he granted the Public Trustee's request for an injunction to stop Stavro from taking the company private, and both sides prepared for a trial. In mid September, Maxwell called Perry Borden and gave him a $1,200 retainer to lead a class-action suit, which sought $13.6 million in damages against the directors of Maple Leaf Gardens. Finally, after three years of playing on the sidelines, Borden had his client.

The remaining gaggle of would-be suitors and disappointed shareholders Ornest and Devellano, would fight their respective battles by proxy, hitching a ride on the Public Trustee's legal bandwagon.

CHAPTER ELEVEN

Overtime

"I'd like to say that I'm glad to see
you all again, but I would be lying."
– MR. JUSTICE JACK GROUND

LESS THAN TWO MONTHS after their day in court, the charities got the velvet boot. In the weeks that had passed since Justice Lederman's decision, the group had been plunged into a beggar's purgatory. Stavro and his co-executors did not appeal the judge's decision—and that meant any hope of collecting money from Ballard's estate was put on hold until after what looked like a lengthy trial.

Worse, the Public Trustee hadn't said a word since her victory in court, even though her legal salvo had unleashed a new sense of purpose among the charities.

The charities' group of ingénues had many questions. Why hadn't they been told about Stavro's option and why had the Public Trustee's lawyer so vigorously supported the executor's right to vote on his own proposal back in 1991? More importantly, they couldn't figure out how the government agency expected a judge not to throw that back in its face. Which, of course, he did by accusing the Public Trustee of "doing an about-face to its earlier position." Luckily for the Trustee (and its supporting cast), Justice Sidney Lederman didn't have to deal with this "apparent inconsistency." He was being asked to rule on a very narrow point of law: the Public Trustee requested that he halt Stavro from amalgamating the estate's MLGL shares with his private company MLG Ventures.

241

"I think ultimately down the road, we would be expected to take over and participate," mused Marie DunSeith, president of the Toronto Hospital Foundation. She'd be disabused of that notion shortly.

In the first week of November during a lunch buffet of sandwiches and salad in one of Borden & Elliot's boardrooms, the group of mostly upper-drawer charity board members were told by Frank Newbould (not Susan Himel, who attended the meeting) that their services were no longer required. As if that weren't enough, they were also told that the Public Trustee wasn't stepping up to bat for them specifically, but rather, her efforts were on behalf of all non-profit organizations in Ontario.

Jaws visibly slung open; a few muttered something about understanding why Frank Newbould hadn't wanted them to bring their own lawyers to the meeting. "I feel like a used hankie," quipped one of the doyennes in attendance.

Newbould's speech was polished but it was wasted on this well-heeled crowd. Delicately sidestepping their shock, he ploughed through his agenda for the better part of the seventy-five-minute meeting, refusing to talk about his client's controversial role in 1991, or answer questions about why Himel's office hadn't tried to halt Stavro's deal before the offer actually closed in May 1994, instead of hoping that a trial judge would unwind it.

"If you are being completely prudent, you would have made sure that you knew, right?" asked a voice in the room. "If you hear rumours that a deal is being done, you send a letter saying, 'We understand a deal is being done. You are on notice that we take the position that this deal can't be done and please, advise us immediately of what is going on.' That never happened. Why?" implored another.

Newbould wasn't entertaining those kinds of questions and he avoided them again later during the pre-trial examinations for discovery of Eric Moore and Himel's predecessor, Hugh Paisley. Newbould said he didn't know how much money was at stake, all the while cautioning the charities that the executors still had the right to decide who would receive money and how much. Although true, it was a self-serving warning; Newbould didn't want the charities running off like a herd of rogue elephants suing the executors on their own. That, of course, would have severely crimped his own case. The reason: Himel's legal case against Ballard's executors, painstakingly pieced together by Newbould and her deputy Jay Chalke, was looking better on paper every day, thanks largely to an unexpected court order allowing Ballard's former lawyer Rosanne Rocchi to hand over her scrupulous files to the government agency. Those documents, previously privileged and confidential, were invaluable in strengthening Himel's position.

Newbould also didn't want the charities cutting any side deals with the executors because that would hurt the Public Trustee's cause, even if she wasn't bargaining exclusively on their behalf.

As for a possible settlement, forget it. Newbould knew that was the charities' preferred method of resolution but his client was still trying to get answers. Besides, a litigator's job is to prepare for trial, not a closed-door signing.

But he may have underestimated his increasingly sceptical audience. "There was a lot not being said," recalled one of those in attendance.

Then Himel took over. Much to everyone's surprise, Himel offered little consolation, let alone gratitude for their timely intervention. But she did serve up plenty of platitudes, including a lecture on the importance of writing a proper will.

"She thought we were stupid," said one who was miffed by Himel's attitude.

Then, as if to cast them adrift permanently, she warned them to keep their heads down. It was all the group could stand. "I feel like I just paid a heck of a lot of money to publicly shoot myself," said one who could hardly believe the nonsense.

Needless to say, it didn't take long for the venomous whispers of that encounter to make the rounds. "I'm told they [the charities] got the straight arm," said a mischievous Bellmore—no doubt, a situation Ballard's executors figured they could exploit.

Within days, the executors extended olive branches to the same disgruntled lot that had just recently appeared to be their adversaries. Each of the named organizations was invited to a meeting with Crump, Kelly and Stavro. Ostensibly, the executors wanted to spin their side of the story and, more importantly, to underscore their resolve to fight the Public Trustee's allegations.

An hour-long gathering was set for 4 P.M. on November 17 in John McKellar's offices. Unlike their meeting with the Public Trustee, the charities afforded these hosts greater deference.

"I'm not going to tear strips off Steve. His behaviour with the Ballard file is something else. But I'm not going to blackball him." That sums up the way most approached the meeting, where, once again, the lawyer did most of the talking. This time, it was John McKellar.

A quick history was given of the Ballard estate and the melodramatic recounting of how the sick, even senile, old man had fallen heavily into debt to buy out the children because he so desperately wanted to keep his company out of their hands after his death. That was why, McKellar said, the scrutiny and the resulting adverse publicity generated by Himel's suit was such an injustice and a personal affront to the executors.

Even the enigma spoke. Stavro reiterated that he and his co-executors had only carried out the final wishes of their good friend Harold Ballard. They suspected the Public Trustee had some undisclosed agenda but they refused to speculate about it.

Stavro knew enough to tell the group, still smarting from their meeting with Himel, what they wanted to hear. He understood their position, Stavro told them, and he would never think of using his clout as an executor and director of the trust to influence whether future donations might flow their way.

"It was cordial and polite. You know you can catch all kinds of bees with that kind of honey," remarked one of the invitees.

Still, others were more practical.

"They've got to understand that we're a business too. The non-profit part is only not to pay taxes. We have responsibilities to our donors too," said another, bluntly adding, "I didn't want to antagonize him at the meeting—he should be mad at the Public Trustee, not me."

Although most came away thinking that Stavro's actions may have been legal, they were troubled because his offer left little on the table for the beneficiaries. But they weren't about to risk saying as much. "There wasn't a charity in the room that wanted to appear averse to anything he said," says one of the honchos. "Most of us came away feeling that he was going to fight like mad."

He proved them right two days later on November 17, 1994, when Stavro launched a countersuit against the Public Trustee and the Attorney General of Ontario. In his suit, Stavro claimed that the government agency had acted in bad faith by not carrying out its responsibilities. More specifically, he accused the government agency of a complete about-face, pointing out that Hugh Paisley had supported his option proposal in 1991. By doing that, the implicit argument went, the Public Trustee had implicitly supported the notion that Stavro would not have to seek court approval when he decided to purchase the shares in Ballard's estate. "The Public Trustee was nevertheless guilty of prolonged, inordinate and inexcusable delay in claiming that the transaction was unauthorized," alleged his court papers. Obviously, the strategy was to put pressure on the government agency heading into the first round of mediation meetings to resolve the dispute before a trial.

Justice James Farley was far more successful doling out sarcastic one-liners in his chambers over two days in late November 1994 than he was getting both sides to agree on a settlement. Judge Farley had brought the two sides together hoping for an early resolution and began the proceedings by scribbling on a chalkboard the title of a collection of short stories written by American author Kurt Vonnegut Jr., called *Welcome to the Monkey House*. The novelist had chronicled his experiences as a prisoner of war and had even written a satire about an idealistic philanthropic foundation and its encounter with greed. Judge Farley encouraged those gathered in his parlour to get a copy of the book. (Crump bought one on his way home that evening.)

As the discussion gathered some momentum, both sides got their first glimpse of how vitriolic this battle would later become. Once the usual positions had been staked and the lawyers had done the talking, Donald Crump asked to speak. He pointed out that Ballard's will allowed any of his executors to buy the estate's shares, but almost in mid-sentence, Justice Farley shot him down, telling Crump rather sarcastically that these discussions had nothing to do with Ballard's will. Chastened, Ballard's executor sat quietly and that's when he noticed that Justice Farley was missing part of an index finger, so naturally he enquired about it. Farley told him he'd cut it off with a meat saw. "I guess judges are human too," Crump consoled himself, "and they can make mistakes."

Next to be mauled by the judge was Brian Bellmore. When the two sides began haggling over possible trial dates, Bellmore objected to any that would interfere with the Stanley Cup playoffs, to which came Farley's caustic reply: "Why, does Steve intend to suit up?" A tentative trial date was set for May 1995 but that was just a formality. Justice Farley made it clear he wanted both sides to reach an out-of-court settlement as quickly as possible. Using his vast powers of intimidation, he described the situation as an "omelette" and said that despite the Public Trustee's attempts, it would probably be impossible to unscramble. But Himel wasn't buying it. She felt bullied and unsure; she was in no hurry to cut a deal.

Meanwhile, Stavro's adversaries away from the judge's chamber continued to grow in number. The class-action suit spearheaded by MLGL shareholder Gwen Maxwell received court certification in January 1995 (and ate up her thousand-dollar retainer in a single morning of lawyers' meetings).

Around the same time, Harry Ornest made a secret trip to Hogtown. His lawyer, Richard Shibley, a veteran litigator who seemed to command the most respect from the judges, had called him in Beverly Hills at least three times trying to convince him to make the trip. The reason: Stavro's camp had extended an olive branch of sorts, although they wouldn't talk about it over the telephone. They wanted to see Harry in person for dinner at Stavro's Teddington Park home. Ornest flew to Toronto on January 5, 1995. During dinner, Stavro complained to Ornest that the media were attacking his integrity. Bellmore broke in, asking, "Harry, what do you want? Let's see if we can't settle this soon." It was an obvious tactic, Ornest thought, intended to divide the various players suing Stavro in the hope of conquering each one individually to secure a settlement. Harry said he wanted $60 a share (even though back then, Ornest admits, he was willing to take $50 apiece). Stavro gave no reply; instead, Harry was taken on a tour of the mansion and the adjacent coach house. All told, the evening cost Ornest a first-class ticket to Toronto and $2,400 in legal fees ($400 an hour) to dine with his adversary at his lawyer's behest, and he received nothing for it. Typical, thought Ornest. "I should have known better."

A month later, the pre-trial examinations for discovery finally got under way. And six months of pent-up frustration and aggression were unleashed during verbal brawls and petty fighting among the hired legal help.

The transcripts of the discoveries read like a script in a soap opera: constant interruptions, thinly veiled insults, badgering, grandstanding and refusals to produce documents, especially from Stavro's side. With every objection, they hauled each other before Justice John (Jack) Ground, the case management judge assigned to fast-track this extremely complicated case through the court's Commercial List. A former commercial lawyer at Osler, Hoskin & Harcourt, Justice Ground is not a litigator and thus was not well-versed in the art of courtroom theatrics that dominated this case. Every time the combatants appeared before the meticulous judge, the trial date would get pushed back even further. It was rescheduled three times during the eighteen-month legal battle.

With each refusal for material from either camp, the litigators' strategy was to file motion records crammed with all kinds of documents putting out onto the public record as much damning evidence as they could. For their part, Bellmore and the small army of other lawyers representing Stavro's various roles with Ballard's estate, Maple Leaf Gardens Ltd. and his takeover company MLG Ventures, forced Newbould to produce two key witnesses—Eric Moore and Hugh Paisley. At first, Newbould refused to serve them up (he preferred deputy Public Trustee Jay Chalke) by arguing Crown immunity. The Public Trustee's lawyer said that as high-ranking employees of government, they could not be forced to testify. At first Justice Ground concurred. But Bellmore would not be denied. He appealed that decision to the Ontario Divisional Court—and won.

By the early spring of 1995—a year after Stavro's takeover offer—Justice Farley took another shot at getting a settlement. If nothing else, the erudite judge considers it sport reaming out high-price legal talent and is especially good at getting lawyers to move quickly, even if it means forcing them to make their clients settle under the threat that he'll do it for them. Still, not even Justice Farley's heavy gavel could secure the elusive détente.

Finally, a break in the stalemate. On September 28, 1995, a spectacular fall day, ten lawyers sat on wooden benches facing three rather sombre-looking judges on the appellate panel. For eight months, the Public Trustee had been demanding that its opponents hand over confidential documents in the TD Bank's files, papers that specifically detailed the relationship between the Ballard estate and the bank since 1990. As well, Newbould wanted to see the bank's version of how it became involved with Stavro's takeover deal. Every time he had asked for those documents the TD Bank's lawyers had steadfastly refused, supported by the battery of other lawyers in Stavro's camp.

Newbould dragged the issue all the way to the Court of Appeal. Based on the number of bodies in attendance on this day, Newbould looked badly outgunned. The room was heavily weighted with lawyers on the Stavro side—about eight in all—taking on the lowly Public Trustee with a supporting role from a junior lawyer representing Ornest and Devellano.

The government agency's lawyer had a simple request: he wanted the documents to be handed over because Stavro seemed to have trouble remembering the answers to many of the questions he was asked during pre-trial discoveries. Newbould argued that it was unfair that all the other parties involved in the case had access to the documents, except his client, and besides, he needed them to prepare for trial. This line of thinking seemed to garner favour with Justice David Doherty.

The lawyers on the other side of the room split the various arguments between them so as not to overlap.

First up, Thomas Lederer. A lawyer for the executors, he bluntly accused Newbould of conducting a witch hunt and expecting the court to give its approval. "This case and this request for information can be reasonably seen as conducting an investigation in a public forum," Lederer argued. "Is it appropriate for a public agent to use this forum to get information?"

It became a recurring theme for Stavro's soldiers of war.

Next came Maple Leaf Gardens hired gun Bernie McGarva (David Matheson's partner). He dismissed the claim as a stalling tactic by Newbould to delay the trial even further, which by now had been rescheduled to begin on February 15, 1996.

During his turn at the lectern, a very tempered Jeffrey Leon, Bellmore's fellow counsel for MLG Ventures, said the whole process was becoming unwieldy. The litigator representing Stavro and his business partners argued Newbould hadn't proven that if he didn't get the documents before trial, justice wouldn't be done.

And speaking of justice, Brian Bellmore had a few thoughts about that. The hydra-head of this story because of the number of hats he wears (as a director of the Gardens, Stavro's personal lawyer and counsel for Knob Hill Farms), Bellmore repeated his mantra for the judges, who'd never heard it before. There were two issues, he argued: one, whether the provisions of Ballard's will allowed Stavro to buy the shares; and two, whether his client had paid fair market value. That was it. The rest was filler.

Bellmore is a fierce competitor and reputedly one of the best cross-examiners around. But it wasn't lost on the judges—or his colleagues and adversaries alike—that Bellmore himself had a lot at stake.

As he picked up speed, he was interrupted by Justice Jean-Marc Labrosse, who delicately pulled his bifocals down to the tip of his nose and asked, "What relevance is all this? That's not what this motion is about!"

Bellmore finally settled down to the nub of his argument, that whatever Stavro told the TD Bank while he was trying to line up capital for his investment was information the Public Trustee could get its hands on at trial. In perhaps one of the greatest understatements of the case, Bellmore argued against handing over the information because, he told the judges, "the Public Trustee's case won't turn on this information."

Still, TD Bank had its own reasons for refusing to oblige. The threat of being named as a co-defendant in such a high-profile and controversial legal battle could severely undermine its credibility with its other clients. Like many in this case, the country's fifth-largest bank feared the media spin. Its lawyers knew how potentially explosive and damaging the sensitive and confidential memorandums (written by some of that institution's highest ranking pinstripes) could be when aired with the manipulative slant of a clever litigator. "When you put them all together," sighed one in the bank's camp, "it's like mixing gasoline with fire." Added another: "We didn't want to hand over sensitive documents to a government agency. The only arguable point was whether you needed Charitable Gift Act approval and our legal view was that you didn't. If you think you're right and it's Maple Leaf Gardens, you'd be asking for trouble by exposing this [the documents] to the public."

No doubt this was the motivation behind TD's eight-month resistance to releasing the papers. In mid-October, the bank finally lost the battle in the Court of Appeal when the appellate judges ruled in Newbould's favour. TD Bank would have to hand over its confidential documents. The trickle of documents slowly began making their way to his office and that's when the battle for Maple Leaf Gardens took on a whole new direction.

Frank Newbould knew that banks are fastidious creatures and that their inhabitants write everything down. When TD's documents were finally handed over to the Public Trustee, Newbould would be proven right. Contained in the pile of papers was the handwritten memo by William Brock to bank chairman Dick Thomson in early January 1994 which said that Stavro "confidentially advises that these [broadcast revenues] will rise from $5 million now to an absolute floor of $15 million."

Today, Brock described that information as merely an opinion that was expressed by Stavro and that it was to remain confidential. "This was not confidential information," he later explained in an interview, "it was confidential to the people he told." That is, it was intended for the eyes and ears of the bank's senior management only—not the pinstripes at the King and Bay streets branch from where the credit would flow.

However, it's still unclear whether the bank actually had a copy of the Mellanby report in its possession. Brock said they didn't; TD Capital's president John McIntyre concurred, saying it never turned up during their internal sweep of documents. But the bank's in-house lawyer, Colin Taylor, told the Court of Appeal in the fall of 1995 that they found the report in their files but didn't know how or when during the three-month process of negotiating the equity position it may have been put there.

Nonetheless, the TD still had Stavro's opinion, which was based on confidential information. More importantly, the bank knew that it had not been disclosed to Burns Fry or RBC Dominion Securities when they assembled their two evaluations. Whatever Brock may have thought about what Stavro had told him, he obviously believed it was knowledge important enough to pass along to the bank's investment arm. TD Capital then considered the information when it decided to take an equity position and become one of Stavro's partners in the takeover of Maple Leaf Gardens.

Dundas and Bellmore said the broadcast issue had been blown out of proportion. MLGL's annual report had been saying there was a new lucrative contract in the wings since 1991. There were also press releases clearly outlining how the Gardens broadcast contracts were undervalued. "If there was a conspiracy theory out there, there sure were a lot of very credible people that were trying to do so many sinister things," Dundas says, shaking his head. "It just boggles the mind."

Given that the Mellanby report would later emerge as probably the single most damning piece of evidence in the Public Trustee's case against Stavro, his own lawyers conceded that the report should have been handed over by Crump with the other materials regardless of whether he thought it was valid. Jeffrey Leon, MLG Ventures' lawyer, would later say that the Public Trustee's lawyer Frank Newbould "did some good lawyering on Mellanby. He changed the view of the case, with Mellanby as the smoking gun."

"Through all of this time, I didn't know of a Mellanby report," says McKellar. When did he find out about it? "When the litigation started. My job was to advise the executors on how to operate an estate. The details of the Gardens isn't my business."

He would ask about broadcast revenues just before the deal closed on May 16, 1994. "I remember before the closing asking David Matheson about McCarthy's. I think they had sent a letter when they were acting for the Gardens for a brief period that there might be some way to renegotiate the Molson contract. And I can remember asking Dave because I didn't see any of that in the report. What happened to that? Was that considered useful or otherwise? And he told me there was nothing to that at all, that when they got into it there was really no practical way, it was a waste of time to litigate that to the point. So that was the only thing that I knew that I didn't see reflected in the reports and that was the answer that I got. So there was nothing further to say on the subject."

In hindsight, Matheson says the omission of the Mellanby report was an "oversight." McKellar is more blunt. "What we all said to Crump was tell them everything that's relevant, give them everything. And so presumably Crump didn't give them something that he thought was either irrelevant or not specifically asked for."

You could have taken the words right out of Crump's mouth. He says he didn't give the report to the valuators because "They didn't ask for it—I didn't try to tell them how to do their jobs. There wasn't any info they couldn't have gotten from me." In any event, the chartered accountant says the report was "at best very poor. I never thought of it as germane to the issues."

Still, the new broadcast agreement hammered out by the Gardens in 1995 called for the company to receive $12.8 million over the course of a four-year deal with Molson. That's not far off the $12.25 million Mellanby called for back in late 1990. "There's no question the Leafs were somewhat undervalued," explained a Molson negotiator. When the old deal ended in 1995, the Leafs should have been getting $5 to $6 million more a year than they were getting because they were a much better team."

But those numbers only covered television rights. MLGL took back the advertising and promotional rights—worth just over $2 million a year—that Molson had enjoyed in the old days under Ballard. For example, the rights to buy thirty-six rink-board spots (known as line-of-sight advertising and the most prestigious of all), the exit signs, even the back of game tickets, all formerly belonged to Molson.

And now that MLGL had more advertising to sell, they bought the Warner Bros. building across the street for $1 million, ostensibly to house the burgeoning marketing department. And Bob Stellick, director of the hockey team's communications, introduced a new mascot in the form of a white polar bear named "Carlton" who roamed around the arena during hockey games wearing a Leaf jersey, number 60.

An important prong in the new marketing strategy was radio, which, until recently, had not been exploited nearly enough by the Gardens. Consider these figures: the Leafs were receiving $300,000 from Molstar (Molson's entertainment arm) for its local radio sponsorship rights from 1992 to 1994 while the CFL's Toronto Argonauts (a much less important marketing tool for advertisers) were getting the same amount from local radio station CFRB over the same period of time.

Once he was comfortably ensconced in his corner office in the southwest corner of the Gardens, Fletcher began comparing the company's broadcast deal with Telemedia Network Radio in Toronto (worth $750,000 a year) with the contract his old team, the Calgary Flames, had signed with a local station. The Leafs were treating radio as an afterthought instead of capitalizing on its promotional potential for the team. So the Gardens' chief operating officer and Molson managed to get a bidding war going between Telemedia ("The Fan"), which had the previous contract, and Westcom Radio Group in May 1995. In the end the upstart Westcom, better known to Leaf fans in Toronto as Q107 (and Y95 Rock in Hamilton, Ontario), won the prize, shelling out an estimated $1.2 million annually for the rights to air and market the Leafs until 1999.

With the TD documents in hand, Newbould seemed to have a dream file. The Public Trustee's lawyer filed what's known as a Fresh as Amended Statement of Claim, which is to say, it was the revision to the list of allegations Newbould originally filed with the court back in August 1994. The latest court documents named the Toronto Dominion Bank as one of the co-defendants, and the Public Trustee took the extraordinary step when she sought $75 million in damages from the executors and an additional $7.5 million from Stavro. It was a bold move. Newbould knew financial institutions are prissy and hyper-sensitive about public exposure. Being lumped in with the so-called bad guys in what was sure to become one of the juiciest trials ever was likely to make more than a few pinstripes squirm.

The timing for Newbould was even more perfect. The court-appointed mediation was scheduled to begin again on November 24, and Newbould was betting his latest salvo would knock his opponents right off their self-righteous blocks.

But his date with destiny would be postponed. Days before the mandatory settlement talks were to begin, the fifty-four-year-old

Newbould complained of chest pains while in court on another case and was hospitalized for a few days. Two other lawyers (Jeffrey Leon and John Morin) involved in the Gardens case would suffer similar fates by the time it was all over.

Once again, the markers were moved: to give Newbould time to recuperate, settlement talks were rescheduled to begin January 15, 1996, and a trial date was set for April 9.

As the months wore on, Stavro maintained a deafening silence as his lawyers continued to poke for soft spots in the Public Trustee's case against him. Stavro appeared to patiently wait for his day in court even though most of his own advisers privately admitted the case would not likely get that far. That strategy grated on some of Stavro's business partners, particularly the Ontario Teachers' Pension Plan Board, which had been operating on the assumption that Stavro's bid fell within the permissible boundaries set by Ballard's will. Stavro and his partners were losing the public relations battle badly, and soon the latter began worrying about the court of public opinion and their own constituents.

After eighteen months of sparring—and almost six years after Ballard's death—the two sides finally arrived in the Shangri-La suite of the Hilton Hotel. The mediation talks officially began on January 15, 1996. Stavro's camp sat across the table from the Public Trustee and the two court-appointed mediators, Thomas Allen, a senior Bay Street lawyer with Davies, Ward & Beck (and former partner at brokerage house Gordon Capital Corp.), and George Adams, a judge with the Ontario (General) Division and former chair of the Ontario Labour Relations Board. Susan Himel spoke first, outlining her agency's position, which, to the fury of her adversaries, had been transformed from the temporary injunction Newbould won back in the fall of 1994 to what Jeff Leon called "the lawsuit from hell."

Himel was feeling emboldened by her new sense of purpose. She had twice resisted strong-arm attempts by Justice Farley to settle, and now she spoke with greater confidence about her position and that of Ballard's beneficiaries. Both sides knew that the Attorney General of Ontario—Himel's ultimate boss—had made it known publicly that he wanted to expand the use of a secretive system, called the Alternative Dispute Resolution, for resolving legal battles that didn't involve violence. Ultimately, the mediation was carried out behind closed doors in the strictest confidence.

Next up to address the masses in Shangri-La was Brian Bellmore. He explained for the umpteenth time that Stavro's takeover followed the blueprint outlined in Ballard's will. Bellmore, who always did the talking for his client, defended Stavro's position again, using his well-worn mantra: "The will allowed it." For him, there were only two issues to be resolved: was there ever a duty to solicit public offers for the estate's block and, at $34 a share, did Stavro pay a fair price?

Yet despite their howls to fast-track the case to a public courtroom, Bellmore and his colleagues on Stavro's side were relieved with the closed-door sessions. The harsh glare of public scrutiny was casting them in the uncomfortable role of fighting benevolent charities. "We're very angry to be put in this position," he said.

What was especially irritating to Stavro was how the public scrutiny seemed so unfair. Stavro, his friends and lawyers protested, was the white knight, the man who had lent millions of dollars to Ballard's estate back in 1991—when no one else would—keeping it from the precipice of bankruptcy long enough for the charities to even consider handouts. (That particularly upset Stavro, who complained to his business partners about how ungrateful the charities had been. Not one had written a testimonial about his past generosity.)

The fact that Stavro had secured a lucrative personal benefit as a result of his largesse as an executor of the same estate was a contentious issue already bared before the court. Bellmore had successfully argued that issue for him twice, in two different jurisdictions, during the first six months of 1991. And, he had what appeared to be unconditional support of the Public Trustee at the time. It was infuriating for Stavro and company to think that four years later, they were sitting across from a different trustee, one who had unleashed one of the most aggressive legal assaults in the province's history in an attempt to unravel the tangle her predecessor had helped create years earlier.

An hour after the plenary session began, the group splintered off into adjoining rooms to begin the verbal trench war with the two judicial mediators engaging in shuttle diplomacy. The two sides had staked out their turf: the trustee wanted the shares put back into the estate and then a public auction to establish a fair market price.

Stavro's bargaining stance was simple: never to concede anything he'd so painstakingly worked to acquire. No rescision, no bidding wars. Everyone had a price and Stavro wanted the Public Trustee to name hers. That was the strategy Bellmore had relayed to his client's business partners during a meeting before the mediation began. "But that went out the window in the first thirty seconds," joked one of Stavro's associates.

From then on, the players at the table began shifting. The lawyers did the talking with only spot duty from their clients, mostly to clarify and analyse the chalkboard diagrams used to explain corporate structures and share price calculations. From time to time, there were even attempts at comic relief. Donald Crump tried to inject a little humour after a particularly gruelling session. "You know, Harold is alive and well and living in the Caymans," he chortled to a fatigued Justice George Adams. "Yeah, you wish," came the response.

Himel, herself a lawyer, showed up every day alongside Newbould, as did Stavro, prompting some to suggest that her presence could have been a strategic error. Instead of employing the typical bargaining ploy of allowing her lawyer to negotiate and return to her for instructions, Himel's daily presence at the bargaining table made her appear vulnerable. She would not have a face-saving option of backing out of any decision with any grace if or when she decided to rethink her position.

Stavro was the only one in his camp who seemed to want a settlement. His partners urged him to tough it out in court. "We were telling Brian [Bellmore] that in many ways, we were hoping the settlement doesn't go through because we have been believers up until this time," said one of the partners. Claude Lamoureux figured Stavro should fight the good fight. "My advice to him all along was to go to court, confess that some things looked bad but don't forget, the Public Trustee didn't look so good either."

After four days in the Shangri-La, they'd hammered out a deal in principle. And by the second week of mediation, a working blueprint was in place. All that remained was to negotiate the finer points of the deal, which would be straightened out during weekend sessions in the glass-walled conference rooms at Fasken, Campbell's thirty-sixth-floor offices in the Toronto Dominion Bank Tower. At least, that's what Stavro's team thought. They celebrated the imminent deal with a steak dinner in the Hilton Hotel's dining room. A dozen businessmen and their lawyers clinked their glasses toasting one another. When the talk turned to issuing press releases, the always cautious legal beagles doused the euphoria by reminding the group that deals often come undone when the final details are still to be negotiated. Still, at least publicly, Stavro began reclaiming the hockey team, appearing with his entourage of directors at a practice and travelling with the team on a road trip to Winnipeg with Bellmore and Terry Kelly.

Appearances were key to the draft proposal hammered out at the Hilton. Stavro would make a lump-sum payment to the Public Trustee, preferably in the form of a charitable donation, which would go straight into the Harold E. Ballard Foundation set up in 1984 for philanthropic purposes. That would effectively transform him from Scrooge to Santa Claus—with a catch. Stavro wanted a tax credit for the donation, even if he was offering it under duress because it amounted to millions of dollars (up to 80 percent) in savings for him.

Himel liked the idea up to a point. Her intention had always been to secure a nice stash of cash for the charities but she was uncomfortable with Stavro's idea of packaging the payment as a donation. The Trustee was preoccupied with newspaper headlines screaming about how taxpayers would be subsidizing a deal that was brokered behind closed doors. Besides, the tax issues fell under the federal government's jurisdiction. It was clear they would have to continue negotiating for a while.

The thorny issue of equal treatment for shareholders was also raised at the mediation table but wouldn't be resolved during these discussions. Only Ornest and Devellano would receive more money for their shares because they were part of the Public Trustee's lawsuit. However, Newbould expected the OSC would step in to protect the rights of the other minority shareholders still clutching the remaining 4 percent of MLGL's outstanding shares. Those who had tendered their shares had already launched the class-action suit led by Gwen Maxwell against Stavro and MLG Ventures. But Maxwell's lawyers weren't invited to attend the peace talks either; they learned about the mediation from the press.

Molson posed another potential problem. The company had tendered its 20-percent stake in the Gardens to Stavro for $29 each two days before his public offer back in April 1994. (That was later bumped up to $34 apiece, totalling just over $25 million.) Ontario Teachers and TD Bank were understandably concerned that Molson might argue the company was entitled to the same consideration as the other shareholders would receive as a result of the settlement with the Public Trustee. But Bellmore and Stavro denied the brewery had any rights to more money for its shares and waved their agreement as proof of that. So sure was Stavro, according to one of his partners, that he never factored in a top-up for the Molson shares when his advisers crunched the numbers in preparation for the mediation negotiations.

According to their April 2, 1994, deal with Stavro, Molson was entitled to a top-up only up to six months after the closing of Stavro's original offer. Still, presumably that arrangement didn't contemplate the legal entanglements and controversy that had arisen since the offer—and the extra cash per share—since Stavro's original bid. Stavro's business partners wondered whether Molson would demand the same treatment as the other shareholders. And if that were the case, Stavro and his partners would have to dole out another $7 million to Molson.

Given that Molson was so concerned about preserving its exclusive marketing and broadcast contracts with Maple Leaf Gardens, one obvious question was whether the company received other consideration for its shares. That collateral benefit might explain why the publicly traded company was still not clamouring for the extra money the others received. And if that were the case, that would pose a problem under securities law, which requires that all shareholders must be treated equally.

The bottom line: it was clear that Stavro was going to have to ante up substantially more than the $125 million he had originally bankrolled to buy the company. Over the next couple of weeks, while the negotiations changed venues on weekend meetings to Jeff

Leon's offices at Fasken Campbell Godfrey, Stavro and Bellmore scrambled to keep their team together while trying to secure the extra financing.

As the weeks dragged on, Ontario Teachers and TD Bank were getting restless, even demoralized, about the impasse, albeit for different reasons. "I've talked to nobody who thinks it's [a settlement] a good idea," explained one of the partners at the time. "The only person who does is Steve."

In fact, a rift was developing in the Stavro camp by the third week of negotiations. Himel, who seemed to be in no particular hurry for a settlement, left town for a two-week vacation, in the middle of the process. As a result, the formal talks went on hold, and that was just fine with Stavro's camp, who used the time to patch up differences between the partners.

Ontario Teachers, for one, was getting tired of the delays and wanted to head straight to court. Although the pension fund was the only member of the group not specifically named as a defendant in the lawsuit, its chairman Claude Lamoureux had nonetheless made it clear to Stavro that his fund would not shell out a penny more than the $44.3 million it had already sunk into the original takeover offer. The giant pension fund was already having enough trouble justifying its original investment.

The problem was that Ontario Teachers didn't have much to show for bringing almost half the money to the takeover table other than two seats on the Gardens board of directors. And although Lamoureux became a staunch supporter of Stavro, the folks in his fund's merchant banking division couldn't justify throwing in more money because the returns wouldn't meet their usual investment criteria. At $33 and change, Ontario Teachers was already paying less for its shares than Stavro. In fact, that's why Stavro secured a $35-million line of credit from TD Bank, to pay the extra 67 cents per share that Ontario Teachers was refusing to ante up. The prospect of a costly settlement would no doubt mean Stavro would at least try to pass along some of the pain to his partners—and Lamoureux's men would have none of it.

More worrisome for Stavro was that he might have to find another investor to take Ontario Teachers' position in the middle of the game. According to the put/call agreement he had signed with the pension plan back in 1994, Ontario Teachers could put the 49 percent of the MLGL shares it owned through MLG Ventures back to Stavro on April 2, 1996, forcing him to buy them back at 110 percent of the market price. Although they never directly threatened to exercise those rights, the pension fund didn't rule it out altogether.

But Stavro's other partner, Toronto Dominion Bank, was desperate for a settlement. Bill Brock, himself a director of Maple Leaf Gardens, was becoming almost apoplectic at the lack of progress from the mediation process. TD Bank wore two hats in this deal: as creditor it had $35 million in a loan, while its investment arm TD Capital had shelled out $32 million in a loan to Stavro and another $9.75 million for 10 percent of the equity of MLG Ventures, the private company that would amalgamate with the Gardens and another $32 million out to Stavro personally. The bank also had another $43 million in loans out to Ballard's estate dating back to the buyout of Harold Jr. in 1989 and Bill in 1991. And now, TD Bank had also agreed to provide the letters of credit to the Public Trustee guaranteeing that it would backstop Stavro in the event he couldn't raise the funds to hold up his end of the settlement agreement.

Susan Himel returned from her vacation on February 10 with even less resolve to settle. While away, Himel had begun to rethink her settlement strategy and to wonder whether she should forge ahead to a trial. Typically, at the forefront were her concerns about public opinion. Himel never lost sight of the fact that she presided over a government agency with 207 employees funded with $21 million from the taxpayers' purse.

She passed along her concerns to Newbould, who, although he was earning the government rate of $240 an hour (paltry when compared to his usual hourly rate of up to $400), had preferred to contend his case in a courtroom.

Despite his natural ardour for a court battle, Newbould was uneasy about the thought of his client walking away from the negotiating table after stringing along the other side for more than a month. It would be hard to justify, especially because Himel had managed to check off most of the items on her wish list.

And she couldn't forget Ornest and Devellano. Their lawyer, Richard Shibley, had been a staunch settlement hawk. The former lecturer at Osgoode Hall didn't have much of an appetite for what looked like a six-month trial in the making. His clients, especially Devellano, wanted to accept the higher share price Stavro offered. After all, they had real money invested in the deal—their own—unlike Himel, who they complained was costing taxpayers an additional $150,000 in legal fees by delaying her decision.

As Ornest, now seventy-three, entered Cedars Sinai Hospital in Beverly Hills in late January to have a faulty pacemaker removed, he was confident he had a deal. By the time he was back home convalescing and well enough to take the excitement of an update from Shibley, the wily tycoon was told they'd reached an impasse because of Himel. Ornest was livid. He knew that a trial is a crap shoot; he didn't want to risk the chance of winning in court if he had a deal in hand.

Still, Himel would become even more paralyzed when the eldest son of the late Harold Ballard finally stepped out from the sidelines.

Bill Ballard had been unusually quiet. For over a year, he had sat by watching the Public Trustee poke and prod at Stavro's offer, all the while rekindling his own dream of one day owning his late father's company. Bill had hoped for a full airing in court, confident that the government agency would prevail, rendering Stavro's takeover null and void. A public auction would ensue and Bill would take a run at the shares. He even thought he'd likely be asked to act as a witness for the Public Trustee. All the while, though, he quietly conferred with his own lawyers about taking his own action against the executors. In the meantime, the multi-millionaire would piggyback on the trustee's case, taking advantage of all the documents that were pushed to the surface at the taxpayers' expense.

Certain that mediation talks would fail, Ballard and his lawyer James Hodgson, along with Dusty Cohl, the sixty-year-old granddaddy of promoters and cousin of Bill's business partner Michael Cohl, boarded a cruise ship in late January for a two-week travelling movie cruise, complete with whiskey and cigars, through the Caribbean. During one of their days at sea, Hodgson slipped into a comfortable deck chair and read the Mellanby report, which had been filed in the court by Frank Newbould. He went "nuts" when he read the document, prompting him to write a letter to all the lawyers involved upon his return in the first week of February.

Hodgson put them on notice that his client had enough cause to force legal action of his own against the estate. Of course he had his own agenda: Hodgson was worried that a settlement might have sealed the invaluable public record, thus cutting his access to the documents—all the while portraying his client, rather fittingly, as the wild card. Stavro wouldn't be in the clear to take over the company if he cut a deal with the Public Trustee because he might still have to fight Bill's claim. Himel, according to Hodgson's letter, couldn't have a public auction because his client would be contesting the ownership of almost 40 percent of the shares up for grabs. In any event, the charities would get less money if Bill prevailed in court.

The missive went ignored, dismissed by both sides as a typical last-minute antic from Billy-come-lately. So he backed up his threat on February 22, 1996, by suing the executors Stavro, Crump and Kelly, and the TD Bank (which financed the purchase of Bill's shares in 1991), claiming they had deliberately withheld the Mellanby report, which outlined information about the true value of the hockey club's broadcast rights, when he sold his shares back in September 1991. Bill was entitled to that information because he was a shareholder, and because Justice Farley had ordered Crump and Giffin to pass along all financial information to Bill in 1991. That information, Ballard alleged, would have increased the value of his own shares, which he claimed he sold for a "grossly undervalued price." In his suit, Ballard asked that his thirty-four common shares in HEBL be returned to him or a lump-sum payment of $100 million be made for his troubles.

Nine days after Ballard fired off his legal salvo, the two sides were back at the negotiating table in Jeff Leon's offices in the TD tower. Interminable hours were spent waiting, so naturally, they delved into gossip; the ailing fortunes of the hockey team, the imminent departure of coach Pat Burns—and the drama unfolding in the private life of general manager Cliff Fletcher. The sixty-year-old president of the Gardens, known to many as the Silver Fox for his white mane, had lost about fifteen pounds in recent months and was sporting a sleek new hairstyle. His thirty-year marriage had come to an abrupt end during the Christmas holiday in Florida when Fletcher informed his wife, Donna, that he wanted a separation. Details of his marital woes and subsequent liaison with a forty-two-year-old former airline stewardess were grist for the rumour mill not only among the lawyers in the TD tower but among sports reporters and hockey rink-rats around the National Hockey League.

On March 5, Himel finally made up her mind. Around six o'clock on that Sunday night, mediator George Adams walked into the small office where Crump, Kelly, their lawyer John McKellar, Bernie McGarva and David Matheson were biding time. Adams could barely hide his disappointment when he explained that, unbelievably, Susan Himel couldn't skate with the only deal they'd been working toward since the early days of mediation. She wanted to fight the executors in a public courtroom.

Stunned, the middle-aged men and their lawyers, all of them touched by the Hope Diamond that is Maple Leaf Gardens, left the room an hour later shaking their heads in disbelief. "You don't change your mind after six weeks and suddenly renege on a deal," miffed one. "Talk about bargaining in bad faith." For several days, there'd be sotto voce insinuations about Himel's lack of authority as the "new kid on the block," and plenty about how out of touch her bureaucratic style was with the rough-and-tumble world of business.

To be sure, the war of words was going public again. Swept aside were the tight-lipped courtesies of the confidential peace talks as both sides began girding to do battle again in the courtroom.

With the six weeks of closed-door discussions having yielded nothing concrete, the group was soon to go back before Justice Ground to clean up some unfinished business. The weightiest was Newbould's request to amend portions of his Statement of Claim, most notably to include the TD Bank as a defendant.

But before they all gathered before Justice Ground, Stavro raised the stakes again.

When Himel had walked away leaving his millions to settle on the table, the grocer made the settlement offer again in writing, one copy for the Public Trustee and another for Ornest and Devellano, who were both seething over Himel's about-face.

This way, if Himel wanted to drag them all kicking and screaming through a lengthy trial, she'd have to score not only a court decision in her favour, but a decisive one that included damages equal to Stavro's offer—or better. If that didn't happen—even if she won the case—the government would be on the hook for most of the legal fees incurred by both sides from the date Stavro made his overture. And at the rate they were going, it would have easily amounted to five or six million dollars.

Not only that, Stavro's latest offer wouldn't be bound by the confidentiality restrictions of the mediation process. That meant Stavro's lawyers could parade the offer in front of the charities—but not the court—letting them know how much money the Public Trustee was leaving on the table—with any luck, inciting them to pressure Himel. Indeed, Stavro had just tied the unofficial score of the game within the game and wiped the smile off Newbould's face—at least for now.

They were all back before a less than enthusiastic Justice Ground on March 13. "I'd like to say that I'm glad to see you all again but I would be lying," was how he greeted them. During the next two weeks, three outstanding issues were argued and the Public Trustee lost every one. It began when Justice Robert Blair, the judge who would have presided over the case if it had gone to trial, shot down Newbould's request to delay the trial until September. Justice Ground sandwiched that decision with two of his own: he forced the Public Trustee to hand over the confidential notes and documents of Richard Wise, the Montreal-based evaluator, and those of David Peterson, who had sworn the all-important affidavit for Newbould back in 1994, kickstarting the protracted lawsuit.

The charities weren't going away either. They'd hired their own lawyer, Edgar Sexton, from Osler, Hoskin & Harcourt, to act on their behalf.

They had been mobilized by Robert Prichard, the president of the University of Toronto, who is also a superb fundraiser. The British-born, Yale-educated academic had called Himel back in May 1995 and offered to play Henry Kissinger to see if he could bring about a truce between the two warring factions. A well-meaning opportunist, Prichard wanted to advance the cause of his own university by taking advantage of a clause in the Ballard Trust documents that allowed for educational institutions to be added to the list of discretionary beneficiaries of the estate. Prichard had hoped to add the University of Toronto to the list if he could broker a settlement.

Himel hesitated and, as usual, referred Prichard's call to her lawyer. Newbould had known the head of Canada's largest university through his identical twin brother, Ian, who is the dean of Mount Allison University in Sackville, New Brunswick. After a brief telephone chat, Newbould agreed to bring Himel along for a meeting with Prichard, during which Himel delivered her standard line: she didn't want to talk about any possible settlement until she had full disclosure.

After the mediation talks failed in March 1996, Prichard was dispatched again as an emissary by the Stavro camp. The charities learned that Stavro was willing to designate them all as beneficiaries in his written offer to Himel and Prichard's job was to get the Public Trustee back to the bargaining table. Prichard met with the representatives from the various non-profit organizations at his office in Convocation Hall with Sexton on March 8.

That Prichard managed to assemble the group was no easy feat. Many of the charities who already had a discretionary designation in the Ballard Trust didn't take too kindly to the idea of someone else cutting into their pie because all that did was reduce their own slice and underscore that their own status was equivocal. Nonetheless, they agreed to hire Sexton to plead their case to the Public Trustee.

At about the same time, Frank Newbould made a pitch of his own. He called the TD Bank's lawyer with an offer: according to TD Capital's John McIntyre, Newbould said that the Public Trustee was willing to settle the dispute if the TD Bank would throw another $3 million into the pot. And, Newbould said, they had only until the end of the day to respond. McIntyre said he and Brock mulled it over for "two minutes and made a decision within three." No thanks, came their response. So both sides prepared for another day in court.

Meanwhile Justice Ground braced for the remaining order of business: debating TD Bank's official entry onto the court card. And for that, both sides sent in the heavy artillery.

Sheila Block, a partner at Tory Tory DesLauriers & Binnington, a highly respected litigator specializing in commercial law, made an entry on behalf of the bank. To her right sat Dennis O'Connor, a senior partner of Newbould's who stepped into his colleague's shoes while he was otherwise engaged in another battle.

O'Connor began two days of verbal warfare that in the end was the closest this case ever got to a trial. As always outnumbered, the Public Trustee's lawyer defended Himel's decision to radically change the allegations against Stavro and company as "cleaning up and refining the pleadings" now that they had the benefit of pre-trial testimony and the TD documents in their possession. "The fundamental case does not change on the amendments," O'Connor argued before Justice Ground. "We're delving into the acts of the executors and asking: 'Did they breach their duties? What happened in the discoveries in greater and more specific detail revealed more serious and more egregious breaches of their duties."

Take the Mellanby report, O'Connor argued from the lectern. Here was an example of how the executors failed to consider revenues that would have been crucial to the cash flow estimates used by Burns Fry and RBC Dominion Securities to evaluate share value. Since their fiduciary duties required them to act in the best interests of those people they were bound to protect—in this case, Ballard's beneficiaries—the broadcast information should have been factored into the price Stavro paid the estate for its shares.

Bellmore jumped to his feet almost immediately to object to O'Connor's interpretation of the controversial document, which prompted the even-tempered judge to ask him to sit down and wait for his turn to speak. "Whether we agree or not on the interpretation of the broadcast revenues is up to a trial judge," the always pleasant O'Connor shot back to his counterpart. "We're not making these amendments idly. They naturally spring from the evidence we've acquired, which suggests that the executors withheld renegotiating the new broadcast deal [with Molson] until after Mr. Stavro bought the shares."

Rubbing his right ear lobe and removing his glasses for effect, O'Connor finally zeroed in on his target: he asserted that the information in the Mellanby report (which said the Leafs should get up to $12.25 million a year for TV rights instead of the $4 million they were getting) was given to TD Bank officials to entice the financial institution into making a $35-million loan for Stavro's takeover and later to take an equity position in his deal. However, the same information was not passed along to the Bay Street brokerage firms who were determining the price Stavro would have to pay for the shares. O'Connor tried to depict Crump, Stavro and Kelly as executors who viewed their role as fiduciaries not as a duty but as a perquisite.

Justice Ground called for a brief fifteen-minute recess before the sparks could fly, which elicited Sheila Block's quip, "We need to pass out some valium in this case."

Back from the break, Richard Shibley argued in support of getting TD Bank on the ticket "as the only way justice can be done." The veteran lawyer for Ornest and Devellano argued that the bank was not an innocent buyer unaware of the securities laws involved in the transaction. "From the moment Mr. Stavro was given the right to purchase under the will, clearly his intention was to complete a takeover of this company," Shibley said. "His conduct was not honest and carried out in good faith. It was calculated to frustrate rather than to increase revenues."

Block countered the next day. She complained that for the TD Bank to be included in a $75-million lawsuit at such a late hour was "unfair," particularly "given that the Public Trustee is attempting to do this on the basis of misread documents that the Public Trustee promised not to use against them [the bank]." She alleged that when he had asked for—and received—the TD documents through the Court of Appeal in the fall of 1995, Newbould had promised not to use them against the bank. "The Public Trustee is suggesting that the TD assisted the executives in defrauding and breaching their trust," Block ploughed on, "but in order to charge that TD became a participant to the breach of trust, it would have known all along, every step of the way, that a fraud was being undertaken. He can't prove that."

Bellmore stood before the judge and bellowed his description of the Public Trustee's case as "allegations. Allegations and allegations. We are ready to test the allegations, Your Honour." Bellmore complained that his adversary Newbould had argued his case in the media while "we have sat quietly and patiently resting with the fact that the court will deal with this in a timely fashion. This trial seems to be preoccupying all of our waking hours." An impassioned orator, Bellmore made a simple argument: the Public Trustee has had all of this so-called new information it was attempting to use to expand its case against the executors sitting in its files since 1991. He expressed concern that all the government agency was trying to do was cast its net wider and that would "open the floodgates to more proceedings if they [are allowed] to amend the pleadings to add new ones."

Estate lawyer Thomas Lederer gave a more understated, but no less compelling perspective. "There is nothing new [in the proposed amendments], except further damage to the reputations of Stavro, Crump and Kelly. There are serious implications from what a public official is saying against three men who were asked to be executors," Lederer implored while Terry Kelly sat at the back of the courtroom. "Who would name these three men as executors in the future?"

While each hired gun took his place at the podium before the bench, the others shuffled in and out of the courtroom to join the peace talks that were coming together out in the hallway. During the second day of arguments, there was enough incentive on both sides to request a temporary adjournment to talk things over behind closed doors. The understated Justice Ground smiled broadly for the first time.

Finally at 4 P.M. on Friday, March 29, Susan Himel called her boss's office to let him know that she'd decided to accept a settlement offer but that there were still a number of small details to iron out. Both sides had met that morning to discuss whether there was any common ground left between them—and wound up shaking hands on a deal.

Nonetheless, another week passed before Himel finally signed her name to essentially the same offer she'd left on the table weeks earlier. According to the settlement, Stavro would pay $20 million directly to the Harold E. Ballard Foundation starting with $4 million on the day of the closing and $4 million plus accrued interest at 8 percent each of the next four years. His partners in MLG Ventures would also commit to another $3.5-million debenture plus interest over four years. Stavro also agreed to personally guarantee $5 million from the TD Bank to protect the Ballard Foundation against a Revenue Canada assessment for unpaid taxes, which were now estimated to be worth up to $7 million. (Whether Stavro would receive a tax break for his "donation" was left up to Revenue Canada.) As well, Stavro agreed to pay up to $1.5 million in legal costs—$1.35 million to the Public Trustee and $150,000 to Ornest and Devellano. Stavro and his co-executors would also resign as directors of the Ballard Foundation but would remain as executors of Ballard's estate.

According to securities laws, the other shareholders were also entitled to the same amount received by the Public Trustee for the estate's shares. In the case of Harry Ornest and Jim Devellano, that worked out to $49.50 for each of their shares—$45 in cash and debentures worth $4.50 for each share tendered. In all, the two major shareholders received $2.5 million more than what Stavro had originally offered.

Except there was a problem. Ornest had changed his mind. It wasn't such a great deal after all. He had given the proposed settlement the thumbs up in January, he said, because his failing health had sapped him of his will to fight. Although he was at first angry about the impasse created when Himel refused to sign onto the deal in early March, Ornest began to view it as a blessing. Still, he was frustrated, even bitter, that he didn't have the chance to sit across the table from his adversary to negotiate directly on his own behalf. "Let lawyers negotiate money? Never."

Devellano, on the other hand, felt differently. He'd called Harry in the hospital. Frustrated with the process and mounting legal fees, the Detroit hockey executive told his cohort that he wanted to give up the battle and tender his shares. Always the spear carrier, Harry went ballistic, barking back threats of his own. He was still angry with Devellano for admitting to Stavro's lawyers that he thought the shares were worth $50 during his pre-trial testimony. He'd just telegraphed his price and they jumped. By the end of the call, Devellano had fallen back into line and Harry called the nurse for a sedative.

By the end of March, the seventy-three-year-old multi-millionaire had regained his strength and was able to leave Cedars Sinai. No longer on heavy medication, he began to think more lucidly about the fight he'd been waging. When his lawyer,

Richard Shibley, called on April 2 to say that Himel had finally signed her name on the proposed offer, he was stunned by his client's reaction. "Dick, we got screwed." Shibley couldn't understand Ornest's apparent change of heart. Harry had always wanted it to end with a victory and besides, he'd been pleased weeks earlier when they first shook hands on the offer. "What are you complaining about, Harry? We got you another $15," Shibley replied.

Actually, that was the problem. Even though Harry stood to gain $6.5 million for his shares, he wanted the actual share price to be net of interest, which meant he wanted $49.50 plus the interest on top of that. And he wanted the provision that entitled them to a top-up (in the event that Stavro dealt the shares at a higher price) to last for five years, not two years as stated in the tentative settlement. That would prevent what had happened to Molson after they cut their deal with Stavro back in 1994.

Ornest complained to Shibley that they were outmanouevred and outgunned by Stavro's attorneys. "They [Stavro's side] were never going to trial. That was a red herring; a negotiating ploy used by lawyers on both sides," he told Shibley. "They knew Devellano would accept $50 a share and Stavro could smell that all the lawyers wanted to settle. It was a cop-out." Shibley knew he had a problem in the making.

He called again later that day and connected Susan Himel, Jay Chalke and Frank Newbould in a conference call. They were noticeably concerned. After all, they knew first-hand about Ornest's ability to stoke the flames of controversy through the media. They wanted Harry to state publicly that he was happy, like Devellano, who was ecstatic at the prospect of getting $1.6 million for his shares. "Jimmy was thrilled to finally be a millionaire," deadpanned Ornest. The Public Trustee pleaded with Ornest to "say nice things about the settlement." Ornest sensed she needed to protect herself from the inevitable criticism in the press and, more importantly, to sell the deal to Justice Robert Blair, who would be asked to give the settlement the court's blessing. Ornest had strong reservations, he told a grateful Himel, but he acquiesced just the same. In an ironic twist, he would receive a similar request weeks later from Stavro.

Still, Shibley wanted to keep his client in step with the others.

His secretary faxed a memo with eight helpful hints on how to deal with the press. Harry couldn't believe his eyes. "She phoned me twice (and charged me, of course) telling me that a fax won't go through.' So I said, 'What does it say?' And she said, 'It's advice from Mr. Shibley to you on how to handle the media when they call you about the settlement.'" Ornest replied, "Don't bother, I know what to do." She sent it by mail anyway—and charged Ornest the postage—but it arrived a week after the settlement was made public. "Can you imagine?" Ornest laughed, "Shibley advising me on how to talk to the media is like sending a tiger to jungle school."

For their part, Prichard and his cohorts would be out of luck. Himel came back to the table all right, but he didn't get a piece of the action. Edgar Sexton would have to join the long queue leading up to the new directors of the Ballard Foundation—Willard Estey, Leslie MacLeod, a former assistant deputy Attorney General with the Ontario government, and Richard Meech, a partner emeritus at Borden & Elliot.

On April 4, two years to the day since first announcing his takeover offer, Stavro had come full circle. But there was no victory party. Himel, Newbould and Jay Chalke celebrated the windfall (which amounted to more than the ministry's entire budget) over dinner at the King Edward Hotel in Toronto. "I think the case has some very important significance for the business, legal and social community because it brought to the public the importance and serious role that executors have and the public scrutiny to which they are subject," was how Himel reflected on the case. Maybe, but the province's taxpayers would have liked that moral to have surfaced earlier, perhaps before their money was used to make the point.

Tom Lederer was more philosophical. "The opponents were coming from this differently. For Stavro, it was a commercial transaction, but the Public Trustee was driven by a political imperative they never really understood."

On April 9, the day the actual trial had been set to begin, both camps gathered once again at Borden & Elliot to sign their own peace treaty, officially ending a bitter twenty-month legal war.

Later in the week, on April 12, the day after the sixth

anniversary of Harold Ballard's death, they would gather in court for the last time. Lawyer after lawyer stood before Justice Robert Blair espousing the virtues of the settlement. "My clients represent the largest individual shareholdings in Maple Leaf Gardens," Shibley told the court. "Their endorsement of this settlement should give comfort to the court that the amount is fair and reasonable. The court could take some comfort that this is not the Public Trustee acting in isolation from normal commercial considerations."

Brian Bellmore couldn't resist another opportunity to allude to Ballard's will, this time as the "smoking gun." As he handed a copy of the document to the judge, Bellmore declared that "what this case came down to was a difference of opinion of what the fair market value of those shares were. The settlement is an attempt to bridge the gap between those differences."

Bernie McGarva, the Gardens attorney, succumbed to a cliché. "The sun is shining on Carlton Street today. We can move the spotlight from the courts to centre ice."

Twenty minutes later, Justice Blair commended both sides for their efforts and then endorsed the settlement. In doing so, he specifically cited—as Harry had predicted—the testimonials from Ornest and Devellano as justification for concluding "that the settlement is fair and reasonable and in the best interests of the charities and all parties." No sooner had he delivered his ruling than an anxious Newbould approached the bench, asking the surprised judge to sign the document then and there "for a speedier resolution of the transaction."

A few weeks later, the class action suit led by Gwen Maxwell also received an equivalent top-up; $10.60 was added to the $34 she and the other shareholders had already received when they had tendered their shares after Stavro made his original offer. That total is the maximum they would likely have received had she proceeded and succeeded with her case in court. Stavro's new offer was also extended to those shareholders who still held the remaining 4 percent of shares that had not been tendered.

Several weeks before the shareholders gathered, Stavro had dialled his pal in California. It was another typical early-morning call for Stavro, who just days earlier had signed the multi-million-dollar deal with the Public Trustee. When the phone rang in Ornest's bedroom just after 6:30 A.M., the "Beverly Hills tycoon" was still sleeping. The initial nervousness of living without a pacemaker after twenty-six years had forced Harry to slow down. "Harry! It's Steve." Ornest couldn't believe it. "He woke me up like we'd been friends for years." Oblivious to his chilly reception, Stavro ploughed on, "Harry, you have a top-up and so do the minority shareholders," Ornest recalled Stavro saying. "Brian will tell you about it but it's a follow-up to the OSC." Ornest tried to decipher the coded request while Stavro continued, "Harry, you'll always be welcome in the Directors' Lounge when you're in town." Ornest could only laugh, "You're a real piece of work, Steve."

Later, Bellmore called to explain. Stavro would like Harry to write a letter to the Ontario Securities Commission stating that he was pleased with the settlement offer he had received from Stavro and his business partners as "fair value" for his shares. If Harry Ornest could say the $49.50 he received in the settlement was reasonable, then the other shareholders would take their cue from him—just like Justice Robert Blair had done weeks earlier. "Forget it," came Harry's reply. "It wasn't fair value. It was a settlement!"

In the end, there wasn't a call to arms. The final Maple Leaf Gardens shareholders' meeting on August 6, 1996, was more like a last request for clemency.

Just as Jim Devellano had pleaded with Brian Bellmore over the telephone two years earlier, eleven-year-old John Torrance stood before thirty-two shareholders gathered in the Hot Stove Lounge for the last time and implored Stavro not to snatch his small stake in the fabled company. "I got my share in Maple Leaf Gardens from my grandpa when he passed away and left it to me. I'd just like to say that I don't think it's fair that it can be taken away from me when I don't want to give it away."

The room erupted in applause but Stavro remained stoic, staring straight ahead while Gardens director George Whyte fumbled with banal platitudes as he desperately tried to move past the awkward moment. Not even the accusing finger of an elderly shareholder demanding that Stavro personally account for his decision to squeeze out the stakeholders was enough to make the chief executive or his directors snap out of their collective aphasia.

Clearly, the final leg of Stavro's odyssey was a nuisance. He and his investment group had already acquired just under 96 percent of the shares, the result of his out-of-court settlement with the Public Trustee and Gwen Maxwell's class-action suit. And since Ontario's corporate governance laws permit anyone with more than 90 percent of a company's shares to force the others to sell, the meeting was a mere technicality—even if it was two years overdue. As the mandatory thirty minutes allotted for "discussion" droned on, the independent shareholders stood one by one to innocently ask questions of Stavro and his entourage. George Whyte, the court-appointed director of Ballard's holding company (and Gardens director), fielded the questions. Company president Cliff Fletcher was conspicuously absent and Donald Crump sat solemnly at the head table as if he were about to give the funeral peroration.

Yolanda Ballard, that constant reminder of the *ancien régime*, sat at the back of the room bobbing her well-coiffed head from side to side, catching glimpses of familiar faces she'd come to know during her reign. When a disgruntled shareholder nearby sighed that it was "the end of the company as we have known it," Yolanda promptly grabbed hold of his arm and said, "No dear, it's not. It's the beginning."

"My Harold would have taken the company private in 1988," Yolanda told this writer as we lingered in the Gardens' front lobby, "because every time he wanted to scratch his—I'll say elbow but he meant butt—he had to talk to the board about it." Given Ballard's indebtedness in the late 1980s, it's anyone's guess where he'd have come up with the money to finance such a deal.

Finally, a blue-collar type took to the microphone located just behind the board of directors. He thanked Harry Ornest and Jim Devellano for the 40-percent increase in the new share offer price. "It's to their credit that we're getting $49.50 a share," he said, eliciting another round of applause. Stavro and Bellmore exchanged smirks.

The voting ballots were finally distributed shortly after George Whyte shut down the microphones. The shareholders, including Stavro and his whopping 96 percent, cast their votes even though there was never any doubt of the outcome. The little guys hadn't much choice: they could either tender their shares and receive a cheque or they could protest on principle, bypass the money and try to convince a judge to award them more as fair value. In any event, the shareholders would receive a consolation prize: in an unusual gesture, Stavro was allowing them to keep their now-worthless stock certificates as souvenirs. But not before Maple Leaf Gardens passed into the private hands of Steve Stavro.

EPILOGUE

Six weeks after he made his final play, Steve Stavro moved into the same corner office that had been inhabited by his two co-executors, Donald Giffin and, more recently, Donald Crump. It was Stavro's first step toward staking his own claim on the Gardens. He was now ensconced in Conn Smythe's old office.

The millionaire merchant had always intended to take the public institution private. That's the way Stavro prefers to conduct his business affairs. Of course, there are a number of compelling reasons for doing that. The cost of carrying a clutch of public shareholders who represented a small float of thinly traded shares made very little economic sense. Those savings, Stavro claimed, would be used to improve the product on the ice for the city's long-suffering hockey fans.

Yet, money was never really the issue, that is until Stavro hit a few legal roadblocks along the way. Still, at first blush, the machinations don't appear to have been for a profitable end: it cost Stavro and his partners about $200 million (including fees for investment bankers and lawyers) to buy an asset that would yield about $6 million annually in profits, one he'd originally bargained for at $125 million.

Even today his financial worries aren't over. Stavro was confident at the time of the April 1996 settlement that his lawyers could negotiate a tax credit for his $23.5-million "donation" to the Public Trustee. That way, Stavro could offload some of the cost of his takeover onto the backs of Canadian taxpayers. However, Revenue Canada has yet to rule on that request and many say it's unlikely, given that the estate has yet to hand over a cheque for the estimated $7 million in unpaid taxes, interest and penalties levied since Ballard's death. In fact, the executors are appealing an assessment recently levied by the government tax man, which should take months to resolve.

Within his own ranks, Stavro's business partners are clamouring for change. Having watched their original business plan go down the drain, they were especially unhappy to see the extra debt incurred as a result of Stavro's settlement boost the cost of their investments to approximately $38 a share from the original $34. Before they dole out another penny, the Toronto Dominion Bank and especially Ontario Teachers are searching for ways to improve the economics of the transaction. "If the business plan hasn't unfolded the way they wanted," admits a Stavro strategist, "it doesn't bode well to get them to ante up more."

The new corporate structure at the Gardens looks like this on paper: the Toronto Dominion Bank and TD Capital have the most at stake financially with about $67 million worth in loans and almost another $9.75 million in equity for an indirect stake of 10 percent; Stavro owns 31 percent on a diluted basis for bringing roughly $7 million in cash to the table and $32 million he borrowed from TD Capital. But he controls the company. Larry Tanenbaum has another indirect 10 percent after his company, Kilmer Sports Inc., invested $21 million in Stavro's holding company—MLG Holdings Ltd.—on June 20. The company, which was set up in early 1994 for the takeover, was originally 20-percent owned by TD Capital, and the remaining 80 percent represented Stavro's interest. However, with Tanenbaum in the picture, his friend's piece of the pie has been cut. (MLG Holdings together with Ontario Teachers make up MLG Ventures Ltd., the private company that owns Maple Leaf Gardens.)

Bellmore admits that Stavro needed the new financing from Tanenbaum to help pay for the extra costs incurred from the settlement. About $5 million of the $21 million Tanenbaum invested will be used to help Stavro retire his $32 million loan from TD Capital. (Toronto Dominion Bank also lent $35 million to MLG Ventures.) Tanenbaum, whose Palestra Group lost the bid for Toronto's NBA basketball franchise back in 1983, probably figures the best way to be involved with basketball, which is his real love, is to start with the Raptors playing in the Gardens and become partners in a joint venture.

The largest shareholder in the new Gardens is the Ontario Teachers' Pension Plan Board by virtue of its direct 49-percent ownership in the company, courtesy of having dropped $44.3 million into the takeover pot.

Wisely, the pension fund has bought some breathing space in

order to assess its most controversial investment ever. During the mediation process, Ontario Teachers agreed to push the original deadline of its "put" from April 2 until the end of the NHL 1995–96 hockey season. When the settlement was finally signed, the deadline was moved only slightly to the end of the calendar year 1996, despite protests from Bellmore and Stavro's financial adviser, Chris Dundas.

In the meantime, the giant institutional shareholder has been flexing its muscle. Its two representatives on the company's board— George Engman and Robert Bertram—have been advocating better management of the company's books and its overall business. "We want to see the company living within its means," explains Engman. He's taking that pragmatic approach to the board's audit committee, where he has been supporting Stavro's charge to pare down costs, particularly $5 million from the players' payroll, which at more than $33 million accounted for almost half of the company's total expenditures. Plans to install a state-of-the-art time clock, complete with video replay, have been nixed in favour of some minor—and cheaper—tinkering with the existing clock's matrix. And hot patrons can forget about air-conditioning.

Still, that may not be enough to satisfy the demanding merchant bankers at the fund. "We still haven't made up our minds," explains Engman. "When we came into this deal, there was an original business but we've fallen short of our targets and that has impacted our returns. So we began to explore other alternatives to make us whole." Ontario Teachers and Toronto Dominion began clamouring for a new arena months ago, prompting the board to send Cliff Fletcher and a gaggle of Gardens employees off on a fact-finding mission to new arenas around the league. Now that Larry Tanenbaum has joined the board, Stavro's business partners are happy because they have a staunch supporter for the new arena.

Tanenbaum first unveiled an elaborate presentation to the Gardens board for a new facility over a year ago. At the time, Stavro was still in legal limbo, waiting for the Public Trustee's suit to grind its way to trial. His cronies on the board weren't exactly forcing the issue either. That of course changed when Stavro finally tied up all the loose ends attached to the lawsuits. Suddenly, his partners weren't being so subtle any more. An executive committee made up of Stavro, Bertram, William Brock and Tanenbaum was created soon after the privatization meeting to begin the process of meeting with groups to discuss constructing a new arena.

Inevitably, that search has brought Allan Slaight and David Peterson from the Raptors and their investment bankers from Wood Gundy and Bank of Nova Scotia to Stavro's door. The basketball team has yet to break ground to build its Air Canada Centre (a new multi-use facility in the old Canada Post building) near Toronto's waterfront. If there was ever a time to build a joint basketball-hockey arena, they've persisted, this is it. But any collaborative effort between the Stavro and Bitove clans would almost certainly see Stavro and the Leafs calling the shots. It's a concept that takes some getting used to for the Bitoves. So far, the best the Raptors could do is to secure rental space at the Gardens for three nights during their next season.

There is, however, one wild card still left to play in this game: Stavro's nemesis, Bill Ballard. Harold's son hasn't backed down from the legal challenge he launched in early 1996. "My dad always wanted to leave the company to the four Stavro daughters. That was his life's ambition," Ballard says, dripping with sarcasm. "He wouldn't have wanted me to sit around watching this without at least trying to do something about it. He ain't resting till I rest, and I won't do that until I get those people out."

To that end, he has hired Earl Cherniak, a tough litigator who has been described as one of the top three trial lawyers in the country. (Jim Hodgson's firm, Blake, Cassels & Graydon was forced to resign from Bill's case because of a conflict.) If it proceeds, Bill's suit would put on trial many of the same issues raised by Frank Newbould on behalf of the Public Trustee.

For its part, the Ontario Securities Commission is investigating the events leading up to Stavro's takeover offer in 1994. Lawyers in the securities watchdog's enforcement branch are paying particular attention to how the evaluations were prepared and later used to buy out the public shareholders. When asked for his opinion, at least one regulator said the brokerage houses were "willfully blind" for accepting unusually restrictive conditions to produce their valuations. However, investment dealers prepare these reports based on a number of assumptions. And that raises the tricky question of who is responsible—the dealers who prepare the valuations or the client, in this case Ballard's executors, who gave the brokers the mandate.

However, now that the dust has settled, there are those who appear contented. Molson, for one, has secured an exclusive four-year broadcast contract with the Gardens, thus preserving its pre-eminent position in Canadian hockey. And Donald Crump finally closed the door of his office for good. After twenty-five years at the company, he announced his retirement in September.

Not surprisingly, a calamitous conflict such as this would yield a few who feel jaundiced by the whole affair. Rosanne Rocchi, for one, still maintains that Ballard never intended to exclude others—especially his son—from taking a run at his company. "He was convinced the only way to maximize value was to create a bidding war, complete with bid books," she says of the long discussions with her irascible client, which often occurred while he was sitting in the barber's chair. "The auction was to be held with sealed bids being opened at Maple Leaf Gardens. It would be televised and open to the public. Admission would be charted, with the gate and television revenues going to charity. All the bids would be opened and the winner announced at centre ice. It was to have been pure Harold and Carlton Street cash box."

Rocchi should know because she was the one who spent the most time with Ballard. However, the will doesn't state explicitly what she now contends. In fact, that seminal document remains the one unsolved mystery in this case; an elaborate piece of legal artistry that some say appears to contradict the uncomplicated style of the testator it was intended to reflect. It's true that Ballard was a rascal to his last breath and, given his net worth and his standing as Rocchi's most lucrative client, no bells and whistles were spared in its preparation.

Yet some observers suggest that Ballard's will provides far too much latitude for others to determine—and ultimately dictate—Ballard's own wishes. His executors saw theirs as a right of exclusion—that the spoils were to be carved up among themselves. In the year following Ballard's death, his trustees would be increasingly motivated by a desire to determine *who* would buy rather than for *how much*.

"This case is about a man's shares," Bellmore explains again as if giving his jury address at the trial that never happened. "His will states the parameters, and those who wanted an auction wanted to change Harold Ballard's will." Then as he tosses a copy of the document across the table, Bellmore, who never met Harold Ballard, says, "The language is very clear. The man wrote in a mechanism to dispose of the assets. His shares were his treasure and he wanted to dictate how they would be disposed."

Bellmore was the ultimate advocate for his client, as any good lawyer would be. Steve Stavro wanted the Gardens badly and his trusted legal sidekick helped him negotiate his way around legal requirements—without breaking any laws—even if it meant using bully tactics.

The paper trail of closed-door meetings and secret deals reveals that much. Ultimately, the events that led to Stavro's ascent to the helm of Maple Leaf Gardens were not all happenstance. The chaos of Ballard's final days presented circumstances and opportunities that a man with Stavro's background could not have resisted.

Years later when the Public Trustee challenged these actions, Stavro and his lawyers claimed it was all "an innocent flow of paper." Either that, or it was a string of the most incredibly timed coincidences in Canadian corporate history. In any event, Stavro delivered his master stroke with utter transparency.

The fact remains that the Public Trustee's office was fully aware of the coup Stavro and his entourage were pulling off. Despite having been the only one to take Stavro to task at the zenith of his power, Himel has been criticized for being too little, too late. Some even argue that her legal campaign against the executors was the height of hypocrisy. To be fair, we must remember that Himel didn't assume the position as Public Trustee until 1993, but she had to carry the burden of the department's past—the government agency that missed its real chance and ultimately became the litigant who never was. "When you're passing out the raspberries in this one," quips one of the lawyers involved in the case, "the Public Trustee's office should get a second serving."

Worse, according to the critics, was that she opted for a deal because it was safe and expedient. Having made such an aggressive statement intending to scrutinize the actions of trustees and executors, Himel preferred to take the money. That was understandable; Himel faced the real possibility that Frank Newbould could never recover the millions her agency was spending in pursuing Crump, Stavro and Kelly. The $23.5-million settlement amounted to the largest donation to charity ever negotiated in the watchdog's eighty-two-year history. It was a bounty that at least to some extent meant the Public Trustee's constituents would be well served.

Ultimately, Harold Ballard didn't decide who would assume his mantle. Instead, he assembled the would-be contenders and played impresario. But having done that, he could only shape the events of this protracted boardroom scuffle. The final outcome was determined by the various combatants, the courts and the regulatory bodies. If, as Louis Brandeis, one of the spiritual fathers of the U.S. securities act, declared over eighty years ago, "sunlight is said to be the best of disinfectants, electric light the most efficient policeman," then the battle for Maple Leaf Gardens should have had a public airing of the complex issues, and cross-pollination of commercial and trust laws argued before a no-nonsense judge who would have broadened the scope of the inquiry beyond the narrow legal interpretations of the past. That would have forced the one event that never happened: everyone would have had to step onside and out from the shadows.

Index

Adams, Justice George, 254, 256, 263
Aird & Berlis, 18, 232
Allen, Thomas, 254
Amell, Robert, 29
Anderson, Marianne, 18
Argus Corp., 4
Asper, Israel (Izzy), 129, 130
Atlantic Packaging Products Ltd., 199
Attorney General of Ontario, 9,
  19-20, 22, 24, 32, 193-94, 219,
  254, 271

Baillie, Charles, 225
Ballard, Dorothy, 31, 73
Ballard, Harold Erwin: biography, 1,
  26-27, 39, 40, 72, 74, 146, 201-2;
  history with Maple Leaf Gardens,
  3, 25, 26, 29, 30, 33, 35, 36, 48,
  60-61;
  relationships with children, 31,
  40-41, 49, 50, 63-64, 159-60; last
  will and testament, 6, 19, 19-21,
  26, 34, 97, 138-39, 219-20, 235;
  Harold E. Ballard Trust, 45, 73,
  101, 167, 190, 219, 265; Harold E.
  Ballard Foundation, 45, 74, 172,
  220, 235-36, 257, 268-69, 271
Ballard, Harold Garner, 30, 34, 42,
  49, 63, 64, 106, 114, 260
Ballard, Mary Elizabeth, 30, 34, 42,
  46, 50, 63, 64
Ballard, William Owen, 30, 34, 37-
  38, 41, 44, 49, 50, 63, 72, 105,
  107, 114, 116, 127, 137, 149-52,
  159, 165, 166, 168, 170-75, 178,
  179-80, 194, 197, 198, 238, 261-63
Bank of Montreal, 121, 210, 222, 224
Bank of Nova Scotia, 30, 81, 166,
  169, 198, 228-29, 234, 279
Banks, Denise, 52, 58, 102

Barrett, Matthew, 121, 122
Bassett, John W., 27, 29-32, 35
Bellamy, Robert, 18-19, 133, 207
Bellmore, Brian, 3, 6, 8, 10, 11, 13,
  14-17, 23, 97, 99, 101, 102, 115,
  118, 119, 127, 128, 132, 133, 133-
  36, 138-41, 144-55, 161, 164, 166-
  67, 169, 174-75, 178, 180, 181,
  208-10, 212-13, 215-17, 222, 228,
  231, 243, 246, 247, 249-50, 255,
  257, 258-59, 266-68, 273, 278, 281
Bertram, Robert, 213, 214, 278, 279
Bettman, Gary, 9, 11, 12, 203, 236
Beynon, Murray, 196
Bickell, Jack, 28
Bitove, Jack Jr., 22, 174, 196, 198,
  232, 234, 279
Bitove, Jack Sr., 195, 196, 198, 231-
  32, 234-36, 279
Blair, Justice Robert, 264, 270, 272,
  273
Blake, Cassels & Graydon, 155, 279
Blanchard, James, 195
Block, Sheila, 265-67
Booth, Norman, 56
Borden, John Perry, 13, 16, 184, 186-
  89, 192-93, 194, 195, 197-99, 236-
  37, 240
Borden & Elliot, 15, 16, 21, 110, 184,
  185, 187, 190, 192, 193, 242, 271
Bosworth, Norman, 58, 61, 71, 76
Bouey, Gerald, 213
Bower, Johnny, 95
Bowman, Scotty, 162
Boyd, Marion, 193-94
Brock, William, 11, 222, 223, 224,
  227, 260, 265, 279
Brooks, Darcy, 110
Burgess, Campbell, 27
Burns Fry Ltd., 18, 19, 132-34, 208-
  99, 215, 223, 229, 253

Burt, Tye, 133

Caldwell Partners, 162
Calgary Flames, 162, 181, 253
Canadian Association for the
  Mentally Retarded, 20
Canadian Broadcasting Corp. (CBC),
  29, 86
Canadian Football League, 1, 58, 66,
  67, 90, 93, 95, 110, 112, 132
Canadian Imperial Bank of
  Commerce, 42, 47, 78, 197, 234-35
Canadian Tire Corp., 90
Candy, John, 108, 112
Canus Containers Corp., 41
Cassels, Brock & Blackwell, 22, 193,
  195, 198, 234
Centre for Canadian Living, 73
Chalke, Jay, 16, 19, 22, 243, 247, 270,
  271
Champagne, Dan, 101
Chapman, John, 61-62, 92, 101, 109,
  126, 131-32, 134, 136
Charlie Conacher Throat Cancer
  Fund, 20, 73, 240
Cherniak, Earl, 279
Cherry, Don, 92, 207
Chicago Blackhawks, 28, 103, 204
Clancy, King, 41, 69
Clark, Edmund, 173-74
Clarke, Ian, 89, 90, 103
Cluff, Bill, 56, 62, 103
Coca-Cola Canada, 170, 229
Coccimiglio, Jim, 224
Cohen, Marshall (Mickey), 5, 43, 47,
  82, 105, 174, 177, 190-91, 198
Cohl, Dusty, 171-72, 261
Cohl, Michael, 34, 44, 49, 72, 149,
  153-54, 160, 165, 170-72, 174,
  175, 194, 197, 261
Concert Productions International
  (CPI), 37-38, 159-60, 174
Connacher, Brian, 164
Cook-Bennett, Gail, 214
Cowan, Paul, 63
Cowper-Smith, Blair, 105, 181
Crombie, David, 166

Crump, J. Donald, 5, 16, 23, 24, 38,
  39, 43, 45, 53, 55-57, 61, 64, 72, 73,
  80, 88, 93, 95-98, 100, 103, 106,
  107, 110-12, 115-17, 120-21, 122-24,
  127-33, 137, 142, 143, 157-58,
  162-63, 164-65, 169, 180-82, 205-10,
  217, 218, 219, 222, 227, 233, 245,
  251-52, 256, 262, 263, 267, 275, 280;
  biography, 66-67
CUC Broadcasting Ltd., 194
Cullity, Maurice, 15
Curragh Resources, 165

Davies, Ward & Beck, 15, 18, 234
Davis Printing Division, 34, 66
Davis, William, 64, 110
Day, Glen, 193, 207, 230
DeFrancesco, Joseph, 53
Del Zotto, Angelo, 95
Deloitte Touche, 18, 163
Dembroski, George, 18, 207, 229
DeSante, Dana, 16, 232
Detroit Red Wings, 8, 201
Devellano, Jim, 8-10, 17, 24, 93, 200-
  3, 230, 237, 248, 257, 260, 261,
  263, 266, 269, 270, 272, 273, 274
Doherty, Justice David, 248
Duguid, Lorne, 68
Dundas, Christopher, 11, 213, 217,
  222, 224, 251, 278
Dunlap, John (Jake), 58, 61, 71, 76
Dunnell, Milt, 39
DunSeith, Marie, 20-21, 242

Eagleson, Allan, 60, 163
Eaton, Frederik, 77
Eaton, John Craig, 77
Eaton, Thor Edgar, 77, 102, 110,
  111, 162, 164, 170, 183, 184-85,
  190, 197, 237
Emerson, George, 234
Engman, George, 211, 213, 214, 278
Estey, Justice Willard, 64, 110, 271
Eyton, Trevor, 196
Ezrin, Hershell, 82, 84, 90, 102, 156,
  190

Farano, Ronald, 97, 98, 101, 114, 131, 135, 142, 144, 147, 150, 152, 153, 172

Farley, Justice James, 21, 106, 137, 141, 144, 146-51, 156, 161, 165-66, 171, 245-46, 247, 254, 262

Fasken, Campbell, Godfrey, 14, 15, 214, 257, 259

Finlay, Bryan, 23

Finlayson, Justice Geroge, 166, 168

Fletcher, Cliff, 162-64, 169, 181, 196, 208, 212, 215, 229, 234, 253, 262-63, 278

Ford Motor Co., 90

Frank, Barry, 212, 223

Freedman, Stanley, 119, 138, 139, 146, 147, 150, 151

Fuller, Robert, 135

Gans, Arthur, 38-39, 45

Garbig, Doug, 146-47

Gardiner, George, 29

General Motors Canada, 86

Giffin, Donald, 36, 38, 43, 44, 45, 47-50, 53, 55, 58, 60, 61, 64; biography, 65-66, 67; option, 70-72, 81, 93-94, 97-100, 103, 107, 108, 111, 112, 117-25, 126, 127, 131, 137, 143, 144, 147-48, 157-58, 160, 164, 168, 172-73, 182, 185, 188, 219, 231, 237

Giffin, Patricia, 53, 65, 100, 120, 180

Giffin, Philip, 185, 186, 188-93, 197, 199, 237

Gillett, Bill, 13, 235, 236, 237

Global Communications, 129

Globe and Mail, 17, 228

Gobuty, Michael, 41-42, 74-75, 101, 193, 205

Goodenow, Robert, 3

Goodman & Carr, 16, 213, 214

Goodman & Goodman, 231, 232, 236

Goodman, Wolfe, 16, 213

Gordon Capital Corp., 254

Gowling, Strathy & Henderson, 22

Grange, Justice Samuel, 160

Granovsky, Phil, 199, 234

Grant, Stephen, 22

Gray, Herb, 18

Gergersen, Darrell, 21, 22, 239-40

Gretzky, Wayne, 108, 112, 195

Grinsky, John, 96

Gross, George, 68

Ground, Justice John (Jack), 241, 247, 264, 265, 266

Haley, Justice Donna, 64, 70, 95, 98, 99, 117

Hamilton Tiger Cats, 66

Harold E. Ballard Ltd. (HEBL), 27, 30, 31, 37, 39-40, 44-47, 49, 70-71, 91, 106, 107, 110, 113, 114, 117-18, 124, 126, 132, 133, 140, 156, 157-58, 160, 168-71, 175-76; 810756 Ontario Ltd., 47, 113; 810757 Ontario Ltd., 70-71, 113, 124

Hatch, William, 29

Haynen, Grant, 18

Haynes, Arden, 84

Hewitt, Foster, 28, 77

Himel, Susan, 10, 13, 14, 15, 193-94, 216, 219, 231-34, 235, 236, 238, 239, 242, 243, 244, 246, 254-59, 260-65, 267, 270-73, 281-82

Hockey Canada, 20, 73, 163, 238

"Hockey Night in Canada," 29, 83, 85, 86, 88, 90, 92, 203, 212

Hodgson, James, 107, 146, 148-49, 166-67, 179, 261-62, 279

Hollywood Park, 1

Honda Canada, 166

Horton, Delores, 187-88

Horton, Tim, 95, 129, 187-88

Hot Stove Lounge, 31-32, 62, 63, 78, 81, 180, 273

Hough, Ted, 87, 92

Huebescher, Linda, 236

Hugh MacMillan Rehabilitation Centre, 20, 21, 73, 239

Hull, Bobby, 163

Hunt, Peter, 187

Ilitch, Mike, 9, 201
Imperial Oil, 84, 86, 87
Innes, William, 21
International Brotherhood of
    Teamsters, Local 847, 13, 235-37
Irwin, Robert, 35

J.J. Barnicke, 95
JJ Muggs, 115, 229
Jackson, Vernon, 51, 52
John Labatt Ltd., 37, 38, 90, 100,
    107, 163, 174, 202
Joslin, Barry, 190, 197
Joyce, Ronald, 95, 129, 130, 187-88
Julian-Wilson, Mary Elizabeth, 10

Kane, Judge Joe, 102
Kassie, David, 198-99
Kay, Katherine, 21
Kelly, Terence V., 5, 23, 24, 169, 206-
    7, 222, 227, 231, 233, 257, 262,
    263, 267, 268
Kelsey, Tasker, 91
Kennedy, Ted, 204
Kilmer Van Nostrad Co., 194, 277
Kinnear, Guy, 78, 79
Knob Hill Farms, 5, 7, 22, 23, 24, 68,
    93, 121, 124-25, 172, 178, 179,
    209, 222, 224, 250
Korthals, Robin, 222, 237

Labrosse, Justice Jean-Marc, 158, 249
Lambert, Warner, 226
Lamoureux, Claude, 11, 213, 237,
    256, 259
Lamport, Allan, 63
Lawrence, Edward, 38, 58, 61, 76
Lay, Michael, 11, 210-14
Leboff, Bruce, 225
Lederer, Thomas, 218, 248, 268, 271
Lederman, Justice Sidney, 20, 21, 23-
    24, 240, 241
Leon, Jeffrey, 249, 251, 254, 258-59,
    262
Lloyd, William Donald, 35

Lloyds Bank of Canada, 42
Los Angeles Kings, 2, 13, 108
Love, Doug, 45, 47, 83

McCamus, Morgan, 87
McCarthy Tétrault, 105, 109, 111,
    126, 251
MacDonald, Dr. Ian, 238
McDowell, Frederick, 76, 77, 102,
    105, 107, 110, 170
McGarva, Bernie, 23, 248, 251, 263,
    272
MacInnis, Lyman, 163-64, 181, 191
McIntyre, John, 250, 265
McKellar, John, 10, 11, 14-16, 46,
    193, 206-7, 208, 216, 217, 218,
    219, 220, 222, 226-27, 232, 233,
    246, 253, 254, 263
McKinnon, William, 76, 81, 93, 109-
    11, 115, 116
MacLaren Advertising Ltd., 86, 87,
    92
McLaren, Jack, 86
MacLeod, Leslie, 271
MacMillan, Anastasia, 62
MacMillan, William, 35-36
MacMillan, William (son), 62
MacMillan-Babic, Yolanda, 34, 35,
    39-40, 41, 42, 43, 47, 51-53, 55-
    58, 62, 64, 73, 81, 102, 112, 180,
    202, 205, 216, 219, 220-21, 274
McMillan Binch, 133, 135, 141, 155,
    170, 238
McNall, Bruce, 13, 108, 112, 162
McNamara, Paul, 39, 58-59, 60, 61,
    75-76
MacNeil, John, 237
Mahovlich, Frank, 94
Maple Leaf Gardens Ltd., 1-5, 7, 17,
    18, 20, 25, 43, 250;
    history of company, 27-28, 30-33,
    48, 277;
    financial statement, 203-4;
    broadcast contract, 86-88, 90, 92,
    113, 140, 203-4, 266-67;
    special dividend, 81, 82, 93, 115,
    116, 202;

shareholders, 7, 18-19, 200-1

Maple Leaf Gardens Scholarship
Fund, 13, 20, 236

Mara, George, 29

Matheson, David, 16, 18, 19, 115,
117, 121, 124, 128, 133-40, 150-
51, 157, 158, 163, 166, 181, 207,
208, 230, 251, 252, 263

Maxwell, Gwen, 24, 240, 246, 258,
272, 274

Mazankowski, Donald, 55

Medland, Edward, 213

Meech, Richard, 271

Meighen, Michael, 84

Melanson, Michael, 214

Mellanby, Ralph, 92;
report, 108, 109, 113, 115, 140,
204, 209, 212-13, 215, 229,
251-53, 262, 266

Metcalfe, Michael, 214

Midland Walwyn Inc., 7, 193

Miller Thomson Sedgewick, Lewis
and Healy, 27, 61, 64, 75, 89, 105,
107-9, 115, 116, 126, 130, 134,
135, 137, 141, 218-19

Milrod, Leslie, 236

MLG Holdings, 7, 277

MLG Ventures Ltd., 6, 14, 19, 22,
241, 249, 251, 253, 260, 262, 268,
277

Molson Companies Ltd.:
history with MLG, 36-37, 43-44,
46, 50, 113, 114, 116, 124, 127,
132, 142, 146-47, 172-77;
Montreal Canadiens, 5, 37, 45,
162, 203-4;
Molson Breweries, 100, 103, 107,
203;
broadcast rights, 87, 88, 90, 92,
121-22, 177, 203, 225, 238, 251-
52, 266,-67 280;
MLG shareholder, 4, 5, 37, 82, 84,
91, 116, 176-77, 179, 189, 190-91,
227, 230, 258;

Moore, David, 165, 169

Moore, Eric, 10, 13, 15, 16, 170, 216-
20, 237, 247

Morgan Financial Corp., 173-74

Morgan Guaranty Trust Co., 187

Morin, John, 254

Mount Allison University, 265

Muckler, John, 164

Mulroney, Brian, 195

Murray, Anne, 41, 163

Murray & Co., 211

National Bank of Canada, 42, 75,
193, 205, 216, 219, 220

National Basketball Association
(NBA), 22, 194

National Hockey League (NHL), 5,
12, 39, 82, 177, 263

National Hockey League Board of
Governors, 11, 82

National Hockey League Players'
Association, 12, 60

Nesbitt Thomson Inc., 209, 210

Newbould, Frank, 15-20, 21, 22,
238-39, 243-44, 247-51, 257, 260,
261-62, 263, 264, 265, 266, 267,
270, 271, 279

Newbould, Ian, 265

Nicholson Island Club, 183

Nikolaou, Ted, 7, 115, 169, 229

Nixon, Joel, 92

Obodiac, Stan, 89

O'Connor, Dennis, 266-67

Ontario Business Corporations Act,
6, 15, 49, 60, 75, 239

Ontario Charitable Gifts Act, 14, 19,
40, 166-68, 219, 237, 239, 240, 250

Ontario Crippled Children's Centre,
20, 73

Ontario Office of the Public Guardian
and Trustee, 9, 10, 14, 19, 20-21,
24, 92, 98, 110, 133, 136, 138,
139, 141, 143, 144, 147, 186, 189,
191, 194, 199, 207, 209, 218-20,
226-27, 232-33, 237-40, 253, 254,
269, 270-73, 274, 276, 278, 281

Ontario Securities Commission
(OSC), 13, 15, 17, 37, 81, 82, 132,
208, 233, 236, 237, 238, 279

Ontario Teachers Pension Plan
Board, 6, 11, 17, 24, 210-11, 214-
15, 222, 223-24, 226, 227, 233,
237, 254, 258-60, 277-78
Ornest, Harry, 1-4, 8, 9, 24, 93, 108,
112, 201, 204, 230, 238, 248, 257,
260, 263, 267, 269-273, 274
Ornest, Ruth, 2, 204
Osler, Hoskin & Harcourt, 46, 179,
189, 247, 264, 266
Osmak, Borden, 198, 234

Paddon, Stephen, 166
Paisley, Hugh, 136, 138-44, 167, 173,
193, 219, 245, 247
Palestra Group, 194, 196, 197, 209,
277
Pash, Jeffrey, 12
Peat, Marwick, Thorne, 18, 66, 76,
79, 80, 89, 93, 103, 115
Perkins, John, 172, 174
Peterson, David, 22, 23, 84, 196-99,
228, 232, 234, 264, 279
Pollock, Sam, 162, 170
Prichard, Robert, 264-65
Princess Margaret Hospital, 20, 73,
189-90, 240
Pringle, Ronald, 7, 170, 229

RBC Dominion Securities, 18, 208,
209, 215, 223, 229, 251
Revenue Canada, 32, 66, 81, 103,
221, 266-67, 269, 271, 276
Rideout, Peter, 238
Robinson, Patricia, 232, 234-38, 235,
236
Rocchi, Rosanne, 27, 34, 39, 40, 42,
58, 74, 76, 79, 82-84, 89-94, 99-
105, 107-9, 111, 113-19, 124, 126-
28, 280;
biography, 53-54;
trust law, 129-31, 135-37, 138-39,
171, 233, 243
Roebuck, David, 144-51, 152-53, 155
Rogers Communications Inc., 76
Rogers, Edward, 76, 102, 105, 107,

110, 111, 115, 143, 161, 162, 170,
180
Rothschild Canada Ltd., 234
Royal Bank of Canada, 90
Royal Canadian Mounted Police
(RCMP), 31, 57
Russell, Robert, 16, 21

Saltman, Lorne, 186, 193, 195-96,
197-99, 234
Salvation Army, 20, 73
Sasso, William, 145-51, 155
Scace, Arthur, 110, 126
Seagram, Norman, 36-38, 43-44, 45,
47-49, 82-84, 90, 102, 110, 121-
24, 129-30, 142, 146, 147, 172-73,
188-89
Sedgewick, Robert, 27, 34, 38, 87, 92
Sexton, Edgar, 264, 265, 265, 271
Shannon, John, 85
Shaw, Wayne, 238
Shibley, Richard, 246, 260-61, 267,
269-71, 272
Sichewsky, Dr. Vernon, 52
Silver Seven, the, 29
Simpson, Ronald, 90
Slaight, Allan, 196, 199, 234, 235,
279
Smith, Floyd, 78, 79
Smythe, Constantine (Conn), 2, 27-
33, 86, 94, 112, 157
Smythe, Stafford, 27, 29-33, 36, 39,
57
Sokol, Stan, 154, 167, 218
Sproat, John, 126, 135, 136
St. Louis Blues, 1, 3, 162
Stadium Consultants International,
196
Standard Broadcasting Corp., 196,
235
Stavro, Sally, 3, 68, 69, 70, 95, 180,
201, 204
Stavro, Steve A., 1-3, 5, 7, 12, 14, 15,
17, 22-25, 39, 40, 44, 58, 61, 62,
64, 71-72, 73, 74, 75, 76, 77, 79,
92, 93, 95, 97, 98-100, 114, 115,
118-19, 120, 121-28;

biography, 67-70;
option, 124-25, 126-31, 142-44, 147, 148, 150-52, 157-59, 163, 165, 166-70, 171, 175-82, 185, 189, 191, 196-97, 200, 202, 206-7, 209-10, 212, 215, 220, 221-24, 227, 228, 244-48, 254, 255-57, 258-60, 263-64, 272-75, 276, 277
Stellick, Gordon, 65, 69, 80, 89
Stellick, Robert, 89, 90, 103, 252
Stern, David, 194
Stikeman, Elliott, 21, 238
Stratton, James, 184

Tanenbaum, Lawrence, 194, 209, 277, 278
Taylor, Colin, 250
T. Eaton Co., 28
Telemedia Network Radio, 253
Theriault, Carmen, 135
Thomson, Kenneth, 197
Thomson, Richard, 76, 222, 224, 250
Toronto Argonauts, 1, 108, 162, 253
Toronto Blue Jays, 90
Toronto Dominion Bank, 4, 6, 7, 17, 24, 33, 36, 38, 50, 91, 93, 123, 124, 143, 178-79, 205, 214, 221, 222-26, 233, 237, 249-51, 257, 258-59, 260-62, 263, 265-68
TD Capital Group, 6, 7, 224, 226, 227, 251, 260, 265, 277-78
Toronto Hospital Foundation, 20, 21, 240, 242
Toronto Maple Leafs, 1-3, 12, 28, 38, 140
Toronto Raptors Basketball Club Inc., 8, 22, 194, 196, 209, 235, 236, 277, 279
Toronto Star, 10, 39, 40, 65, 193, 219, 228
Toronto Stock Exchange, 6, 81, 83
Toronto Telegram, 27
Torrance, John, 273
Tory, John, 110
Tory Tory DesLauriers & Binnington, 54, 64, 110, 226, 265-66
Trainor, Justice Richard, 153, 154, 160, 166-68
Tridel Corp., 95
Trudeau, Pierre, 18
Turner, John, 64, 110, 126

Ullman, Norman, 163
University of Toronto, 264-65

Van Alphen, Tony, 10, 193, 194, 219
Vancouver Canucks, 17
Vesely, George, 179-80
Vonnegut, Kurt Jr., 245

Waitzer, Edward, 13, 238
Walton, Mike, 94
Warren, John, 21
Warren Paving, 194
Watchorn, Jeff, 18-19
Waters, Bill, 103, 234
Weir & Foulds, 10, 174, 179, 221
Wellesley Hospital, 20, 21, 26, 73, 189-90, 237, 238, 240
Westcom Radio Group, 253
Weston, Galen, 197
Whiteside, Judson, 107, 110, 136
Whyte, George, 7, 18, 165, 166, 169-71, 228-30, 274, 273, 274
Wirtz, Bill, 103
Wise, Richard, 18, 19, 238, 264
Wood Gundy Inc., 82, 198-99, 213, 234, 235-36, 279
Wood, Howard, 156
Wright, Larry, 186, 187, 190, 192-93

Young, Scott, 86

Ziegler, John, 5, 38, 47, 75, 83, 84, 103, 132, 163, 201
Zimmerman, David, 13, 14, 237